CW00746971

# The Violin Explained

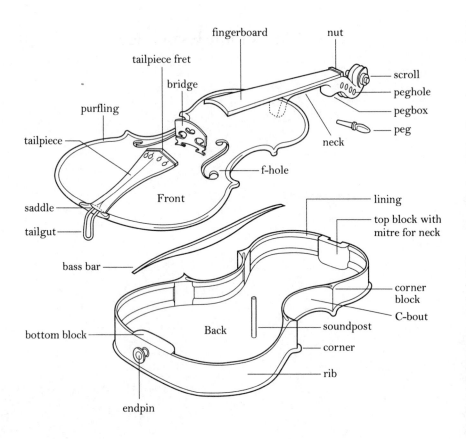

An opened violin with the parts named as used in the text.

# The Violin Explained

◆◆◆◆◆◆◆

## Components, Mechanism, and Sound

JAMES BEAMENT

CLARENDON PRESS · OXFORD

Oxford University Press, Great Clarendon Street, Oxford OX2 6DP

Oxford New York

Athens Auckland Bangkok Bogota Bombay
Buenos Aires Calcutta Cape Town Dar es Salaam
Delhi Florence Hong Kong Istanbul Karachi
Kuala Lumpur Madras Madrid Melbourne
Mexico City Nairobi Paris Singapore
Taipei Tokyo Toronto Warsaw

and associated companies in
Berlin Ibadan

Oxford is a registered trade mark of Oxford University Press

Published in the United States by
Oxford University Press Inc., New York

© James Beament 1997

First published 1997

All rights reserved. No part of this publication may be reproduced,
stored in a retrieval system, or transmitted, in any form or by any means,
without the prior permission in writing of Oxford University Press.
Within the UK, exceptions are allowed in respect of any fair dealing for the
purpose of research or private study, or criticism or review, as permitted
under the Copyright, Designs and Patents Act, 1988, or in the case of
reprographic reproduction in accordance with the terms of the licences
issued by the Copyright Licensing Agency. Enquiries concerning
reproduction outside these terms and in other countries should be
sent to the Rights Department, Oxford University Press,
at the address above

This book is sold subject to the condition that it shall not, by way
of trade or otherwise, be lent, re-sold, hired out or otherwise circulated
without the publisher's prior consent in any form of binding or cover
other than that in which it is published and without a similar condition
including this condition being imposed on the subsequent purchaser

British Library Cataloguing in Publication Data
Data available

Library of Congress Cataloging in Publication Data
Beament, James, Sir.
The violin explained : components, mechanism, and sound / James Beament.
p. cm.
Includes bibliographical references (p.   ) and index.
1. Violin—Construction.   2. Music—Acoustics and physics.
I. Title.
ML802.B25   1996
787.2'19—dc20   96-35558
ISBN 0-19-816623-0

3 5 7 9 10 8 6 4 2

Printed in Great Britain
on acid-free paper by
Bookcraft Ltd, Midsomer Norton, Somerset

# Preface

◆◆◆❖◆◆◆

THERE are few inventions like a violin: an improbable object which has not changed significantly since it was evolved by trial and error more than three centuries ago. The violin family and the sounds they make seem to have intrigued more people than any other instruments: makers, players of very different kinds of music, and almost every serious composer. Fiddles and fiddlers have been associated with the occult and myths; mystery and surprising beliefs persist to this day.

I have had the privilege of knowing several skilled makers, of playing with fine performers, and of hearing them play some of the music I write. Many of them would like to know more about how their instruments work; some want to know whether science can tell them anything useful, or substantiate the beliefs. In fact, over the past fifty or so years, physicists have discovered a great deal about how violins work mechanically and produce sound. There are also some excellent textbooks for those studying acoustics, which include chapters on sound and stringed instruments. Most of these friends will not mind my saying that if they open any of those books, they see mathematical equations—and close them again. They don't think like that. They don't need to think like that to make fine instruments or to play them. To most people, the mystique of mathematics is just as obscure as the mysteries surrounding violins. I am lucky because I also have some acquaintance with several branches of science and I believe that most of the discoveries can be sufficiently explained in simpler ways.

So this book has no equations. It might have included the simple one found in every acoustics book, which supposedly shows how the length of a string determines the pitch—but it doesn't. A theoretical string may behave like that but if you played any of the violin family according to that equation, you wouldn't get into an amateur orchestra. We don't play by physics; we play by musical hearing. And that seems to provide the key to assessing the relevance of most of the physical discoveries, as well as the myths and beliefs. A physicist's description of violin sound is

v

only half the story because it is a poor indication of the sensation it produces. We don't all own oscilloscopes; we do all have ears, and a violin
exists only because of what we hear. But what science knows about our
hearing system is probably even less accessible than acoustics to most
people.

I have tried to explain how these instruments work and how we hear
their sounds, without assuming readers have a background in any of the
sciences involved. They need to know the names of a few musical notes,
including those to which the instruments are tuned. I am of course
indebted to all those whose discoveries I interpret. There are some of
my own findings too, which might well be somewhere in the literature if
there was limitless time to search. Anyone professionally engaged in
physical research on violins will know more than there is in the first five
chapters. The discussion of what features of construction appear to be
significant and those which are not, but to which some people attach
importance—like the outline shape—is not intended for professional
makers. I expect the account of how we hear string sound will be new
ground to many readers and also the basis of two important components: glue and varnish. I feel sure that many players and, I hope, some
parents and teachers of players will find the information about the bow,
real strings, maintenance, and selecting an instrument useful. And there
is an explanation of that puzzling phenomenon the wolf note!

Science is about discovery, and real scientists are usually content just
to discover. Many of them are like Lothar Cremer, who made some outstanding discoveries about violins and was very humble about his work.
There are unfortunately a few who, at the end of a report which would
mean as much to the average violin maker if it was written in Sanskrit,
say, 'and therefore makers should . . .'. People have been making fine
violins very successfully for three hundred years, obtaining all they
need to know in the time-honoured way that a skilled craft is handed
down from master to apprentice; that is also true of players and playing.
Violins are not like cars, television sets, computers, and other desirable
objects where the emphasis is always on supposed advances and
improvements by modern technology. If you ask any player what he
wants for Christmas, he wants one like Stradivarius, Guarnerius,
Testore, or Goffriller made. There are many thousands of instruments
of that playing quality and more are added every year, all made by the
same methods that they used. The insuperable problem which faces
science is that it may discover things about instruments in isolation, but
they are inextricably submerged in what we hear when an instrument is

controlled by a skilled player. You can learn to drive a car in six lessons; acquiring full control of a vibrating string takes much longer than learning to talk. Science can only deal with things which are amenable to its methods of investigation.

So nothing in this book is intended to suggest how instruments should be made or played, because it is very doubtful if science can contribute anything to either; its contents might possibly change the way in which some readers listen to them. The only reaction I seek from the reader is: so that's what happens. Knowing how something works does not alter the fact that it does. Hardly any of the wonderful music which has been composed to make use of the sound of the bowed string has been written by people with the vaguest idea of how violins work, and that may also be said about most of the great players. But they were the kind of people whose hearing determined the instruments, and they had a profound understanding of how the sound would intrigue our minds.

The discussion applies equally well to violins, violas, cellos, and basses unless otherwise stated. Because of the friendly rivalry between proponents of the four instruments it would be nice if there was a neutral collective word but, with apologies, it has to be 'violin'. There are many makers and players of both sexes and no discrimination is implied by masculine pronouns. There are a very few places where the justification for something is given in greater detail; the reader may pass over them without loss to the argument.

I am indebted to John Green, Brian Harvey, Jan Kaznowski, Christopher Longuet-Higgins, John Mather, Malcolm McLeod, Ben Milstein, Jim Prentis, Dennis Unwin, Robin Walker, Rob Wallach, and Jim Woodhouse, from whom I have sought advice or who have read and offered comment on parts of the manuscript, and to Christopher Beament and Richard Wilson, who also played instruments for some of my experiments. Any errors or misinterpretations are entirely mine. Figure 6.5 is redrawn from E. A. G. Shaw in *The Auditory System Handbook of Sensory Physiology Vol. 5, 1974* by kind permission of Springer Verlag, Berlin. I have received unstinting help and advice from Bruce Phillips, Helen Foster, and the staff of Oxford University Press.

But this book really owes everything to my wife Juliet Barker. In her workshop in Cambridge, Juliet and our son Christopher teach a hundred amateurs to make instruments in day or evening classes from autumn to spring; every summer over a hundred people from all over the world come to residential classes there, when they are helped by other professional makers. In discussion with these many friends from all walks of life, I learned how to explain complex science. My knowledge of making is entirely derived from Juliet's remarkable expertise; the several hundreds of good instruments which have been made in the classes, together with the fine instruments she makes herself, provide a unique background. This book would not have been written without her knowledge, encouragement, and cogent criticism. Everything in it has had to pass the test that it agrees with her experience.

J.B.

*Cambridge*
*November 1995*

# Contents

◆◆◆❖◆◆◆

*List of Figures*                                                      x

1  Sound and Vibration                                                 1

2  The Vibration of Strings                                            7

3  The Bridge, Soundpost, and Tailpiece                               33

4  The Violin Body                                                    51

5  Resonance and Response                                             70

6  Hearing String Sound                                               96

7  Under the Ear and Far Away                                        144

8  The Bow                                                           156

9  How Glue Works                                                    165

10  Varnish and Varnishing                                           179

11  Real Strings                                                      210

12  Purchase, Maintenance, and Children's Instruments                219

13  Conclusions                                                       234

*Further Reading of Several Kinds*                                    241

*Index*                                                              243

# List of Figures

◆ ◆ ◆ ❖ ◆ ◆ ◆

| Fig. 1.1 | A dynamic scale for sound | 6 |
| Fig. 2.1 | The pure tone | 8 |
| Fig. 2.2 | A harmonic series | 9 |
| Fig. 2.3 | An early theory of a bowed string | 11 |
| Fig. 2.4 | Pizzicato vibration | 12 |
| Fig. 2.5 | Bowed vibration | 15 |
| Fig. 2.6 | The path swept by the corner | 15 |
| Fig. 2.7 | Increasing dynamic by bowing speed | 17 |
| Fig. 2.8 | Sticking and slipping times | 19 |
| Fig. 2.9 | The bridge and bow from above | 19 |
| Fig. 2.10 | Wave forms | 19 |
| Fig. 2.11 | The dynamic levels of the harmonics | 21 |
| Fig. 3.1 | The violin bridge | 33 |
| Fig. 3.2 | The triangle of forces | 35 |
| Fig. 3.3 | Bridge pressure | 35 |
| Fig. 3.4 | Bowing forces on the bridge | 37 |
| Fig. 3.5 | Cello bowing angles | 39 |
| Fig. 3.6 | Soundpost mechanics | 41 |
| Fig. 3.7 | A variable mute | 46 |
| Fig. 4.1 | Sawing wood for instruments | 53 |
| Fig. 4.2 | Deforming wood | 53 |
| Fig. 4.3 | Flexibility of edge regions | 54 |
| Fig. 4.4 | The behaviour of a flexible arch | 56 |
| Fig. 5.1 | A typical response curve of a well-made violin | 76 |
| Fig. 5.2 | A typical resonance curve of a well-made violin | 77 |
| Fig. 6.1 | The sensitivity of hearing at different frequencies | 99 |
| Fig. 6.2 | The distribution of harmonics on the ear's coding device | 100 |
| Fig. 6.3 | Vibration on the coding device | 101 |
| Fig. 6.4 | The clarity of perceived harmonics | 102 |
| Fig. 6.5 | The resonance of the ear tube | 106 |
| Fig. 6.6 | Schematic representation of the system sensing sound | 107 |

| | | |
|---|---|---|
| FIG. 6.7 | The loudness of pure tones | 109 |
| FIG. 6.8 | Signalled amplitudes of harmonics | 113 |
| FIG. 6.9 | The harmonics of real instrument sounds | 118 |
| FIG. 6.10 | Nerve pulses and pitch | 120 |
| FIG. 6.11 | Harmonic interference | 132 |
| FIG. 7.1 | Distribution of sound from a vibrating surface | 145 |
| FIG. 7.2 | Sound pressure and distance from a small source | 145 |
| FIG. 7.3 | Maximum sound reception by a human ear | 150 |
| FIG. 7.4 | Identifying the direction of pitched sound | 151 |
| FIG. 8.1 | Bow mechanisms | 158 |
| FIG. 9.1 | Liquid adhesion and cohesion | 166 |
| FIG. 9.2 | Atoms and molecules | 167 |
| FIG. 9.3 | The symmetry of molecules | 168 |
| FIG. 9.4 | The polarity of water | 169 |
| FIG. 10.1 | Symmetrical non-polar substances | 181 |
| FIG. 10.2 | Ring substances | 182 |
| FIG. 10.3 | The normal alcohols | 183 |
| FIG. 10.4 | Plant oils and animal fats | 188 |
| FIG. 10.5 | Saturated and unsaturated chains | 188 |
| FIG. 10.6 | Linseed oil | 189 |
| FIG. 10.7 | Chains of linseed oil | 189 |
| FIG. 10.8 | How linseed oil dries | 189 |
| FIG. 10.9 | Reflection with varnish and figured wood | 192 |
| FIG. 10.10 | Changing surface properties | 200 |
| FIG. 10.11 | Surface tension | 204 |
| FIG. 10.12 | Varnish in concavities | 205 |
| FIG. 10.13 | Sealers in tubes | 207 |
| FIG. 12.1 | A double bass tail wire | 222 |

# 1

# Sound and Vibration

♦ ♦ ♦ ❖ ♦ ♦ ♦

## 1.1. *Introduction*

There are three simple ways of producing pitched sound: hitting something, making air in a tube vibrate, and plucking a stretched string. The string started with a disadvantage, for on its own it produces tiny sound, but this was sufficiently intriguing for man to experiment for thousands of years, to find ways of increasing the sound by attaching strings to pieces of wood. Bowing was invented only hundreds of years ago, and gave the string an ability long the preserve of using air in tubes: producing a sustained sound. At first it was bowed on instruments evolved for plucked strings; the violin emerged from them.

The form of the violin became stable long before people had concepts to think about how one worked, and it is not surprising that they imagined the pieces of wood were using the *sound* produced by the strings. What little sound a bowed string produces is drowned by the sound coming from a violin's body. Instruments use the *vibration* of the strings. Understanding them is concerned with how strings vibrate, how they vibrate bridges, how bridges vibrate bodies, and how bodies vibrate. Sound is not produced until the body vibrates the air around it. Sound is also a vibration, so is this splitting hairs? Don't we want to make the air vibrate just as the strings vibrate? That is not quite what happens.

## 1.2. *Sound*

Sound is a peculiar phenomenon. Once sound has been produced, there is little that can be done to manipulate it. We hear it and it disappears into the environment. Sound is produced by almost any vibrating object, and vibration is simple enough. Something moves backwards and forwards. We can see that the strings of a cello are vibrating. We know

1

that sound travels from the thing producing it but we cannot see sound moving because it travels *through* things. Animals discovered millions of years ago that sound is produced when almost anything moves, and could be used to discern that something was happening in their surroundings. They discovered ways of producing sound so that it could be used to send and receive information. That is the origin of our hearing and of speech, and eventually of music. The legacy we have inherited is that hearing is, fundamentally, a continuous means of detecting danger. We can shut our eyes but we cannot prevent ourselves from receiving noise when others generate it.

Sound travels in the following way. If we tap a piece of wood, we apply a small force momentarily to its surface. The wood at the surface is compressed. Think of this as compressing a minutely thin layer. That layer returns to its original shape of its own accord: sound only travels through *elastic* substances which restore their own shape as soon as the force deforming them is removed. In restoring itself, the compressed layer also pushes against the next layer in the substance, compressing it, and this process goes on layer by layer right through the substance. The 'layers' are so small that they are the actual molecules of the material. The information that the surface on one side has been tapped is passed *through* the wood. The piece of wood as a whole has not moved at all.

The same thing happens if the surface of the wood is pulled and expanded. It pulls on the next layer and so on. If the force on the surface alternates, the pattern of the alternation travels through the substance. That is sound. We call the alternation a wave—simply, something which moves backwards and forwards—and by using electronic instruments we can see how the pattern of expansions and contractions changes with time; we call the picture the wave form of the sound. We can learn about the nature of some sounds, particularly those produced by solo musical instruments, by looking at the shape of the waves. This helps us to understand how instruments work; what sensations we might obtain from listening to sound with such patterns is a very different matter.

The bigger the alternating force which starts the sound wave, the bigger the wave. But the *rate* at which the pattern of changing force travels is entirely determined by the substance through which it is passing. A simple analogy is to set a row of wooden dominoes on end and push the first one over so that it pushes the next one. The 'push' travels down the line. The only way to make the collapse travel faster is to move the dominoes closer together. Sound travels faster the nearer the particles of a substance are to each other—in other words, the more dense it is. Through steel sound travels at about 5000 metres per second (m/sec). Through spruce it goes at around 3000 m/sec along the grain, but at about half that speed across the grain because the wood is less dense in that direction. Sound travels through air in the same fashion, each bit pushing and pulling on the next. But because the particles of a gas are far further apart than those of a solid, sound travels much more slowly through it: at about 330 m/sec, roughly 1,000 feet per second. Sound travels at the same speed regardless of how rapid the vibration is; all the sounds from an orchestra arrive at our ears at the same time, fortunately.

To create sound in air we must push and pull on the air. The amount of sound depends both on how big the alternation is, and how much air can be pushed and pulled. The larger the area which is vibrating, the more sound. A string vibrates through a greater distance than a violin body but produces very little sound directly because it has such a small surface. The whole of the front of a stringed instrument has to vibrate to be an effective radiator of sound.

## 1.3. *Transferring Vibration to Air*

If a whole cello front is made to vibrate, there is so much energy involved that one might think there would be no problem in making air vibrate. There is a serious one. You cannot vibrate air as you can a piece of wood, unless it is in a tube or box. All you can do is expose a vibrating surface to the air and let it produce sound. The air moves away very easily when pushed and is sucked back very easily. A piece of A4 cardboard is about the size of a violin front; very little force is needed to move it backwards and forwards a fraction of a millimetre. In comparison it requires huge force to make a heavy stiff violin front move in a similar way. In that sense, a stringed instrument is very inefficient, but it appears to be the best mechanical way to obtain sound from the peculiar business of bowing a string.

The energy in sound in air is so small that the average output of a string orchestra is about a tenth of a watt; it would need the sound of twenty-five such orchestras to light the front lamp of a bicycle. It is not tactful to mention this to performers after playing Tchaikovsky's Serenade for Strings. Players may be pacified by explaining that they use far more energy in moving their arms than they can put into the

instrument. A pianissimo solo violin note rates at less than one mil-
lionth of a watt. The sensation produced by such a sound depends on
the phenomenal sensitivity of normal human hearing, though sadly
average human hearing today has much-reduced sensitivity, because of
the permanent damage caused by listening to loud amplified music.

## 1.4. *Limitations*

We can explain the principle of a violin's mechanism by picturing in
various ways, firstly, the form of vibration of a string, then of the
wooden parts, and finally of the sound produced. That tells us how a
violin works. We have to begin by describing this for uniform unvarying vibrations and sounds because that is the only way to get an idea
of how the mechanism works. When a violin is played it does not produce completely uniform sound, even when a skilled player is trying to
make it do so. The sound is changing continuously, and that is a vital
part of what we perceive; it may be the critical difference between hearing a real instrument played and attempts to produce such sound electronically. We can explore how that vital component arises; the same
mechanism produces and sends that sound into the air.

That brings us to the biggest limitation on any description of the
sound which is produced, and it is a thing with which this book is particularly concerned. A physical picture shows the way the air is vibrating; how does that relate to what we perceive when we hear it? A
superficial problem is the difficulty of describing any sensation from
sound. Listen to musicians discussing tone; language does not have a
vocabulary for hearing, corresponding, for example, to sight. The serious problems are of a rather different kind. The physical description of
the sound does not represent the messages sent to the brain. Many false
assumptions and misconceptions have arisen from the naïve belief that
it does. The moment the sound enters the hole in the ear it is changed,
even before the hearing mechanism begins to sense it. Some things
which are obvious in the physical description we cannot sense; some
things which appear trivial we do. What makes bowed string sound
even more intriguing is that it also produces sensations which are not
there *at all* in the sound, but which are characteristic of hearing bowed
strings.

Those matters are discussed in detail in Chapter 6. One simple way
in which we can get the wrong impression from a physical description
applies to all sound, and we need to understand this before we discuss

how instruments work. It would seem reasonable that if we double the amount by which a string vibrates, that doubles the amount by which the violin vibrates and doubles the amount by which the sound in the air vibrates, and that is broadly true; but we do not perceive that the sound has become twice as loud. Very roughly, the vibration has to be increased just over three times to be perceived as having become twice as loud. That seems a simple enough rule—until we realize that our hearing works like that whether we are judging an increase in loudness with very soft sounds or very loud sounds. Whatever the size of the vibration we hear, it has to be increased about three times to sound twice as loud. This is a very real matter in playing music. We don't measure vibration; we judge *dynamic*. Music is one of very few activities in which we do have to judge levels of loudness. The way that our judgement works is that if we start with a low-level sound, we will perceive that it increases in similar steps of loudness if the amount of vibration increases by about three times, then another three times to about ten times the first vibration; the next step needs about three times that, which is thirty-odd times the first one, and the next step is up to a hundred times.

It is easier to appreciate the effect of the sizes of vibrations on our hearing if we can show them in diagrams in a way which gives a sensible musical impression of their loudnesses. Suppose there are two vibrations, one a hundred times bigger than the other. If we draw two lines to represent their size, with one a hundred times longer than the other, this gives a completely false impression of how relatively loud they would be. A better way of representing the vibrations is shown in Fig. 1.1. The scales on the two diagrams, *a* and *b*, show that the values of the vibrations are the same in both pictures. But the lengths of the lines in *b* indicate how relatively loudly the sounds with those vibrations would be heard, and that is what we want to know about musical sound. We could say that *b* shows the sound vibrations on a **dynamic scale** because it shows roughly how we would compare the sounds in music.

Similarly, in the following chapters, the description of how the strings and the rest of the instrument behave are related wherever possible to playing and to what we hear. Once we can see how the sound is produced and what the sound is like, we can approach the reason for bowing strings: in so far as it can be explained, why we obtain the sensations we hear when these instruments are played.

We start without any assumptions. That is important, because one

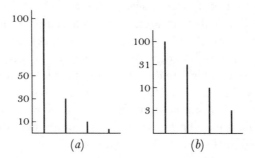

FIG. 1.1. A dynamic scale for sound. The lines represent how much four different sounds vibrate (*a*) on a simple scale, (*b*) on a *dynamic* scale, suggesting how they compare in loudness.

very big assumption pervades almost everything written about violins, and not only by players and makers. Several scientists have investigated and measured the characteristics of these boxes in great detail, such as their dimensions, the pattern of vibration of the front, and the elasticity of the wood, and have suggested how these things may determine the specific sounds we hear, some of them even proposing how a box should be made, without having asked themselves a fundamental scientific question. The idea that the box has any special role in the nature of the sound we hear is an assumption based on popular belief, just as much as is the notion that Stradivarius had a magic varnish. Before we can assume that any particular feature of what is heard is due to some property of a particular violin, we have to show that the box does play a specific part in what we perceive; it may only have a passive role, and the bow, the strings, and the bridge may be the significant things which determine the particular nature of what is heard. There is only one thing which is absolutely clear at the beginning of our investigation: the player determines whether we receive pleasing sensations from members of the violin family. We do not need any scientific tests to realize that.

# 2

# The Vibration of Strings

◆ ◆ ◆ ❖ ◆ ◆ ◆

TERMS have these meanings until developed further in the text:

**Amplitude:** how big a vibration is; the distance between the extremes of movement of a vibration (see Fig. 2.1).

**Cycle:** the repeated element of a regular vibration (see Fig. 2.1).

**Frequency:** the rate of vibration; the number of repetitions or cycles in a second. The frequency of violin open A is 440 cycles per second.

**Pitch:** the characteristic of musical sound which enables the hearer to refer it to a scale of pitches.

**A note:** the complete played sound of the simplest unit of music as produced by an instrument, which consists of a **starting transient** at the beginning followed by a sustained sound of constant pitch and loudness.

## 2.1. *History*

The way in which varying the length of a plucked stretched string produces sounds of different pitch, and the relationship of lengths to pitches which were agreeable when heard simultaneously (in musical terms, consonant), were known in classical Greece. Before the thirteenth century the Arabs had developed sophisticated fretted instruments based on these relationships. By 1640 Mersenne and Galileo had independently discovered how the diameter and tension are related to a plucked string's pitch. Although it was obvious to these pioneers that sound generation was concerned with vibration, they had no way of measuring vibration and no means whatsoever of discovering what sound actually was. All the early discoveries had to be described in terms of pitch—what was heard—and many of the words we use in music today continue this way of describing things. It was not until early in the nineteenth century that Savart demonstrated a precise relationship of musical pitch to a rate of vibration which we call frequency. He matched

the pitch of sounds from instruments with the pitch of the sound produced by holding a piece of flexible material against a toothed wheel
rotating at known speeds. This only proved that what we call pitch can
be described as a rate of vibration. Why musical sounds of the same
pitch differ from each other in what most people call 'tone', and how
instruments produce such sounds, proved much more difficult problems.

## 2.2. *The Basis of Tone*

The presumed basis of tone was discovered in the middle of the nineteenth century by the great scientist Helmholtz. Blowing across the
opening of a bottle produces a pitched sound. The pitch is determined
by the volume of air in the container. When a spherical globe is used,
the pitch obtained is very clear. If a tiny listening-hole was added to the
globe and held to the ear, Helmholtz heard its clear note when an
instrument sounded a note of that pitch. But he also heard that note
when some lower-pitched notes were played. He realized that if he
heard the sound in the globe, a sound of that pitch must be present in
that musical note. Such a globe is called a Helmholtz resonator.

Helmholtz listened to various musical instruments with these globes
and concluded that each pitched sound was made up of several sounds,
which were appropriately called partials. But when he listened to the
note of a tuning-fork, one only of his resonators would respond to that
sound; it contained only one pitch. He could draw the form of vibration
of a tuning-fork by attaching a tiny bristle to one arm of the fork and
holding it so that as it vibrated, the bristle marked paper on a revolv-
ing drum. The wave it draws is a **sine wave** (Fig. 2.1.). Sound with this

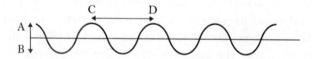

FIG. 2.1. The pure tone is a sine wave vibration. Its amplitude is A–B; one cycle
is C–D.

form of vibration is called a **pure tone** because it cannot be dissected
into anything else. To musicians this tone also has less character than
any other sound, and if heard continuously, is a form of torture comparable with the incessant beat of neighbouring pop music.

Helmholtz then discovered that the frequencies of the partials (the pure tones) he detected in a musical sound, appeared to be very simply related to each other. Their rates of vibration were given by multiplying the pitch rate, the slowest rate of vibration present, by small whole numbers such as 2, 3, 4, and so on. This explains why the pitch frequency is also called the **fundamental**. One mystery about our hearing is why we ascribe the pitch of a musical sound to the slowest rate of vibration present, regardless of the many higher rates of vibration which are also there, and, as we shall see in due course, it has led people to attach far too much importance to the fundamental in the sensations we hear.

Helmholtz had found a way of measuring a property of this invisible mystery, pitched sound, long before there were methods for seeing what the vibration was like. Forty years earlier, the French mathematician Fourier had looked theoretically at wave forms and had shown that each regularly repeating wave of whatever shape was equivalent to a particular set of sine waves, which belonged to the same series that Helmholtz had discovered: small whole-number multiples of a fundamental rate. It was realized that the vibration of a musical pitched sound could be described by the pure tones of which it was composed. The components—the partials of the sound—were called the **harmonics** of the wave. A complete set of pure tones which vibrate at twice, three times, four times, and so on as fast as the fundamental, often extending to twenty or more times as fast in a musical sound, is called a **harmonic series**; their pitches are represented musically in Fig. 2.2. We call the

FIG. 2.2. A harmonic series is any set of pure tones with frequencies in simple multiples of the lowest frequency. The notes show the perfect intervals of one such set; some, such as the 7th, lie between notes on the tempered scale.

fundamental the first harmonic, and it is useful to call the other harmonics the 2nd, 3rd, and 4th, or to say, for example, the even-numbered harmonics, 2, 4, and 6.

String players may recognize that the intervals of the notes in Fig. 2.2 are the same as those produced by bowing whilst touching strings lightly in particular places and may call those notes harmonics. Brass instruments produce the same series of pitches by making the air in a tube vibrate in different ways, and they may be called harmonics. The series of pitches is also produced by whales, who are very intelligent animals, and for all we know they might call them harmonics too. But in this book, the word 'harmonic' means what Helmholtz discovered: *a pure tone component of a pitched sound.*

By listening with his globes, Helmholtz found that instruments differed in which harmonics appeared to be present in their sounds. Wind instrument sounds, he said, contained only some of the harmonic series; the bowed string produced the complete series. He concluded that the differences in the harmonics caused the sounds to have different tones to our hearing. His discoveries are in a large book, *On the Sensations of Tone.* This is still a gold-mine of information about the basis of musical sound and music, and Sedley Taylor, a Cambridge physicist and musician of the period, rightly said that Helmholtz did for acoustics what Newton did for astronomy.

Today we can look at the form of a musical sound's vibration on an oscilloscope, and we have devices which will analyse and print out the sizes of its component harmonics; such a process is called harmonic or Fourier analysis. Tone is not simply due to the presence or absence of particular harmonics; the same harmonics can be present in two sounds which have different tone. *Tone depends on how strong or weak the harmonics present in a sound are.* This statement is correct; it is also deceptive. The tone sensation of a sustained musical sound is entirely determined by the amplitudes of the harmonics which are present, but it is not true that the physical sizes of the harmonics directly represent the tone we hear, or that we can discern some of the differences apparent in physical descriptions of two tones (see Chapter 6).

'Tone' is one of the most confusing four-letter words in the musician's vocabulary (leaving aside its meaning as an interval, and its use in terms such as tonal and tonality), but the harmonic content specifies the tone of each note for sustained pitched sound; this means that if we generate simultaneously pure tones, each having a frequency of one of a harmonic series, and each of a particular amplitude, everyone will hear one particular tone. That is precise—and more informative than any of the many adjectives used to try to describe tone. Tone is one of the characteristics of a sensation which occurs in the brain. You don't know what I hear, and I don't know what you hear (and it seems likely that not everyone hears the same thing from the same sound). But a specified set of harmonics will produce a particular sound which each person will recognize as having the same tone every time.

The bowed string sound contains all the harmonics of the series: the fundamental frequency and each of its multiples, typically extending to those which are twenty or more times its frequency. How did a string produce all these vibrations simultaneously? A strongly bowed or plucked string appears to vibrate from side to side as a single smooth loop. But the frequencies of the harmonics seem to correspond to the pitches of the string when shortened to a half, a third, a quarter (and so on) of its full length. Thus an obvious possibility was that a string vibrated in loops of these lengths as well, even if it could not be seen (Fig. 2.3). This also provided a simple explanation for the sounds pro-

FIG. 2.3. An early theory of a bowed string suggested that it vibrated simultaneously in loops which were simple divisions of its length, such as 1, 1/2, 1/3, 1/4.

duced by just touching the string in appropriate positions whilst bowing; the string would then vibrate in only those loops which have a stationary point (called a node) at the touching position. So touching half-way would give the loops producing the octave of the open string. This explanation is wrong, though it was still given in 'respectable' music reference books published a hundred years after the discovery in 1863 of the extraordinary way a bowed string does vibrate; indeed, even the pitches obtained by normal bowing do not correspond to simple proportions of string length (see Section 15 below), so peculiar is the behaviour of the bowed string.

It was also Helmholtz who discovered how a bowed string does vibrate. In essence, his ingenious method was to attach to the arm of a tuning fork a piece of opaque material with a slit in it. Using a microscope, he looked through the vibrating slit at a spot of light shining on a bowed string, tuned to a pitch very slightly different from that of the fork. It is, to say the least, impressive that he worked out the whole system from the vibration of a single point on the string and then wrote in his notebook, 'the movement of a string is really quite simple'. Today we use a stroboscope flashing a light at any chosen speed to watch the whole vibration in slow motion.

## 2.3. *The Form of Vibration: Pizzicato*

Pizzicato helps to explain why, when a string is forced to vibrate artificially, it does not do so in loops. If an open string is plucked at about one-quarter-distance from the bridge, it starts as a shallow triangle (Fig. 2.4). When seen by a stroboscopic light, the peak of the triangle

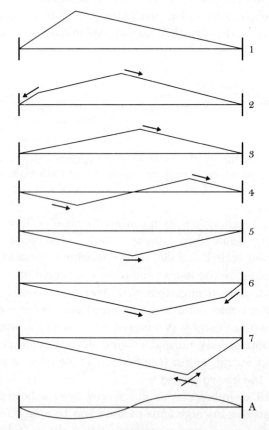

FIG. 2.4. Pizzicato vibration. When released (1), two corners travel in opposite directions along the string (2 → 6) and pass each other (7). The pattern repeats in reverse (6 → 2), returning to shape 1. As vibration (exaggerated in the diagram) dies, the corners are rounded: e.g. shape 4 becomes shape A.

appears to split into two 'corners' running in opposite directions along the string. They appear to be reflected at the bridge and nut, come together on the opposite side of the string's silent position, pass each other, and continue running up and down the string. 'Peak' might seem a better word, but corner is the term always used.

A string is under tension, and a straight line is the shortest distance between two points; tension makes the parts of an artificially displaced string stay in straight lines. When we pull it aside, we make two straight lengths of string. We can think of this as a sort of catapult in which the missile being projected is the bit of the string which forms the point of the corner. As the missile is thrown across, the arms of the catapult fold in, but string tension pulls them into straight lines. At every stage of the initial movements each portion of the string is virtually straight. As the vibration decreases, the shapes become more continuously curved (Fig. 2.4A). The natural way in which a string would vibrate is in curves; bowing and plucking make it vibrate artificially.

Each corner travels along the string to one end, then along the whole length of the string, and back from the other end to reach the point where it was plucked, in one cycle of the fundamental frequency of the note; if the note is A = 440, each corner makes the round journey 440 times a second. The bridge continuously removes energy from the string, transfers it to the body to vibrate it, and that creates the sound we hear. The sound dies away quite quickly, but the string is vibrating very many times a second, so that the bridge does not remove very much energy from each cycle, and most of that energy is used up in vibrating the wood.

To a large extent, the vibration of the string happens because it is *elastic*; its tension is increased when pulled aside, and it is mainly the forces so produced which control its behaviour. Strings must also be *flexible*, which describes a different property. Compare a violin gut A and a steel E string by bending them in curves: gut is flexible, and steel is much stiffer. Our general discussion of how strings behave must be in terms of an ideal string which is elastic and has no stiffness, but the stiffness of a real string has an effect on tone and accounts for the big difference between the sound of gut or gut-imitating strings and steel strings. This is discussed in Chapters 6, 7, and 11; if you are a player, the characteristics of real strings are of considerable practical importance.

The reason for looking in detail at the various contortions of the string when plucked or bowed is that the sound which is produced depends on how the *angle* which the string makes at the top of the bridge changes as the string vibrates, as explained in the following paragraphs. It is fortunate that tension does make the string move more or less in a series of straight lines; it would be more difficult initially to get an idea of how instruments work if we had to think of what happened at the top of the bridge with a string vibrating in curved shapes.

### 2.4. *How a Bow Vibrates a String*

**The bowing position** on a string is taken to be the position of the middle of the ribbon of hair, assumed to be about 10 mm wide.

**Pressure:** the players' term for the force applied by the bow downwards onto the string. See also the Introduction to Chapter 3.

**Frequency:** The rate of vibration is nowadays expressed in Hertz (abbreviated Hz). 50 Hz means 50 cycles per second. Frequencies in thousands of cycles per second are in kiloHertz (kHz).

**Hearing** spans from about 15 Hz to between 9 and 20 kHz depending on age.

So that **forces** and **pressures** can be related to everyday experience, some unconventional abbreviations will be used; those unfamiliar with physics will not know the units now used, such as Pascals and Newtons.

$$
\begin{aligned}
\text{m} \quad &= \text{metre} \\
\text{mm} \quad &= \text{millimetre} \\
\text{gm} \quad &= \text{gram} \\
\text{kgm} \quad &= \text{kilogram} \\
\text{sec} \quad &= \text{second}
\end{aligned}
$$

Once a string is released in pizzicato, the string itself determines how it will go on vibrating. When a string is bowed, the bow maintains it in an artificial form of vibration the whole time (Fig. 2.5). The string sticks to the bow by friction. The bow moves it in the direction of bowing. The bow lets go. The string slips and flies back, whereupon it sticks to the bow again and the process is repeated.

Bowing produces one corner running up and down the string. It goes from the bow to the nut and back to the bow while the string is stuck to the bow. When the corner gets back to the bow the string unhitches; the corner goes to the bridge and back to the bow while the string is slipping past the bow hair. The bow creates the corner, and reinforces its shape in each cycle. The path swept by the corner produces the appearance that the string is swinging in a loop (Fig. 2.6). Many things

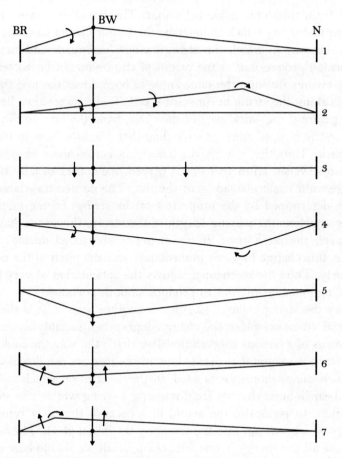

FIG. 2.5. Bowed vibration. A bowed string sticks to the bow (1), and as it is moved, a corner travels to the nut (2 → 3), is reflected, and returns (4). The bow releases (5), and the string slips while the corner travels to the bridge and back to the bow (6 → 7), the string sticks (1), and the cycle repeats.

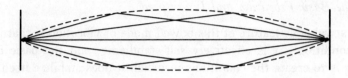

FIG. 2.6. The path swept by the corner produces an envelope, making it appear that the string vibrates as a single loop.

result from this remarkable behaviour. The travelling corner is a convenient feature by which to describe the string's behaviour, but it is the particular way in which the string swings backwards and forwards at the bridge groove that is the origin of the sound. In broad terms, the string swings through the same angle in both directions and the corner travels along the string at constant speed. The distance travelled by the corner during the 'stick' part of the cycle, from the bow to the nut and back to the bow, is much greater than that from the bow to the bridge and back. Thus the bow moves the string across more slowly than it flies back. When an instrument is played, the corner usually travels to a finger and back, instead of to the nut. The corner travels at a fixed speed, determined by the properties of the string. So the moment the player shortens the playing length of the string, the corner has less far to travel; the pitch rises. If the string is shortened during one bow stroke, this change happens immediately and the pitch of the note rises similarly. Thus the mechanism allows the articulation of very fast passages, and enables players to produce smooth portamenti.

Why the string behaves like this is another matter. It is the form of artificial vibration which the string adopts when suitably bowed, and in the words of a famous English novelist, that's the way the cookie crumbles. Once we know that that is how it vibrates, we can discuss the way in which the phenomenon is used. In the description which follows, we must bear in mind that we are discussing a string which is in *maintained* vibration. In pizzicato, the sound dies because the body removes the energy which was put into the string by the initial pluck. The body does not take all the energy in one fell swoop, or all we should hear is a bang and the string would immediately become stationary. Stringed instruments would not work unless the body removed only a very small amount of the energy in the string from each oscillation, and it is this amount of energy that has to be put in by the bow during the 'stick' part of each cycle if it is to maintain level sound.

### 2.5. *The Basic Vibration and Bow Speed*

The first valuable feature of this bowed mode of vibration is that in the right conditions, it is effectively self-stabilizing, and the basic art of bowing is to create the conditions in which it does stabilize itself. The key factor is that the friction of the bow fails to hold the string at the moment the corner returns from the nut. We can see that this must be so in uniform bowing. If the bow released before the corner returned,

the string would slip across, but by a smaller amount than in the previous cycle, and the bow would start a new corner earlier than the previous one, which would then arrive back at the bow at the right time,
but this would have created a smaller vibration. If, when a corner
returned, the bow did not release, the bow would move the string further. When it was released it would swing further and start a new corner later than the previous one; that would produce a larger vibration.
If bow speed is constant, the circumstances are the same for every cycle,
and the vibration remains constant in amplitude.

In principle, if the rate of movement of the bow is changed to a new
faster constant level, the string is moved further in the time the corner
goes to the nut and back, the system adjusts to these new conditions,
and the amplitude of vibration increases (Fig. 2.7). The vibration of the

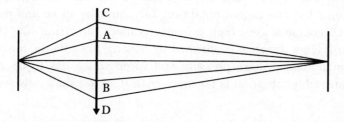

FIG. 2.7. To increase dynamic at one bowing position, the bow must move the
string further (C–D instead of A–B) in the time the corner travels to the nut
and back.

bridge and of the violin body is proportional to the amplitude through
which the string swings, and the sound level accordingly increases. It
is said to be common experience that one can increase the sound by bow
speed alone. The idea is correct, but the system also depends on bow
pressure, and players cannot produce exactly the same bow pressure
over a range of bow speeds. It has been demonstrated, using an artificial bow with constant pressure, that bow speed and vibration are
directly related, but the range of amplitudes obtained by bow speed
alone is small compared with that which is used in normal playing.

## 2.6. *Bow Pressure*

As the string is moved across by the bow, the pull on the bow increases,
and in practical terms, that pull is proportional to the angle the string

makes with the bridge. The bow lets go when friction can no longer hold the string; therefore, in principle, if the speed of the bow remains constant but the friction is greater, the string is moved further before it is released, and the amplitude is increased. As with a change of bow speed, the string settles down to a new stable state with larger amplitude and therefore a higher level of sound. The only way in which friction can be increased is by applying greater bow pressure.

## 2.7. *Combining Bow Speed and Pressure*

As every player knows, bow speed and bow pressure are not independent of each other; they have to be used in appropriate combination. When bowing towards the end of the fingerboard (at about 1/5 string length), a reasonable range of both pressure and bow speed can be used to obtain the stable vibration, and this is the best position to play pianissimo, but one cannot obtain high dynamic by speed and pressure there. Of course if very high pressure is used, the string hits the fingerboard. High dynamic is obtained by bowing towards the bridge, but the combination of high pressure and speed which has to be used to maintain stable vibration is far more critical, as we shall now see.

## 2.8. *Bow Position and Vibration*

The stable form of vibration produced by bowing is a corner which runs round the string, its path creating an envelope (see Section 4 above). This stable mode is independent of where the string is bowed (Fig. 2.8), provided suitable speed and pressure are used. If the string is always vibrating in this same pattern, it is always moving backwards and forwards in the same way at the bridge (Fig. 2.9), and so in principle the same form of vibration is always operating on the bridge. It may help to understand the form of this vibration if we look at the ways in which different points along the string move during the string's cycle. The mid-point of the string moves for half the time in one direction and for half in the other. If we plot how this movement occurs in time (Fig. 2.10), we get a wave which is a symmetrical triangle. A point at 1/5 distance from the bridge flies back more rapidly than it moves across; at 1/10 distance, the wave becomes even more asymmetric. At the bridge itself, the string moves in the bowing direction throughout the time in which the corner makes a complete circuit of the string, and as the corner goes past the bridge, the system jumps and starts the long

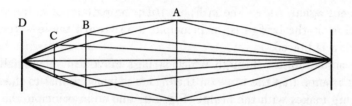

FIG. 2.8. Sticking and slipping times. The width of the envelope depends on how strongly the string is bowed (Fig. 2.7), but otherwise, the path of the corner is the same wherever the bow is applied. At A, the string moves in each direction for half of each cycle. At B, the string moves in the bowing direction for 4/5 of the cycle, and at C for 9/10 of the cycle. Thus at the bridge (D) the string moves in the bowing direction for almost the entire cycle.

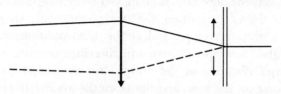

FIG. 2.9. The bridge and bow from above. For the very small vibration of strings, the force applied to the bridge is proportional to the angular movement of the string and its tension.

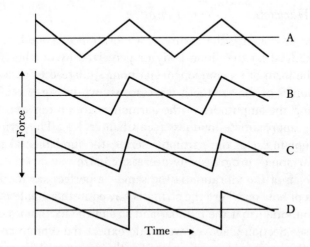

FIG. 2.10. Wave forms. How different places along the string move with time (corresponding to Fig. 2.8): A, at mid-point; B, at 1/5 string length; C, at 1/10 string length; D, the sawtooth wave which the string imposes on the bridge.

movement again. As we see in Fig. 2.10D, the pattern of movement of the string at the bridge is, in principle, a **sawtooth wave**—wherever the string is bowed.

The actual angles through which strings move are very small, and we can assume that the force on the bridge is proportional to the angle the string makes with the bridge (Fig. 2.9), and so in principle the force changes in the pattern of a sawtooth wave. For all practical purposes, this is also the force on the bow.

A second feature of bowing can now be seen. At the 1/5 string position (Fig. 2.8) the bow must move the string a relatively long way to produce a given envelope: a given vibration at the bridge. If the bow is moved slowly, and the string is moved a short distance before it unhitches, the vibration envelope can be very small and a pianissimo can be obtained. But the bow cannot be moved fast enough to obtain a large vibration. At the 1/10 position, the string is moved a shorter distance to produce a given envelope, and at the 1/20 position, a still shorter distance; higher bow speeds here will therefore produce a large envelope and large vibration at the bridge. But the larger the swing, the larger the force on the bow, and therefore the greater the bow pressure must be. The nearer the bow gets to the bridge, the narrower are the tolerances of speed and pressure which will produce a stable string vibration. This is discussed again in Sections 10 and 11 below.

## 2.9. *The Harmonics of String Vibration*

It is easier to visualize the nature of a vibration or sound, and how it may be changed by the violin body or perceived by our hearing, if we see it in the form of its component harmonics, instead of as wavy lines. The harmonics of the sawtooth wave are shown in Fig. 2.11. The lines representing the amplitudes of the harmonics are on our dynamic scale suggesting approximate loudness (see Chapter 1.4). The string generates a complete set of the harmonic series; the fundamental is largest, and the harmonics progressively decrease in size.

If the form of the vibration is the same—a perfect sawtooth wave— regardless of how or where the string is bowed in this stable mode, then on the assumption that the number and size of the harmonics determine the tone (see Section 2 above), we would expect the tone to be the same wherever the string is bowed, except for the dynamic. This is obviously untrue. The sharp angles on the theoretical sawtooth wave would only be produced if the corner on the string were similarly sharp. The cor-

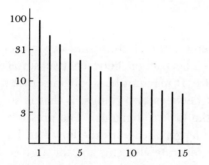

FIG. 2.11. The dynamic levels of the harmonics of an ideal sawtooth wave (Fig. 2.10D), from which bowed sound is generated. The harmonics extend beyond those shown, but the higher harmonics will always be smaller than suggested by this theoretical picture (see text).

ners are always rounded, and the more round they are, the smaller are the higher harmonics in the vibration. The bow is not a narrow wire, but has width. A real string is stiff and cannot be bent into a sharp corner. But the corner is increased in sharpness by bow pressure. Thus when light pressure is used at 1/5 string length, the corner will be much more rounded than when strong pressure is used towards the bridge, and this is the main reason why bowing near the fingerboard produces what we may call a rounder, sweeter sound, while bowing with the high pressure required nearer the bridge produces a richer sound with more edge. This obvious difference in the sound, due to the levels of the higher harmonics, survives all subsequent changes in the vibration produced by the bridge or violin body. Also, whatever shape of corner is generated by the bow, reflection from a soft finger rounds the corner further, compared with the more precise reflection from the hard nut; open string tone has noticeably more edge. Players try to avoid open strings unless the music indicates otherwise. On the bass, open string tone can be softened by holding the finger lightly on the string by the nut, which reduces the high harmonics. There is more precise reflection from the frets of viols, but the inherent edge is mitigated because only light bow pressure is possible.

In addition to the modification of the corner, a number of secondary factors make the vibration, and consequent sound, slightly irregular. These are discussed in Sections 16–19 below.

## 2.10. *Friction*

The ability of the bow to move the string depends on friction, which is provided by rosin. The friction between two surfaces is directly proportional to pressure. It may not be so obvious that it is independent of the area of contact between two things. If that is so, why use the edge of the ribbon for the lowest dynamic? The pressure of the bow would be the same on the larger area with the bow flat. Each bow hair has to be considered as a separate element, and for a given bow pressure, the pressure per hair in contact is higher when on edge; if very low pressure is distributed across the entire ribbon, the friction per hair is so low that the bow skates. So for maximum friction, all the hair should remain attached throughout the 'stick' phase. If the bow is rotated—the bow hand is moved towards or away from the player's head during the stroke—the hair on one or other side of the ribbon must move relative to the string and become unhitched, and it will not contribute to holding the string until it reattaches. The total sticking during the stroke will be smaller, and the bow will release earlier so that the displacement will be smaller. Bowing should be in a straight line. It follows that the chance of bowing at the same distance from the bridge will also increase if the straight line is at right angles to the string, which is a characteristic of good bowing.

However, even if the bow is moving in a straight line across the instrument, the angle of the string changes during the 'stick' part of the bow stroke, so that there must be some unhitching and rehitching of the string. This appears to be accommodated without much noticeable effect when bowing between the end of the fingerboard and lightly at the 1/10 position, but when the bow is used at high pressure, the angular change during the stroke is significant, and the string may jump in steps, creating large random 'spikes' on the vibration wave. This effect is sometimes produced by skilled soloists playing at the highest dynamic close to the bridge, and, curiously, it seems to add brilliance to the sound. It is in complete contrast to what happens when the wrong pressure is used in normal bowing.

If too-high speed is used with low pressure, the bow skates instead of gripping the string and produces a variety of high-pitched noises which are a combination of frictional whistles and the string vibrating in different modes. If too-high pressure is used with low speed, a different kind of nasty noise is produced. This is characteristic of beginners who assume that pressure alone will go on increasing dynamic.

The explanation lies in the 'slip' part of the action. There is friction between bow and string while the string flies back. If you try to slide a weight along a surface, it requires a larger force to start it moving than to keep it moving, but there is still friction when it is moving. The static friction between surfaces is always greater than the sliding friction between them, otherwise the bow would not work. The string is stationary relative to the bow while they grip—static friction—but during slipping there is sliding friction. Pressure increases both kinds of friction with the added disadvantage that, like the brakes of a car, the slipping friction takes energy out of the string and if too great, may make similar noises to brakes. The bow in its energizing stroke has to replace both the energy lost to the body and the energy lost through sliding friction.

One especially significant matter concerning bowing can now be appreciated. Any variation in speed or pressure during a stroke will vary the amplitude of the vibration and of the sound produced *from instant to instant.* The uniformity which expert bowing can produce is a very large factor in the attractiveness of the sound heard. On the other hand, if a note of one pitch is expertly bowed, the measured rate of vibration remains surprisingly similar whether the string is lightly or very strongly bowed. Why surprising? If you place a left-hand finger half-way along a string to get the octave of the open string, is not the same length of string vibrating, however hard it is bowed? Yes—except that if you put your finger there you will not get an octave! For an octave, the string must be stopped appreciably nearer the bridge than half-way; the length of string from the stopping finger to the bridge is only one of the factors which determine the pitch. That is why we should not automatically assume that pitch will be the same for light and strong bowing. This phenomenon is discussed in Section 15 below.

## 2.11. *Noise*

'Noise' is a word with many meanings; here we are using it for random pitchless sound. However well a string is bowed, the friction during slipping always generates some noise, which is best described as a slight hiss. It is often thought that the characteristic buzz of the lower strings of cello and bass is due to friction, but it is not present in the sound and there is no way of eliminating it. It is explained in Chapter 6 that this is created in our hearing mechanism by string sound. Noise does increase at very high pressure when bowing close to the bridge, but part of this is generated by the changing string angle. The instruction to bow *sul pont.*, which literally means 'on the bridge', is used casually by composers. It can mean that the player should bow very closely to the bridge with very high pressure and acceptable tone. If it is combined with tremolo and the bow is moved rapidly back and forth, the string vibrates abnormally and generates only its higher harmonics mixed with noise.

## 2.12. *Starting a Bowed Note*

Starting a string from stationary is one of the many difficult things a player has to learn. The bridge only takes a small fraction of the energy out of the string in each cycle, so that to start the string and get it up to the required steady level, the rest of the energy has to be put in, built up by increased bow input, which has then to be reduced when the required level has been reached. There are some illuminating figures for starting a violin D string from silence. With slow bowing close to the bridge it takes nearly half a second to build up to full vibration at 30 gm bow pressure, but only 1/20 second at 120 gm bow pressure. Bowing at the fingerboard, 30 gm pressure will get the string to full vibration in 1/50 second. Any sound of less than 1/20 second duration can be regarded as a starting transient: the period when hearing is much more concerned with identifying the changing sound than with its tone. Anything longer than that becomes a weak starting sound or a crescendo on the note.

It follows that in most circumstances when starting a note from silence, the player has to produce greater initial pressure and speed to get the string up to the required dynamic. This is unlikely to be a problem on the violin at high dynamic at 1/10 string length. Starting a low-dynamic note is a more difficult matter, and it is essential to give the string an initial starting impulse. This is more readily achieved with the heel or tip of the bow, where the hair is less flexible than in the middle.

Starting from silence is a bigger problem on the cello and bass because much more energy must be fed into a heavy high-tension string to get it up to the required amplitude. Cellists often talk about 'picking up the string'. The obvious thing would be to give the string a strong tweak to kick it into vibration. But the precise way in which the string is started has other consequences (see Section 16 below). Starting technique is especially important in ensemble playing whenever notes should begin 'on the string', that is, with the bow already touching the string. A problem in teaching the more subtle aspects of bowing is that they are not easily described, and demonstrating something which takes only a fraction of a second, like starting a cello string note, does not always work; there may be a future for slow-motion video tapes, such as are used in golf schooling.

A complex situation arises when the bow stroke is reversed on a string already vibrating normally. The direction of the 'stick' phase is reversed, and the corner has to travel in the opposite sense, but this does not mean that the stored energy in the string is removed. It is bound to produce a larger transient sound than changing the pitch during a bow stroke, but good players can reduce the discontinuity to a low level or emphasize it for phrasing and rhythmic purposes by bow control. This is an essential skill when a bass instrument has to produce a long sustained pedal note and the stroke must be reversed repeatedly.

### 2.13. 'Touch' Harmonics

Players use the word 'harmonic' for the sound produced by bowing whilst touching the string lightly at places such as half, one-third, and one-quarter of the way along it, giving pitches at roughly the octave, octave and fifth, and double octave of the open string. The sound is thin, and sometimes called silvery. Players can also produce what they call artificial or false harmonics (musical jargon can be quite illogical) when the string is normally stopped and touched simultaneously in an appropriate place towards the bridge. This phenomenon was, and usually still is, explained by the 'loop and node' theory (see Section 2 above), but it does not happen that way. It will avoid confusion if we use the Italian term *armonico* for this phenomenon, so that we can restrict the term harmonic to a component of a sound (which the Italians sensibly distinguish as *armonica*).

When an octave *armonico* is strongly bowed on a cello and observed by stroboscopic light, it appears as though a corner runs up the string in the usual way, but when it reaches the touching finger, the corner is partly reflected and part runs past the finger to the nut. The touching appears to be light enough to allow passage but firm enough to produce some reflection. There is a corner on each half-string, both moving at normal speed. The corners reach bridge and nut simultaneously and return to the finger simultaneously. A corner arrives at the bridge twice as often as on an open string; the string swings at the bridge with about twice the frequency of the open string, so the pitch is about an octave above the open string. And all the harmonics in the sound have about twice the frequencies of the harmonics of the open string.

Similarly, when a finger touches the string at one-third-length from the nut, each corner seems to be part reflected and part transmitted there. In the time in which the reflected corner gets to the bridge, the transmitted corner has been to the nut and back to the finger. When that corner arrives at the bridge, another is up to the finger again. There are three equally spaced corners travelling along the string at normal speed, and they arrive at the bridge three times as often as for a bowed open string. The bridge is therefore vibrated at about three times the rate of the open string and the pitch is therefore about an octave and fifth above the open string.

## 2.14. *The Pitch of 'Touch' Harmonics*

Almost every experienced player says that *armonici* are out of tune and that they are flat. They are. By the old 'loop and node' explanation, one would expect *armonici* to be in perfect intervals; nor does it help that a normally bowed stiff string's harmonics are not quite in perfect intervals, because the higher harmonics are sharp and not flat. This behaviour of *armonici* introduces some rather puzzling things about both playing and instruments. If we limit discussion to the octave *armonico* we can avoid argument about perfect and tempered intervals; an octave is a doubling of frequency. In the experiments decribed here, the pitches were measured in the following way. A pure tone was sounded, using a variable-frequency oscillator, and it was matched to the fundamental of the bowed open string by elimination of beats. The oscillator frequency was read on a frequency meter. The oscillator frequency was then similarly matched to the bowed octave *armonico*. On gut or synthetic cored strings of a cello, this *armonico* was about 2 per cent (nearly a third of a semitone) flat compared with the theoretical perfect octave of the open string. A similar result was obtained with the bottom two strings of a viola. These results eliminate another suggestion sometimes made, that *armonici* seem flat because people like sharp (often called stretched) octaves, or have been acclimatized to them by pianos; if that is so, *armonici* will seem even flatter.

Touching around the mid-point switches the string from a one-corner to a two-corner mode of vibrating; that has something in common with the 'loop and node' idea. But on a cello it can be switched by touching it anywhere over a band of about four centimetres. The string determines that vibrating with two evenly distributed corners is one of its stable forms of vibrating. Indeed, having started the string in the two-corner mode, one can sometimes maintain it in that mode by continuing to bow after the touching finger is removed. There is a 'best place' to touch it, which can be found by using the edge of a piece of card. But it is not in the middle of the string. Depending a little on the material of the cello string, it is 10–12 mm *nearer* the bridge. A similar thing is true for all four members of the family in proportion to their size. If the string length from the 'best place' to the bridge determined the pitch, the *armonico* would be sharp, not flat. The phenomenon is not my discovery. In 1867 Sir William Huggins demonstrated to Helmholtz that the 'best place' for the octave *armonico* on his violin was not mid-string, and indeed it differed by nearly 5 mm between the four strings (which places he marked with Chinese white on the fingerboard of his Stradivarius *Lady Huggins*!).

Some cellists have told me that they are not happy about using the same touching-place for bowed and pizzicato *armonici*. By testing with the edge of a card, one finds that the string must be touched within a band of less than 10 mm, instead of anywhere over 4 cm. If similar circumstances occur in proportion on the higher instruments, the margin of difference is probably so small as not to be noticed, but on the two lower instruments the difference in position appears to be real. These phenomena emphasize a fundamental point about playing instruments with bowed strings.

## 2.15. *Playing by Hearing*

We have been mainly concerned with bowing so far, and have said little about the left hand. When we want to bow a note which is the octave of an open string, we put a finger on the string where our hearing says that the note is at the octave. The fact that that is not half-way along the string, but some millimetres nearer the bridge than half-way (the amount depending on which instrument is played), does not appear to be widely known amongst players, nor do they need to know—though if they teach classes anything about strings, they might hesitate about saying that the octave is produced by a half-string length, for it is not that difficult for a junior budding scientist with a good sense of pitch and a tape-measure to discover on a cello or bass that it is not so. None of the pitches produced by a bowed string appear to correspond exactly with the simple theory of lengths of string; the left hand creates the lengths which produce what hearing says are the right pitches, and if hearing doesn't, there are instruments with fixed or with indefinite pitch which can be recommended.

We can only suggest that a bowed string behaves like this because the bridge vibrates. A string certainly produces pitches corresponding to its measured length if it vibrates between two rigid bridges. A bowed instrument works because the bridge rocks with the string; if the bridge end of the string moves, the string apparently behaves as though it had a 'fixed' end beyond the bridge. This does not mean that there is a stationary place somewhere along the tail of the string connected to the tailpiece. A plucked string appears to behave slightly differently, but still behaves as though it is longer than its measured length. The behaviour of the electric guitar, with a rigid bridge on a rigid body, conforms closely to theory, which is why its frets can be positioned with mathematical accuracy, though even there, the best bridges have individual adjusters so that small corrections can be made to the different strings.

The bowed octave *armonico* appears to confirm the reality of the phenomenon, because the player has no control over the effective length of the open string, and the left hand is not stretching it or interfering in any way. The 'best place' is, presumably, at the mid-point of the effective length of the string. We do not know where the effective end is, but the half-length must be the distance from the nut to the 'best place'. The measured pitch appears to be produced by that length, which would indeed make it flat compared with a perfect octave of the bowed open string, but of course the bowed open string must have a pitch determined by its effective length too. In normal playing, the player is unaware of effective lengths; all such phenomena are accommodated in the process of placing the left-hand fingers where hearing dictates that the pitches are appropriate to the music. The effective length does appear to depend to some extent on the kind of string, on the pitch played, on the way in which the string vibrates the bridge, and therefore perhaps on the body too. In view of all that, perhaps it is a little surprising that the effective length and therefore pitch remain virtually the same, however lightly or strongly one note is bowed. It is also fortunate for the player; some brass and wind instruments are not so accommodating.

This obviously provides one of several reasons why the violin family are not fretted; perhaps if Mersenne actually did have as remarkable hearing as his writings suggest (described in A. Wood, *The Physics of*

*Music*; see Further Reading), and if he had used bowed strings, we might even doubt whether he would have formulated the simple laws relating the length, weight, and tension of strings to their pitch early in the seventeenth century (see Chapter 11). But it is fortunate that *armonici* can be elicited over a small range of touching-positions, because players inevitably touch at places corresponding to the normal stopping-positions. And most important, we don't play bowed instruments by physical laws; we play them by hearing.

### 2.16. *The Twisting String*

Amongst the minor variations imposed on the basic vibration of a real string, one of the more important is that the bow twists the string as well as moving it sideways. The string is a cylinder; the bow pushes on the upper side of it and 'winds it up'. At high bow pressure it can be twisted through a considerable angle, and it spins back by a similar amount in the other direction when it is released. This produces a 'ripple' on the wave form of the string. It may also vibrate the bow hair. Twisting takes energy from the bow which would otherwise go into moving the string sideways to create normal force on the bridge. Theory and practice offer contrasting views about this. On the one hand, it is said to be helpful if some of the string energy is removed, and that it assists in stabilizing the bowed mode of vibration. On the other hand, the larger the diameter of the string, the greater the twisting; advanced players can sense string diameter by bowing, which is said to be sensing twisting, and modern string manufacturers are devoting considerable effort towards finding further ways of reducing string diameter (see Chapter 11.7).

### 2.17. *More about Pizzicato*

The sound of pizzicato is quite different from that of the bowed string. It is a very characteristic sound, but we cannot really describe its tone, because the harmonics are continuously changing as the vibration rapidly decays (see Chapter 6). We can, however, apply the same ideas about the sharpness of corners to them. The string may be displaced far more than in bowing, but the soft part of a finger cannot produce a sharp corner. What we hear when a string is sharply bent is demonstrated on the upper instruments by the rarely used nail pizzicato, which makes a sharper triangle and a sound with more high harmonics. The 'attack' of the pizzicato sound does depend on the initial high harmonics, and since a stiff steel string cannot be bent sharply, this is one of the reasons why pizzicato on a steel strung bass is a dull noise compared with the magic of a gut string. In all pizzicato, as the vibration decays and the string shape becomes smooth loops, the high harmonics disappear and the 'edge' disappears with it. Vibrato with pizzicato absorbs string energy, and contrary to the belief of some conductors (even bass-playing ones) vibrato curtails rather than extends the duration of pizzicato sound. Pizzicato also involves another property of the vibrating string: precession.

### 2.18. *The Precession of Strings*

So far we have assumed that a string vibrates entirely in the plane of the bow hair. Even without the problem of 'picking up' the string (see Section 12 above), the very act of putting the bow on the string can give it some displacement other than in the bowing plane. This will cause the plane in which the string vibrates to try to rotate as the corner travels up and down. If this were unrestrained, the direction of swing could change until the string vibrated at right angles to the fingerboard, then parallel to the bow and so on. This behaviour is called **precession**. It happens in every pizzicato, and if one watches a light-coloured cello or bass string against the dark fingerboard, the envelope of vibration appears to contract and expand as its plane rotates. The vibration of the bridge is different—and smaller—when a string vibrates at a different angle to the bowing line, and for maximum attack, pizzicato should always start the string vibrating parallel to the fingerboard (unless a slap is required). Since all plucked strings precess, it is only the rapid rate of decay that prevents them from hitting the fingerboard as their plane of rotation changes.

In normal bowing, if the string tries to precess it will 'fight the bow'; the bow will damp the vibration and the elastic bow hair will interact with it. This is another feature of the irregular sound produced by beginners who apply uneven bow pressure. Experiments carried out with the cellist Caroline Bosanquet, using both stroboscopic observation and time-exposure photographs of strings whitened with chalk, showed marked differences in the extent of precession, depending on how the player started the string in motion. Starting on the string reduces the tendency to precess. Precession is bound to occur in spiccato bowing.

## 2.19. *Regularity and Variation*

Detailed investigation of the bowed string seems to suggest a paradox. The basic art of bowing is the production of the mode of vibration which creates the sawtooth wave at the bridge, with greater or less emphasis of its higher harmonics. This can then vary in three ways: in amplitude, frequency, and an irregularity superimposed on the individual cycles of the waves. The most important single feature of skilled bowing, which takes so much practice to develop, appears to be the control producing smooth uniform pressure and speed throughout the stroke, which is remarkably even over the wide range of speeds and pressures employed, even when compared with the bowing of a moderately competent amateur player. In other words, what we might colloquially describe as the quality of the sound seems to be associated with minimizing amplitude variation during the sustained part of a note.

Frequency variation from cycle to cycle appears to have a different role. Players purposely introduce pitch change by vibrato, which is held to increase the attractiveness of the sound when it is at a level of around 1/6 semitone, which some listeners do not perceive as an actual pitch change, but wider vibrato can be obtrusive. However, random frequency variation occurs all the time. Two investigators found that when a very skilled player specifically tried to maintain an absolutely constant note, the fundamental varied irregularly by slightly more than 1/20 semitone on an open violin G, and by more than 1/10 semitone on the same string finger-stopped; the variation in normal skilled playing would of course be somewhat greater. A mechanical bow is said to produce more variation still. My own observations of some expertly bowed notes suggest that the frequencies of all the harmonics continually vary irregularly in this fashion. Frequency variation is a characteristic of making any string vibrate in a forced way and has been measured on strings of several different kinds of instrument. There are then the variety of small and apparently random irregularities on each successive wave; the causes of some have been mentioned, though the largest amount appears to be due to the unhitching and reattachment of the string as its angle changes under the bow. As we shall see in Chapter 6, these continual small irregularities and the frequency variation, produce a vital part of what distinguishes real bowed sound from a sound with constant frequencies, which has an unvarying wave form exactly the same as that of any string sound over any one cycle.

## 2.20. *Coda*

The reader who is interested in the complex details of string behaviour
(and mathematically competent) will find a comprehensive discussion in
*The Physics of the Violin* by Lothar Cremer, which includes accounts of
some of the fine research by workers such as McIntyre, Schelleng,
Schumacher, and Woodhouse. Explaining the many irregular variations
imposed on the basic mode of vibration is an intriguing subject to physicists. Fortunately, what they specifically are does not appear to matter,
musically speaking—as long as they do happen.

It is not suggested that a skilled player need know anything in this
chapter, but bowing is a most difficult technique to acquire, and it is not
always easy to explain to pupils what the right limb has to do. There
are some learners who can be helped to overcome problems if some of
the things which happen when a string is bowed are explained to them.
One must be very careful, however, to avoid any suggestion that playing is a mechanical process; we play by musically sensitive hearing.

# 3

# The Bridge, Soundpost, and Tailpiece

◆◆◆❖◆◆◆

## 3.1. *The Bridge*

The bridge transfers the vibration of the string to the body and plays a much larger part in determining tone than is often recognized. We saw in the previous chapter that it is also involved with pitch. A well-cut, perfectly fitting bridge of the right weight is essential. Would that every player appreciated that a good professionally cut bridge is also precious. The bridge has one foot near the point where the front is supported internally by the soundpost; the other foot is over the bass bar, a beam along the inside (Fig. 3.1). In the playing position the violinist and violist see the soundpost side on their right; the cellist and bassist see it on their left. In the figures the bass bar is marked Bb and the soundpost Sp.

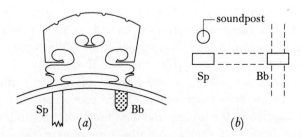

FIG. 3.1. The violin bridge: (*a*) Face view with section of bass bar; (*b*) from above, showing position of soundpost towards the saddle.

## 3.2. *Physical Terms*

The strings produce two kinds of force on the bridge: *static* forces, present in the silent instrument, and *dynamic* ones, due to bowing, which rock the bridge. We shall use words for the forces as people normally think of them—which will be different from the terms used in academic physics. Physics defines force as that which accelerates a mass through a distance, but the force of silent strings pushing down on a bridge is not moving anything anywhere. Most people think of it as pressure. That is what we shall usually call it. It means pressing directly downwards, and avoids the need to say 'a force acting directly downwards' every time. It is easiest to think of it as a weight in kilograms on the top of the bridge. Similarly, the bow pushes down on the string, and everyone calls that **bow pressure**; when we say a bow pressure of 20 gm, it means a force equivalent to putting a 20 gm weight on a *horizontal* string, in order that gravity acts in the direction in which the bow presses. **String tension** is also a force; if we say the tension of a cello string is 20 kgs, it means the tension that would be produced if the string hung like a pendulum with a 20 kgm weight on the end. Finally, we are going to say that objects have **weight**. In physics, a violin bridge has a mass of 2 gm, because it would still require force to move it if it was in space, where there is no gravity, and it did not have any weight. We are only concerned with playing a violin on planet Earth.

### 3.3. *Calculating Forces*

To understand the bridge we need to know what kind of pressures the strings produce on the body, and the force the bow produces on the top of the bridge causing it to rock. Values are given in the text below. The reader need not be concerned with how these are obtained, but for those who may be interested there is a simple method by drawing, known as the triangle of forces, explained in Fig. 3.2. If we know the size of a force and its direction, such as the tension of a string, the method provides values for how much of that force acts in another direction, such as downwards on the bridge, and how much of it is pulling at right angles to the bridge at the top, in the direction of the nut or the saddle.

What often surprises those unfamiliar with splitting a force into the forces it produces in two other directions is that, for example, a string with 10 kgm tension produces 9.9 kgm at right angles to the bridge top and 1.5 kgm bridge pressure; they 'add up' to more than the original force. If two people tow a car by pulling straight ahead, each provides half the force. If they are foolish and each pulls at 45° to the direction

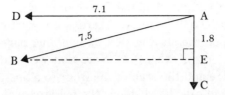

FIG. 3.2. The triangle of forces. The pressure produced on the bridge by a string of known tension, and the force applied at the top of the bridge, can be obtained by a scaled drawing. Suppose we have a string with tension of 7.5 kgm. Any suitable scale can be used: if we choose 1 kgm = 1 cm, we draw a line (AB) 7.5 cm long in the direction of the string. Draw a line (AC) in the direction of bridge pressure. From the other end (B) draw a line making a right angle (at E). If AE is 1.8 cm, bridge pressure is 1.8 kgm. The length of EB gives the size of the force (AD) pulling at right angles to the top of the bridge. In this example EB is 7.1 cm = 7.1 kgm.

in which the car moves, each has to pull nearly one and a half times as hard to produce the same force straight ahead.

## 3.4. *Static Forces on the Bridge*

The static forces on the bridge are large. We can calculate them (using triangles of forces) from the angles which the strings make on either side the bridge (Fig. 3.3). The dimensions used for calculations here are from a full-size scale drawing of the Stradivarius *Messiah* as set up by Messrs Hill in 1926, but violins are very much alike in these dimensions, and we want to know magnitudes, not milligrams. And if we find the forces produced by a string with 10 kgm tension (typical of a steel

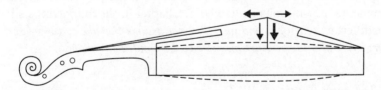

FIG. 3.3. Bridge pressure. A line from nut to saddle and a line continuing the bridge to it (the bridge+arch distance) make two triangles with the strings and tailpiece system. Each triangle gives the bridge pressure produced by the strings on that side; these must be added. They also give the forces in either direction at right angles to the top of the bridge, which are not the same (see Section 20 below).

violin E), we can assume that the forces produced by a string with 5 kgm tension will be half of these. There is one part of the static force due to the string on the playing side, and another part due to the string tail and tailpiece on the other side. Note that we must use a line down through the bridge and the arch of the front to a line joining the nut to the saddle; we shall call this distance the **bridge+arch** height. **Arching** is used descriptively for the general convexity of the front (and back), and specifically for the maximum height of the surface relative to the edges. The string pressure on the bridge is determined by the bridge+arch height, not just by the bridge. A string with 10 kgm tension produces a static pressure down on the top of the bridge of about 1.5 kgm due to the playing side, and 2.8 kgm due to the steeper angle on the tailpiece side, a total of about 4.3 kgm. A string with 5 kgm tension produces half that pressure on the bridge.

The force at right angles to the bridge at the top in the direction of the nut is about 9.9 kgm—in other words, it is so close to 10 kgm that the bridge+arch height does not affect it significantly. Theoretically, it is the 9.9 kgm force of the string whose change in angle produces bridge vibration. It would hardly be changed if the bridge were 5 mm higher, but that would increase the pressure on the front from about 0.43 to about 0.48 kgm for every kilogram of string tension. The bridge+arch height is very important. On the other hand, because the tailpiece side is at a steeper angle to the bridge, it produces less force at right angles to the bridge top than the playing-side strings; there is a permanent static force trying to tilt the bridge towards the playing side. We consider this towards the end of the chapter.

Typical tensions of most violin and viola strings are less than 10 kgm; for cello and bass they are greater. Table 1, at the end of the chapter, gives some typical string tensions and bridge pressures for all the instruments. For reasons explained in Chapter 4, the four strings should be at different tensions, *and one must not assume that the static pressure on the bridge is also the pressure on the bass bar and the soundpost.*

### 3.5. *Dynamic Forces on the Bridge*

The dynamic forces rock the bridge in the plane of the bridge. Because of the very small angle through which the string swings, these forces can be assumed to be proportional to the string's angle with its resting position (Fig. 2.9). We do not need to know the size of these forces, but they are very much smaller than bridge pressure. (If we displaced a 10 kgm tension string from its resting position to half a millimetre, at 20 mm from the bridge, the force on the bridge would be about 250 gm.) The string vibration force acts *along the line of bowing* and changes in the pattern of the wave we discussed in Chapter 2. If we halve the string tension, a given bow speed and pressure moves the string about twice as far before it unhitches. The rocking force is proportional to tension and to distance moved, so it remains about the same. This is a self-compensating system. The strings should have quite different tensions, but the same bowing produces about the same rocking force along the line of bowing, whichever string is being played.

### 3.6. *The Bowing Angle*

Fig. 3.4 shows the bowing lines for the strings on a violin bridge. The actual bridges measured were a violin bridge cut by W. H. Luff for a 1780 Gagliano (price £280!), a viola bridge cut by J. & A. Beare for a Stradivarius, and a cello bridge cut by Withers of Leicester Square for a Testore; alas, we own only the bridges. The bowing lines are determined by the positions of the strings, the height of the bridge, and the edges of the instrument body (and to a degree, the player). To work out how bowing rocks the bridge, we consider the bass bar side first. The soundpost foot is a pivot and the bridge rocks about it, causing the bass bar foot to move up and down, vibrating the bass bar. We can think of this as being rather like using a spanner on a very small scale. To obtain the full effect of pushing or pulling, the force must be *at right angles* to the handle of the spanner. The string would only apply the whole

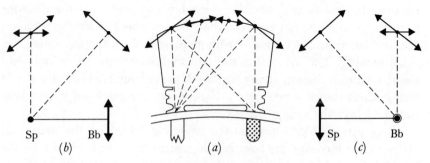

FIG. 3.4. Bowing forces on the bridge: (*a*) bowing lines of the four strings; (*b*) rocking forces of top and bottom string about the soundpost as pivot; (*c*) rocking forces about the bass bar as pivot. (See text.)

vibration force to rocking if it was bowed at right angles to a line join-ing the string groove to the pivot, that is, to the soundpost foot. At any other bowing angle, the portion of its vibration force applied to rock-ing is correspondingly smaller.

Fig. 3.4 shows that the bottom string can be bowed roughly at right angles to its line to the soundpost foot; all its vibration force is applied to rotating the bridge about that foot. The other strings are bowed along lines which depart from a right angle to their lines to the pivot, and the departure gets greater as one goes from the D to the top string. Their contributions to rocking are reduced accordingly. In round terms, the G, D, A, and E respectively apply about 100, 95, 85, and 75 per cent of their vibration force to rocking about the soundpost foot.

### 3.7. *The Bridge Ratio*

If all the strings were the same distance from the soundpost foot, those figures would give the forces on the bass bar foot for equal bowing; but each string is a different distance away from the soundpost foot (Fig. 3.4). Rocking round a pivot works like a see-saw: a small boy can raise a large boy because a small force a long way from the pivot produces just as much force as a large one close to it. So the effect of a string's force will be greater, the further it is from the pivot: the soundpost foot. On a violin, the top string is about the same distance from the sound-post foot as the distance between the centres of the bridge feet. The vibration force it applies to the bass bar foot is its force at right angles to the pivot line: 75 per cent of its total vibration force. The bottom string is much further from the soundpost foot; its full force, because it is bowed at right angles to the pivot line, is multiplied by about 5/3. Putting the two factors together—the bowing angle and the distance from the pivot—the net result is that there is about twice the force on the bass bar from the bottom string as there is from the top string, for equal bowing. The values for the two middle strings are in between: about 1.3 times the top string for the A, and about 1.7 times for the D string. Equal bowing produces progressively greater force on the bass bar, the lower the string.

These ratios hold, whatever the sounding length of the individual strings. The force on the bass bar is greater from an E played on the bottom string than from an E of the same pitch played on the D string, for equal bowing. The ratios have a significant effect on the vibration of the body; as we shall see (Chapter 6.26 and 27), they cause the four strings to have different sound outputs from each other. All the values for the viola are almost identical to those for the violin.

We call the figure for the distance from foot to string, divided by the distance between the centres of the feet, the **bridge ratio**. These ratios, and therefore the forces produced on the bass bar, are smaller if the bridge is low because the arching is high. And they are much bigger on cello and bass because their bridges are high, compared with the distance between the centres of their feet.

The bowing angles for the cello and four-string bass are very similar to the angles at which the corresponding strings of a violin are bowed (Fig. 3.5). On the other hand, the bridge ratios, the amounts by which

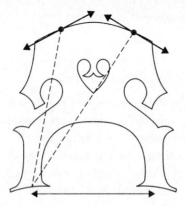

FIG. 3.5. Cello bowing angles. The bowing lines of cello strings are similar to the violin. The bridge is high compared with the distance between the feet.

the effective forces are multiplied, are about 1.25 for the top string and 1.55 for the bottom string. These larger bridge ratios enable the bow to produce greater force on the larger thicker front. There is of course a price to be paid. A small boy may be able to lift a boy twice his weight on a see-saw, but when he does, he moves through twice the distance. Cello and bass bows have to produce larger string vibration for this reason quite apart from the weight of string and wood involved. A bass bow is short because one cannot produce adequate pressure at a tip any further from the wrist.

A five-string bass needs careful design. To avoid a high bridge the waist must be narrow. Obtaining adequate bowing lines may lead to less force from the outside strings compared with the force available on the four-string variety.

## 3.8. *Forces on the Soundpost Side*

The vibration force on the soundpost bridge foot produced by bowing, can be obtained by considering the bass bar foot as the pivot about which the bridge rocks. The situation is almost a mirror image of the way forces act on the bass bar foot (Fig. 3.4). The top string can be bowed roughly at right angles to its line to the bass bar foot. In round terms, for equal bowing, the top string produces just over twice the force on the soundpost foot that the bottom string applies to it.

Overall, the bridge system distributes string vibration force with a considerable differential to the two sides of the instrument. More force from the higher strings is applied to the soundpost side, and more from the lower-pitched strings to the bass bar side. But all bowing produces force on both feet.

## 3.9. *The Direction of the Rocking Forces*

The feet of the bridge would not act as pivots if the bridge was sitting freely on the surface and was subjected to rocking forces. If that were the case, when the bridge was rocked towards the bass bar, the sound-post foot would lift off the surface instead of depressing the bass bar side. The static string pressure makes the respective feet act as pivots.

In one cycle of string vibration of, for example, down-bowing, the 'stick phase' produces a force downwards on the bass bar and at the same time an upwards force on the soundpost foot. *How much* each foot moves, and therefore how large the vibration is under each foot, depends on the behaviour of the wood under the respective feet. But rocking moves the feet in opposite directions, which suggests that the two sides of the front are being vibrated the whole time in opposite senses. Since this is the movement which produces sound, it appears to be counter-productive, one half producing a rarefaction in the air when the other half is compressing it. The outcome is more subtle.

## 3.10. *The Mechanics of the Soundpost*

The soundpost has been described as the soul of the instrument, but what matters is whether it is in paradise or purgatory—in other words, in the right place. It is at an empirically determined distance towards the bottom of the instrument from the soundpost foot. This is empirical in the sense that the luthier tries various positions on a new instrument or when fitting a post in others, and also because it may be moved to the customer's taste (and sometimes then surreptitiously moved back to its original position, which may be greeted with a delight that can only be explained by a poor memory, or by psychology, in Chapter 6).

The soundpost transmits little vibration to the back; the main role of the back is to provide support for the post to be a rigid point on which the front bears (see Chapter 4.6). The movements of fronts when loaded in different ways are discussed in the next chapter. The soundpost, as well as helping to support the soundpost foot so that the bridge can vibrate the bass bar, is a pivot for another see-saw kind of movement. The front may not be stiffened by a bar on the soundpost side, but the long arch of the front running from saddle to neck over the top of the soundpost is adequately stiff. If pressure on the soundpost foot depresses the front on its side of the post (Fig. 3.6), the front on the

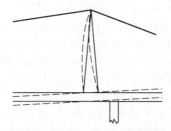

FIG. 3.6. Soundpost mechanics. In principle, the soundpost foot depresses the long arch in each cycle of vibration; the front rocks about the soundpost. When the arch is depressed, the bridge foot follows it (see Section 13 below), but the strings anchor the bridge and it bends.

other side of the post is *raised*. In Section 9 above we saw that when the soundpost foot goes down, the bass bar foot goes up. The result is that in principle the whole of the bass bar side of the front and the lower soundpost side of the front tend to move in the same direction, and only the upper soundpost area of the front moves in the opposite direction to them. How much the soundpost side moves depends on the vibration frequency.

The two kinds of force acting on the front from the soundpost foot are the static string load and the vibration from the string. The further the soundpost is from its bridge foot, the larger are both forces on the long arch towards the top of the front. If the post is close to the bridge, most of the static pressure is on the post, but the vibrating force has very little leverage about the post. If the post is far away from the bridge, the static force on the arch is large and the wood strongly stressed, but the leverage of the vibrating force is also large. The static force of violin strings on the soundpost foot may be about six kilograms, but this is not the size of the force supported by the soundpost and the long arch. If it were, one could never move the post in the way that one can with a soundpost setter, and there would be far too big a force pushing the post into the inside of the back. This apparent contradiction is resolved in the next chapter when the mechanics of the box is discussed.

What we have described in very simple terms is a mechanism by which the force of a string, acting along its bowing line, is changed in direction to operate downwards on two small areas of the front of the box. And broadly speaking, because of the different flexibility under the feet, the low-frequency vibration is introduced on the bass bar side and the high-frequency, on the soundpost side. There is little low-frequency vibration around the soundpost; that is what a good physicist writing for the general reader meant by 'at low frequencies the soundpost induces a node in its vicinity'. The vibration resulting from this system is far more complex than simply that the bass bar side vibrates at low frequencies and the upper soundpost side does so at high frequencies. Investigations using a special method of illumination, called holography, reveal which parts of instruments vibrate strongly and which parts are relatively stationary when the bridge is vibrated by a pure tone of a particular frequency. This method suggests that if one examined the vibration in steps of a few semitones, the pattern would be different at each frequency. When an instrument is played, its front is vibrated simultaneously by a large number of pure tones—all the harmonics of a note. The vibration resulting from this must be expected to bear some sort of resemblance to a pattern which would be created by superimposing the holographs of each of the harmonic frequencies on top of one other, but it is very unlikely that it would be precisely that: a point to which we return later.

The way in which the bowing angle and bridge ratio cause the vibration from the respective strings to produce different vibration of the front can be demonstrated by some simple experiments which are described and discussed in Chapter 6.25 and 27. Altering the conditions under the soundpost foot, by moving the post slightly, does not significantly affect the way in which the soundpost foot acts as a pivot for the bridge to vibrate the bass bar at low frequencies. It affects the sound produced at higher frequencies, and as explained in the following chapters, if the high frequencies in the bottom string's sound are changed, it may appear from listening that the low frequencies have changed too.

## 3.11. *Soundpost Size and Material*

The length of the soundpost is discussed in the next chapter. As to its diameter, Otto, luthier to the Court of Hanover in the middle of the nineteenth century, believed the soundpost should be 'just of such size as could be inserted through the *f*-hole'. Perhaps he never fitted one to a Gaspar da Salo; there is no rationale for putting a gatepost in an instrument with large *f*s. If the island (the area between the *f*-holes) is weak because the wood is thin or the *f*-holes encroach too far, the instrument may need a stronger bass bar, but there is little one can do on the soundpost side. Within reason it does not matter what the post is made of, as long as it is stiff. Spruce is straight-grained; along the grain it is as stiff as most hardwoods, it is lightweight, and if there is a dowel plate to hand, quality waste spruce is available in every maker's workshop. The mechanism suggests that it should produce a 'point' pivot: it should have as small a diameter as it is prudent to bear against the thin front without danger of rupturing and splitting it. Claims have been made for hollow soundposts, waisted soundposts, and so on. If any of these 'improved' an instrument which had no worthwhile resting-place for the soul of a conventional post, perhaps one should suspect the instrument. As with so much else about the violin family, tradition is a nice word for the result of innumerable experiments which selected the best practical soundpost.

## 3.12. *Secondary Forces on the Bridge*

The description given above outlines only the basic principles of what happens. For example, we have taken an average position for the line of the bow when working out the forces rocking the bridge, but when the player moves the bow from string to string in a single bow stroke, there will be small changes in the angle and corresponding changes in the forces operating. Any variation in the bowing-line will introduce further minor variations into the sound.

### 3.13. *Bridge Bending and Twisting*

Provided the bridge is upright, the pressure on its feet from the strings acts directly down on the front, but how the wood under the feet moves depends on the way in which the front is supported. On the soundpost side, any force causes the wood to tilt about the soundpost pivot (Fig. 3.6). The static pressure of the strings ensures that the bottom of the foot follows this tilting movement. The top of the bridge is held in place by the strings. The bridge must therefore bend—and it does. Although the movement of the bass bar side is much more 'up and down', loading experiments show that when the front is depressed at the bass bar foot position, it tilts slightly towards the saddle end of the front. This will tilt the bass bar foot in that direction and cause bending, so that the combined effect is to twist the bridge. One of several important functions of the tailpiece system (see Section 17 below) is to anchor the top of the bridge and minimize the effect of this tilting and twisting on the length and tension of the strings, but this is yet another source of minor variation in string vibration. Because of these complex stresses on the bridge, it is essential that the soles of the feet make an exact fit with the surface of the front. However, a bridge can only be fitted to an unstrung instrument, and as soon as it is strung the static pressure will produce some twisting.

### 3.14. *The Shape of the Bridge*

In order to minimize the effect of bending and twisting, the bridge is made in what may appear to be a highly decorative shape, but this is critical to its function. It must be rigid in the rocking plane, but be flexible from front to back; to achieve this, bridges are made with the grain of the maple running across them. Most of the bending and twisting takes place at the narrow waist. An increase in thickness produces a disproportionately large increase in stiffness, so that bridge thickness is important. It is said that when the bridge bends and twists, some of the energy is absorbed by three little pendulums: the wings on either side and the pendant which hangs down in the middle of the heart. They are certainly flexible enough to vibrate independently. If you hold the top of a bridge between thumb and finger of one hand and press *gently* on one of the wings with the thumb of the other hand, it is flexible in the front-to-back direction, even on a cello bridge, but the wing is quite rigid if you press towards the heart.

The pendant in the heart is similarly flexible (but don't try it; it is very easy to snap it off).

Some luthiers pare the wings: this would raise the frequency at which they naturally vibrate, and one investigator suggested that on a violin bridge they resonate at about 12 kHz, which is well above any sound in which we are interested. It is also said that if they vibrate at different rates they can produce beats (sound with a frequency which is the difference between the frequencies of the two). If this is so—and it is hard to believe—any paring must be done most carefully. However, if an instrument 'screams' (has an over-powerful high-frequency sound), this can sometimes be reduced by cutting away wood from the sides of the bridge waist. The probable reason for screaming is that the bridge and the body have strong resonance at the same frequency (see Chapter 5); reducing the waist would move the bridge resonance away from that of the body.

### 3.15. *The Weight of the Bridge*

Even if the bridge had no strings on it and was standing on an air-cushion, it would still require energy to vibrate it. It requires force to move it in one direction, and when it reverses direction, that energy is lost and a force has to provide energy to move it the other way. The energy used up in vibrating, bending, and twisting the bridge is lost string energy. (One of the main sources of energy loss in a car engine is the continual reversal in the direction of the pistons.) A violin is an inefficient engine and any energy loss is serious. The heavier the bridge, the more energy is lost. If something is rocking, the parts furthest from the pivot, moving through the greatest distance, waste more energy than the parts nearer the pivot. This is why bridges should taper towards the top as much as is prudent. As well as creating pendulums, holes in the bridge reduce weight; the feet of the bridge blank should also be reduced as much as possible in shaping them.

Some remarkable objects purporting to be bridges have been marketed, ranging from lumps of perspex and metal tripods to devices with hinged and screw-adjustable legs. There is no substitute for a properly shaped exactly fitting bridge of high-quality maple. A violin bridge weighs between 2 and 2.4 gm, cut from a blank of 2.8–3 gm. A bridge for a 16 inch (407 mm) viola is 3–3.5 gm, much heavier than a violin bridge. A good cello bridge weighs 17–19 gm, and a four-string bass bridge is 95–110 gm. Otto wrote that he had a bridge of the lightest possible construction, made so that he could attach any of ten tiny box-wood weights to it. He put the bridge on each violin he was asked to set up, and added weights until he found the minimum weight which produced (to his hearing) the best sound. He then cut the violin a bridge of that weight. There is not necessarily virtue in having the lightest bridge one can make; the reason follows.

### 3.16. *The Mute*

If energy is lost in vibrating a bridge of normal weight, more is lost by increasing its weight, and this happens when a mute—a small weight—is added to the top of the bridge. The further the weight from the feet, the greater the muting should be. To demonstrate this, I made a mute of aluminium with two pivoted arms which could be set so that they were either below the bridge top or well above it (Fig. 3.7). The device

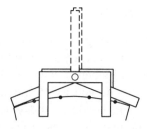

FIG. 3.7. A variable mute. Its weight is fixed, but muting is greater when the arms put more weight above the bridge.

was far more muting when the arms were high above the bridge than when they were at bridge height, though the total weight added to the bridge was constant. It is obvious from the volume of sound produced that a mute absorbs energy, reinforcing the need to make the normal bridge light, but the tone also changes dramatically. Harmonic analysis shows that when a four-gram mute is added to the top of a violin bridge, almost everything above the fourth harmonic disappears. This produces a thinner, 'ethereal' sound. A composer specifying 'con sord.' usually also asks for lower dynamic, and will get it anyway. Muted instruments also produce much less change of tone with bowing position. It follows that a luthier can modify tone to some extent, as Otto did, by selecting the weight of the bridge and, if thought necessary, leaving more wood at the top. A mute is very effective on a bass: rumour to the contrary has been voiced by players who do not possess one.

The weights of commercial violin mutes range from three to five grams; Victorian ones could be ten grams. Although a cello bridge is eight times the weight of a violin bridge, it does not follow that its mute should weigh around 30 gm. The cello bridge is high, and a mute of about 10 gm is sufficient. A mute must grip the bridge firmly. Sliding mutes, secured between two strings on the tailpiece side, are convenient. It should not be assumed that anything wedged between strings on the tailpiece side has no effect on the tailpiece system.

## 3.17. *The Function of the Tailpiece*

When every other part of an instrument seems to be reduced to the minimum weight compatible with function, a hunk of ebony, other hardwood, or nowadays cast metal seems out of place. Yet there are illustrations from as early as the eleventh century, and possibly the ninth, of instruments with a solid object, presumably of wood, connecting the string or strings to the bottom of the body. Viols have always had tailpieces, though usually held at the bottom by a peg rather than a tailgut. Some virtue in attaching the bottom end of the strings in this way must have been discovered at a very early stage in the evolution of instruments with a pressure-operated bridge.

The tailpiece system has a sophisticated and vital function in modern instruments, but we need the principles outlined in Chapter 5 to discuss it. It seems probable that a form of tailpiece came into use for a number of simple reasons and was then found accidentally to have a most beneficial effect which could not possibly have been understood—not the only thing about the violin family which has a touch of a fairy godmother about it. It must have been discovered with early instruments that the bridge ought to be roughly in the middle of the soundingboard, and thus a good distance from the bottom end of the board. Long tails stretch under tension, and if a string does not slide over the bridge when it is tuned, and make the tension the same either side the bridge, the string will slide during playing and the pitch will drop. The shorter the tail, the easier it is to tune and stay in tune. That applies to the modern instrument too. The tail of the string between bridge and tailpiece is conventionally one-sixth of the open sounding length and extends by only one-seventh of the amount by which the string moves over the top nut when tuned.

How much the tailpiece can affect the playing strings was demonstrated by François Chanot, who patented a combined tailpiece and chin rest. Certain difficulties were experienced in tuning, let alone playing. It was his nephew Georges Chanot who taught Heron-Allen, and what is described in the latter's well-known book was his teacher's system, meticulously recorded by Heron-Allen after each lesson.

Because the tails are short, they provide a better anchor on the top of the bridge against the effect of tilting and twisting. It is for other reasons that the bottom strings should have lower tensions than the top ones (see Chapters 4 and 11), but because of this, the tailpiece system applies a stronger anchor to the soundpost side where the bridge is subjected to the greater tilting forces. But otherwise, one's superficial reaction to a tailpiece is that it is 'all wrong'. The tails are at string tensions. They are vibrated by the bridge and could resonate. They pass over an ebony fret on the upper side of the tailpiece which defines their length precisely and makes resonance more likely. Because they are attached to a floating weight they could vibrate at other frequencies too. At least, the tails are wrapped in silk or similar material which will dampen their vibrations. In fact, all these things and the length and weight of the tailpiece are essential to its hidden function, discussed in Chapter 5.14, without which a player would have serious problems controlling the behaviour of the strings. But we may be quite sure that those who introduced a tailpiece a thousand years ago didn't know they had a problem, and that those who arrived by trial and error at something akin to the modern tailpiece a couple of hundred years ago didn't know what problem they had solved. They simply knew that a particular kind of empirically evolved tailpiece produced a great improvement for the player. Although the bridge would appear to be the most likely thing causing the adjustment of the pitch produced by the bowed string (see Chapter 2.15), one cannot discount the possibility that the tails and tailpiece could be involved in that curious phenomenon.

## 3.18. *Double Stops and the Bridge*

The violin, viola, and cello produce unique sound when bowing octaves across a pair of adjacent strings. Two sets of vibrations simultaneously drive the bridge, one of which has component frequencies almost identical with all the even-numbered harmonics of the other. The sound is extremely rich. The phases of the two strings' vibrations (i.e. the times at which the bow sticks and slips) are independently determined by each string's interaction with the bow. The majority of players will not stop the strings to produce an exact octave, but one does not hear beats. The bridge is forcing the strings to vibrate exactly in octaves. A succession of octaves of different pitch is dramatic and has an exceptionally rich sound. The interaction of the two strings can be felt by the player.

With double stop thirds, fourths, and, on the smaller instruments, sixths and sevenths, there is much less coincidence of harmonics; the second harmonic of the upper string of a major third matches the fifth harmonic of the lower string, and there is very little interaction. The sound is far more like that of two independent instruments. It is often said that composers should avoid the double stop fifth because of the difficulty of stopping two strings accurately with one finger, but it is no more difficult than making any other double stop precisely. The reason for avoiding fifths is that players do not like the sound. It causes a reaction of the hearing mechanism and has nothing to do with playing. An explanation is offered in Chapter 6.

### 3.19. *Bridge Creeping*

In Section 4 above we saw that the tailpiece side produces nearly twice the downward static pressure on the bridge that the playing-side strings produce, because of the difference in the angles either side the bridge, and, correspondingly, there is a smaller force perpendicular to the bridge top towards the bottom of the instrument than towards the nut. The difference between the two creates a constant force towards the nut, which can be nearly a kilogram on a violin bridge, depending on the strings' tensions (see Table 1). It is this force, together with the movement of the strings over the bridge when tuned and the vibration of playing, that causes the top of a bridge to creep imperceptibly but continuously towards the nut. A bridge cannot function properly if it leans forwards, but more seriously, if it is not inspected regularly and pulled upright, it will warp and be ruined. Some luthiers rub a little dry soap into the bridge grooves to ease the movement of the strings, but it must be done with caution, as the following experience shows.

On a gut-strung double bass the pressure on the top of the bridge is over 40 kgm and the static force towards the nut is about 5 kgm. A colleague who saw the difficulty I had in pulling a bass bridge upright because of friction in the string grooves proposed an elegant scientific solution: a set of saddles to go under the strings, which he made from the polymer PTFE, a material with extremely low friction. We fitted these and had almost tuned the bass up to pitch when the bridge was projected across the room like a bullet, demonstrating the truth of the definition: force is that which accelerates a mass through a distance. It is only the friction between string and bridge groove which prevents such things from happening to all bridges.

## 3.20. *Coda*

The grain of maple prevents a thin string from splitting the bridge, but also provides the flexibility which is so essential to bridge function. Maple was chosen because it worked, but it would be virtually imposs-ible to produce a synthetic bridge which has all the necessary mechani-cal properties in each direction and also the same weight.

In this chapter we have discussed two items which cost a few pounds and one which costs a few pence. They may not turn a bad violin into a fine instrument, but they will make or ruin a good one.

TABLE 1

Some Typical Values for String Tensions and Forces on the Bridge

---

String tensions of polyamide-cored strings (kgm):

> Violin  G 5; D 5.3; A 5.6; E (steel) 9
>
> Viola  C 5.2; G 5.5; D 5.7; A 8–10
>
> Cello; C 10; G 11; D 12.5; A 14.5
>
> Bass (gut) E 22; A 23.5; D 24; G 26
>
> (steel) E 50; A 56; D 58; G 60

*Note*: Tensions will be appreciably higher for steel-cored strings; the highest quality gut strings for concert performance may also have higher tensions.

Typical static pressure on the bridge from the strings (kgm):

> Violin 10.7; Viola 11.7; Cello 23; Bass 42 (gut) 107 (steel).

Typical static force on the bridge top towards the nut, due to the difference in the angle of the strings either side the bridge (kgm):

> Violin 0.85; Viola 1; Cello 2.1; Bass 4.5 (gut) 11 (steel).

---

# 4

# The Violin Body

$$\blacklozenge\blacklozenge\blacklozenge\maltese\blacklozenge\blacklozenge\blacklozenge$$

## 4.1. *Introduction*

To many people a violin is a beautiful object; to a physicist it is a hideously complex shape. It would be difficult enough to predict its behaviour if it were made of uniform material symmetrically stressed. The complexity of its vibration is revealed by the striking pictures obtained by holography, but these do not explain anything. When the electron microscope first magnified fragments of animals many thousands of times, the pictures were enthralling but they did not explain how the bits worked or whether the structural complexities were significant in how they worked. We find in Chapter 5 that bowed instruments could not work unless they did vibrate in complex ways; that does not mean that any particular way is necessarily significant. Indeed, Cremer concluded that whereas an aviation engineer can generate predictive models of beams, plates, and shells, no such models will ever be possible for the box of a violin. Without pre-empting the conclusions of Chapters 5 and 6, I am quite sure that the most valuable things we know about the violin body were discovered by trial and rejection by the early makers, and that is the origin of everything which makers know from experience are likely to produce a good box. To prevent any misunderstanding, I stress that this chapter is a dispassionate view of the structure and mechanics of the violin body, and not an account of how one should be made.

## 4.2. *Spruce*

The front of the body is the main vibrating structure producing sound in the air. Spruce or similar wood is used for the sounding-board of almost every type of sophisticated stringed instrument. It has a cellular structure of tubes made from enormously long molecules of cellulose wrapped in spirals layer upon layer; more dense materials, including lignin, provide adhesion between the tubes and resistance to compression. This gives wood remarkable strength for its weight. Larger tubes are made in spring growth, while the smaller tubes made in the late summer have more of the dense material between them. This produces the characteristic annual rings across a section, and the alternating darker and paler lines of the grain. Since almost all the tubes run in one direction, up and down the trunk, the mechanical properties along the grain of spruce are very different from those across it.

Instrument spruce is obtained from places where annual growth is slow, such as the north side of mountains above eight hundred metres, but there is little evidence that grain width in adequate-quality spruce affects its mechanical properties significantly. If the fibres are more widely spaced, the tree compensates by making them stronger.

The tubular structure causes two difficulties. One concerns varnish, which is discussed in Chapter 10. The other is that in the tree the tubes are also the main transporting system for water, and their walls are comparatively impermeable. When wood is sawn, the cut ends of the tubes lose water faster than it can move sideways through the timber. It can therefore shrink unevenly as it dries, and split. The drying or seasoning of quality spruce is slowed by sealing the ends with wax. Ideally, wood for fronts will have been cut about five years before it is carved. This is ample time for significant changes to take place. Surprisingly, a well-known maker wrote recently that wood over fifty years old is no good for making violins. There are some fine instruments which are very much older than that. If we use the heartwood of spruce, we often forget that it was biologically dead a hundred years before the tree was felled.

### 4.3. *Arching*

The front is obtained from wedges (Fig. 4.1) which must be sawn so that the grain lies straight along this sawn face. Usually, two adjacent wedges are joined outside to outside to produce a symmetrical front, but violins and violas can have a one-piece front made from a single wide wedge. The fronts of instruments are *carved* out of the solid with the grain running the long way of the instrument, to make shells of more or less uniform thickness. The contour of the front (and back) is called the **arching**. A section through the shell in every direction has the

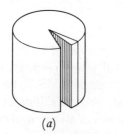 

(a)  (b)

FIG. 4.1. Wood is quarter-sawn (a) for two-piece fronts and backs; one-piece fronts and quarter-sawn one-piece backs are made from a long wedge. Wood is slab-sawn (b) for whole-piece backs.

shape of an arch. If the term goes back to the eighteenth, or even the seventeenth century, when makers could have had little knowledge of mechanics, it was an inspired one.

A violin front is about three millimetres thick, and even before the bass bar has been put in, it is quite stiff along its length, but is very flexible from side to side. When a bending force is applied in the long direction (Fig. 4.2) the fibres on one side are stretched and resist this.

FIG. 4.2. When wood with long elastic fibres is deformed, the fibres on the side away from the load are stretched; the material on the load side is compressed.

There is also resistance to bending on the other side, which is being compressed. Most of the elasticity which causes the wood to regain its shape when the stress is removed, comes from the stretched fibres contracting again; the compressed side could contribute. But there are no long fibres across the grain of spruce; the wood consists of alternate fibre and softer material, and it is therefore flexible and readily deformed and, in comparison, not so elastic. This construction principle was discovered by plants and animals millions of years before man did, and produces the most efficient mechanical system with a minimum of material for the particular organism, but it requires structures many many times more complex than anything man can contemplate making.

## 4.4. *Controlling Flexibility by Carving*

The most important single process in making an instrument is to carve
the spruce of the front to make it stiff where required and flexible where
that is needed. In principle, as much as possible of the front on the bass
bar side should move up and down as a unit. The other side needs to
be sufficiently stiff in the long direction to pivot about the top of the
soundpost, as explained in Chapter 3.10. Bearing in mind that the front
becomes a shell of relatively uniform thickness, the spruce will be
stiffest where the fibres are long, and most flexible where the fibres are
short. Provided the plate starts with the grain parallel to its edges in
the first place, the main area of the front can be made stiffest if it is
carved so that the central part between the *f*-holes is straight, and so
far as possible like part of the surface of a cylinder. If it then slopes gently towards the saddle and nut, the wood will still contain relatively
long fibres. A long thin unsupported arch like this would nevertheless
deform if heavily loaded in the middle, and it is stiffened by the bass
bar, which also has its fibres running its entire length; the bar is thick,
so that there are many fibres to resist stretching. From under the
bridge foot, the bar extends to about three-quarters of the distance to
the top, and three-quarters of the distance to the bottom of the front; it
makes that length of the long arch comparatively inflexible.

The unstrengthened regions beyond both ends of the bar provide the
main flexibility in the direction of the grain. Their flexibility is
increased by carving the wood so that it curves down more steeply
towards the edges, producing wood with short fibres (Fig. 4.3*a*). The
transitions between the straight and curved parts of the arch must be
smoothly made, because any sudden discontinuity is likely to introduce
similar discontinuities in the way the front vibrates. Since the whole
reason for carving a front out of the solid is to determine its properties

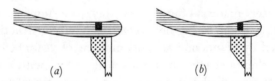

(a)                              (b)

FIG. 4.3. Flexibility of edge regions: (*a*) section through the edge at the bottom of the front, showing short fibres, purfling, and lining; (*b*) the 'scooped'
front is thinner and has even shorter fibres.

by the way the fibres lie and are cut through, an adequate front cannot be made out of laminated wood, or by steam pressing a flat sheet. A small number of makers bend the two spruce wedges into a hollow shape after boiling them in water for some time, and join them when they have dried for a month or so. Whether or not these instruments behave as well as those made in the usual way, it is obvious that the long fibres will run in a curve, and to use them to control flexibility, the wood must be carved to a different shape from a traditional front. One can make things in many ways, but one cannot bend the laws of mechanics.

The flexibility of the ends can be further increased by a 'scoop' inside the perimeter (Fig. 4.3b): this makes the surface lower than the upper edge of the plate, both because it produces more short fibres and because it actually thins the plate in this region, though the shape on the inside obviously also enters into this. In so far as one can rely upon published drawings of sections through fronts of instruments by classical makers, it appears that the Stradivarius pattern of front has a pronounced scoop, whereas the Guarnerius pattern has less and would be less flexible. That may be much more significant than, for example, that the Guarnerius outline is slightly narrower than that of the Stradivarius. There is an interesting LP record with the violinist Ricci playing fifteen famous violins in turn. In a blind test, some listeners picked out three instruments with 'richer tone'; they were all Guarnerius violins of the same period. Players say that Guarnerius-pattern instruments 'require more work' (see Chapter 5.25). This would make sense. A front without much scoop will be stiffer and require more input from the bow to make it vibrate; a stiffer front will favour higher harmonics (see Chapter 6). But one of the three 'richer' violins was Ricci's own favourite Guarnerius, and the player's contribution is more important than the instrument; moreover, on the record, Ricci played different pieces on each violin, so this was not a properly designed scientific test.

Since spruce is so flexible across the grain, there appears to be no physical reason for scooping at the sides of the front. A similar scoop is usually continued along the sides, and may be appropriate for aesthetic reasons, though obviously the scoop cannot extend as far inwards from the purfling where the arch rises from the C-bouts.

## 4.5. *The Flexible Arch*

In the direction of the grain, the front has to be carved to provide adequate flexibility where it is needed; across the grain the question is, rather, what gives the front adequate strength? A violin front looks as though it would collapse under much less force than the many kilograms applied through the bridge by the strings. An isolated front can be tested by placing it on a flat surface and applying forces by means of loaded pivoted arms, pressing via rods of wood about the size of a bridge foot. Before the *f*-holes have been cut or the bass bar put in, a load of only a kilogram placed on the centre line at the bridge position spreads the sides alarmingly (Fig. 4.4*a*). If the C-bouts are constrained with shaped blocks so that they cannot spread, the arch will support 6 kgm applied on the centre line of the bridge position (Fig. 4.4*b*). But if 2 kgm is applied at the bass bar foot position, the soundpost foot area rises, and vice versa. A weak arch with fixed ends distorts if loaded off-centre (Fig. 4.4*c*). After the *f*-holes have been cut and the bass bar put in, it is still spread sideways by a small load if the C-bouts are free, but if the bouts are firmly constrained, the bridge position will support 10 kgm, equally distributed as 5 kgm on the bass bar foot position and 5 kgm on the soundpost foot position (Fig. 4.4*d*) without any form of soundpost substitute under that side of the front. 10 kgm is roughly

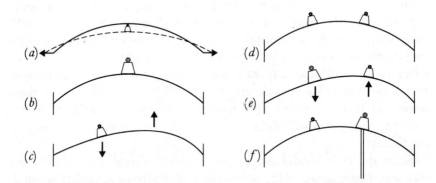

FIG. 4.4. The flexible arch: (*a*) an arch with free ends spreads if lightly loaded; (*b*) with fixed ends, it supports a large load centrally; (*c*) a moderate load depresses one side and the other side rises; (*d*) it supports similar loads symmetrically placed, but (*e*) it is distorted if they are unequal; (*f*) an arch is stable if pinned to a pillar (the soundpost), provided the pinning load is greater than any load on the other side.

bridge pressure on a violin strung with gut or equivalent strings. The island between the *f*-holes communicates its load via the bass bar and the stiff fibres running lengthways along the front to the weak complete arches across the front above and below the *f*-holes, and thence to the sides. But if an extra 1 kgm is then added on the bass bar side, the soundpost foot position rises (Fig. 4.4*e*); an extra 1 kgm added on the soundpost side makes the bass bar side rise.

Although the front has weak arches across the grain, they can support the static string load on the bridge without a soundpost, but the arch is unstable in the sense that any change in the downward force on one side produces a corresponding reaction on the other side. If, however, a support corresponding to a soundpost is placed under the front, *and* an additional 1 kgm is applied over it, the arch behaves entirely differently. Provided the soundpost side is significantly more heavily loaded, changes in loading on the bass bar side which produce depression there have very little effect indeed on the soundpost side. In this sense, the soundpost stabilizes the arch across the front (Fig. 4.4*f*) and makes the two sides comparatively independent of each other under static loads.

What height the weak arch should be above the sides has been argued ever since people thought that they could correlate some simple characteristic they could see, with the sound they heard from an instrument. Leaving aside that one cannot tell anything without knowing, for example, the thickness of the shell, there is no property to which anything can be attributed in isolation. To take the simplest of points, the higher the arch, the lower the bridge must be, which changes many factors. Every property interacts with every other in this empirically discovered mechanical system, which gives rise to very complex behaviour when the box is stressed and vibrated. Other than playing and listening to a violin, the most informative thing is to hold the box in both hands and squeeze the front with the thumbs. That will tell an experienced person far more than anything one can see. It is worth enquiring whether the violin is insured before doing so.

## 4.6. *The Real Pressure on the Soundpost*

Clearly under all circumstances of bridge loading, if one forces a soundpost in it will depress the bass bar side and introduce additional stresses; if the post only just touches the inside of the front, the front will lift off the post with each vibration. For the top of the soundpost to act as described in Chapter 3.10, there must be somewhat greater pressure on the soundpost foot than on the bass bar foot. String tension should be least on the lowest-pitched string and be greatest on the highest-pitched string to produce a difference in pressure on the two feet. It is this difference which is, and indeed should be, the main pressure acting on the soundpost.

Makers very reasonably react with disbelief to the suggestion that the force on the soundpost of a violin is 6–7 kgm while on a cello it may be 12 kgm or more. Those are the sort of forces on the bridge foot, but the force on the soundpost which is pushing it against the back is only one or two kilograms because, broadly speaking, it should be the *difference* between the higher and lower strings' tensions that produces the load shared between the soundpost and the long arch running to the top of the front. The back is an unsatisfactory shape to support a point force of any real magnitude. A flat back on an instrument, usually strengthened by a strut, can work adequately. There is at least one Stradivarius cello with a flat back which is said to have a good voice, and many double basses are made this way. The back is discussed further below.

Sir William Huggins actually demonstrated to Helmholtz in 1870 that the pressure on the soundpost was small, but neither of them realized this from his experiment (see the Dover edition of Helmholtz's *On the Sensations of Tone*, listed in Further Reading). Huggins was concerned to show that the soundpost must be a rigid support for the front, so he removed the post, put a thin layer of rubber on it, and replaced it. This reduced the sound output to a very low level. He then restored much of the sound by applying a force equal to several kilograms across the poor instrument (the 1707 Stradivarius *Lady Huggins*) with a large clamp which crushed the rubber. If the soundpost had been carrying the full pressure of the bridge foot, that would have crushed the rubber anyway and the experiment would not have worked. I related this to Charles Beare, who said that the violin shows no sign of having been treated in this cavalier fashion.

### 4.7. *The Role of String Tensions*

The soundpost mechanism requires the higher-pitched strings to have greater tension than the lower ones, and on the earliest instruments this was almost inevitably the case. One assumes that winding the lower strings with wire, which began well before 1700, was adopted because the sound was more attractive. Wound strings have much less stiffness than large solid gut ones, with correspondingly improved harmonicity (see Chapter 11.5). All this is sophisticated reasoning. Mersenne and Galileo may have discovered the relation between tension and pitch by hanging weights on wires, but the actual tensions of real strings on instruments was not known. It does look as though the asymmetric soundpost system was found to work because, coincidentally, the tensions of the strings happened to be appropriate—another gift of the fairy godmother? Interestingly, when string tensions were measured in the nineteenth century, it was suggested that all four strings ought to be at the same tension, in the mistaken belief that it would produce an even dynamic throughout an instrument's range.

A set of strings from today's reputable makers normally has graded tensions from bottom to top, but players often experiment to discover what strings they like to play on: a combination of what they 'feel' like to bow and what they sound like when bowed in particular ways. That means a great deal to a player—and very little to a scientist. Players may select strings because of their diameter, core, and surface, without knowing their tensions. To make clear the significance of the distribution of tensions, let us take an example. If the tensions of violin strings G–E were 5, 7, 9, and 11 kgm, the total pressure downwards on the bridge would be 14.4 kgm. The differential which the top of the soundpost and the long arch would have to support between them would be 2.7 kgm. If the strings were 6, 7, 8, and 9 kgm tension, the total pressure would be slightly less—13.5 kgm—but the differential would be almost halved to 1.5 kgm. Such situations can certainly be produced with arbitrarily selected mixtures of strings. Although the tensions of cello strings are much higher than those of the violin, the difference between the pressures on the two feet is surprisingly small. This is because the outside strings of the violin are directly over the middle of the respective bridge feet, and each foot carries the full pressure of the string above it. Cello strings are comparatively closer together, and the outside strings are not directly over the feet. Thus a cello with string tensions of 10, 12, 14, and 16 kgm would have a total pressure on the bridge of 23.5 kgm, but the pressure difference operating on the soundpost side would be only about 2.5 kgm. Because the main pressure on the soundpost is this differential, a soundpost can be adjusted easily after lowering the tension of the top pair of strings by a few kilograms.

## 4.8. *The Balanced Front*

Our picture of the mechanism of the front now makes more sense. We saw in Chapter 3.10 that increasing the distance between the soundpost and the bridge foot increased the leverage about the soundpost pivot of both the static force and the vibration force acting on the long arch. If the vibrating force from playing operates in the presence of a static force of only a couple of kilograms, the mechanism appears much more reasonable. Another way of looking at this is that if strings of a different kind are put on an instrument and they produce a different balance across the bridge, the effect on the sound can be somewhat akin to moving the soundpost. In principle the post should be of such length that it fits exactly when the strings on the soundpost side have been brought to the same tension as the strings on the bass bar side of the bridge. When the top strings are then brought up to pitch, the post will bear only the pressure difference due to the higher tension of the upper strings. That is a doctrine of perfection, but it is a situation towards which one might aim.

## 4.9. *The C-Bouts*

The C-bouts perform much of the task of anchoring the ends of the arches supporting the bridge load. One can believe that a waist was introduced simply to facilitate bowing, just as a waist makes a guitar so much more convenient than a lute shape. The first bowed instruments appear to have been flat-fronted; bridge pressure would depress their front and pull the sides in, but as soon as fronts were arched, the shaped rib structures necessary for bowing were also an ideal shape to prevent the front from spreading and cracking under load. We do not know whether anyone understood this dual function, but the waist structure performed an increasingly important mechanical task as string tension, bridge height, and bridge pressure were increased throughout the evolution of the instruments.

## 4.10. *More about Bass Bars*

The bass bar is usually shaped with a slightly greater curvature than the inside of the front, so that it bows the front up very slightly when it is glued in. That apart, one of the absolute rules of making is that every part must fit perfectly before it is glued; if instruments are not so made, they are more likely to come apart during their life because of unusual stresses on the glue, and they are more difficult to repair. If bass bars are not stressed, or if, as one occasionally finds, the inside of the front is carved to leave a piece of the original wood as a beam (called an integral bass bar), the front slowly sinks; in fact fronts with stressed bass bars almost always do sink in the very long term and have to have new bars put in. After gluing, the bass bar is shaped and the ends are chamfered. This prevents a sudden discontinuity in the mechanical properties of the front where it ends, and lessens the possibility of it coming unglued.

It could be suggested that the distortion produced by the bar should be such that the front comes back to its original shape when under the bridge load, producing the natural shape in which it was carved. Every form of stress which is imposed on the box does change its modes of vibration, but it is futile to argue whether one should tension bass bars on acoustic grounds, because, as we shall see, it is one of many things which are unlikely to make any difference to what one hears. There are good practical reasons for springing it.

The strength and thickness of the bar are far more important. When instruments were converted from the baroque to the modern form in the nineteenth century, with higher bridges and string tensions, it is understandable that stronger bass bars had to be fitted, but it is puzzling that they were extended in length—or that they were so short in the baroque design. The modern bass bar must change the flexibility and resonances considerably when a baroque instrument is converted. Other structural changes were made, including a different method of attaching the lengthened neck, but they are unlikely to have significant acoustic consequences. But it is not so remarkable that the classical instruments withstood all these changes so well. Their sides were substantially over-engineered, as so many things in the past sensibly were. It is only today, by what some are pleased to call advanced computerized designing, that the strength of systems is reduced to leave only the smallest margin of safety—or perhaps to build in sufficient self-destruction that articles have to be replaced, sometimes a suspiciously short time after they have reached their guaranteed life.

## 4.11. *The Back*

Temperate hardwoods such as maple are stiffer than spruce in all directions through the wood. They have finer tubes with much more dense material between them and complex transporting structures across the grain called rays. Such wood is much stronger because it has to support a huge weight of leaves and to withstand the stress of wind on them. Although maple and sycamore are the traditional material, beech is sometimes used, especially for basses; there is no reason why other temperate hardwoods of similar density should not be used, and classical makers used a variety of woods. The cost of hardwood is almost directly proportional to the figure and potential beauty, but as a rule, the more complex the structure, the harder the work of carving and the greater the problems which can arise in planing and bending ribs made from it. Some classical instruments have very plain hardwood.

A back can be made from two wedges similarly to a front, or in one piece either from a wedge or from a slab (Fig. 4.1). It is often said that a two-piece back is stronger, but that is the wrong term; it is usually stiffer, and one-piece backs often have to be thicker, making heavier instruments. The back does not have to support an enormous pressure from the soundpost. Usually, the surface of the back is carved as a smooth continuous curve both from top to bottom and across the waist. It may be slightly scooped inside the edges, but the actual shape is largely aesthetic. However, the region between the C-bouts which supports the post should not be scooped to an extent which introduces more flexibility to this region. The back also plays an important part in helping the waist to resist the thrust of the bridge arch. This force tries to push the top of the C-bouts outwards and to tilt the frame of blocks and linings, which is stabilized by the rib (in engineering terms, a web); any actual movement would bend the back.

### 4.12. *Thicknessing*

The external shapes of front and back are determined by carving, and they are then hollowed. For reasons unknown, thinning these plates is called thicknessing. The front is initially uniformly thinned: to 3 mm for violin and viola, 4.5 mm for cello, though the wood between the *f*-holes and the edges is often left a little thicker; it contributes little vibration. Across the area between the C-bouts which supports the post, the back is made nearly twice as thick as the front, and graded uniformly down to thicknesses similar to the front over the upper and lower areas. The plates are then 'tuned': they are suspended as freely as possible and tapped to obtain their resonance pitch. Received wisdom is to thin the front uniformly until it sounds F for violin, middle C for viola, and C an octave lower for cello. This is an empirical recipe for making pieces of wood with a pronounced resonance at roughly 350, 256, and 125 Hz respectively. The pitch is determined by the elasticity and density of the particular piece of wood of that size and shape. It provides just as much as a maker needs to know and in a rapid and simple fashion, but experience takes precedence over resonances or any electronic testing system. If a violin front is likely to attain F before it is thinned to 3 mm, a good maker will already have sensed this while carving it. If a viola front is thinned to 2.5 mm and is still a tone sharp, it is not thinned further. There is no ideal thickness or tap note because there is no ideal piece of wood. One is reminded of Thomas Mace's memorable exposition in *Musick's Monument* when asked how thick the front of a lute should be, that you pare it and pare it until it breaks, and the thickness you should have had was the thickness just before it broke.

Published measurements say that the isolated fronts of some well-known instruments by the finest Cremonese makers have tap notes today spanning a range of a tone either side of the pitches quoted above; we do not know whether they were tested by resonance pitch. (When *f*-holes are cut and bass bar added, the front returns to almost the same resonant pitch.)

Wood is also evenly removed from the back until it approaches an accepted resonance pitch, but if discretion must be used about when to stop thinning a front, it applies *a fortiori* to backs. Some makers believe that backs should sound a semitone sharper than fronts, some that they should have the same pitch. The difference between front and back tap notes of some fine old instruments which have been dissected varies from less than a semitone up to a minor third. This suggests that classical makers decided thickness on sensible grounds; experience is the best judge of adequate flexibility for a front, and warns against reducing the rigidity of the back beyond practicality. Of course once these shells are glued to the ribs and blocks and the instrument is strung, their resonance pitches in isolation have no relevance.

### 4.13. *Symmetry*

It may be thought that the purpose of creating the front from adjacent segments of a tree is to make it physically symmetrical about the centre line. There is no scientific support for this, because in the completed instrument the front is supported, stressed and vibrated entirely asymmetrically, and it does vibrate in that manner at all frequencies. Savart

is reputed to have tested whether such physical symmetry was important by separating the front central joints of two Stradivarius violins and
joining halves from two different instruments together. He said they did
not sound as good as the originals. There are no prizes for criticisms of
his experiment. It would be interesting to know what happened to the
pieces, for there are a number of 'part Strad' instruments in existence.
Some fronts made from two adjacent wedges do not match because a
piece for the bass bar was removed from one of them. It may be important to avoid any sudden changes of thickness, but uniform thickness
certainly does not matter; some of the finest classical instruments'
fronts vary randomly from about 2.5 to 3.4 mm. Some violins and violas with fronts of a single piece of wood, work perfectly well, and at
least one modern maker uses whole-piece fronts, apparently because he
believes they are stronger—whatever that means.

Since there appears to be no good reason for making the front exactly
physically symmetrical, one questions the value of covering a two-piece
front with powder and seeing whether the Chladni patterns which the
particles make when it is vibrated at various frequencies are symmetrical. The remark that this is 'reading the tea-leaves' is probably closer
to the truth than its originator intended, and assiduous use of a measuring calliper will reveal precisely where thickness is uneven far better than irregular Chladni patterns. Something might be revealed by
Chladni patterns on a one-piece front, but if it is asymmetric in behaviour when uniform in thickness, that can only be corrected by making
it asymmetric in thickness. If someone made ten violins with traditional
uniform-thickness two-piece fronts but irregular Chladni patterns, and
showed that none of them behaved well *when played*, there might be a
case for electronics in the luthier's workshop. The many hundreds of
instruments made by amateurs in the Cambridge classes using traditional methods almost always behave very well and in several cases,
outstandingly. Indeed, Cremer says that factory-made instruments
ought to work just as well as hand-made ones. In fact they are made to
a standard thickness regardless of the properties of the individual pieces
of wood, there is no testing of parts to ensure that they fit exactly
before gluing—so that they have a variety of stressing from being
forced together—and the internal surfaces are often left in a relatively
rough state. Smooth inner surfaces improve the air resonance (see
Chapter 5)—and woodworm gain access more easily through a rough
surface.

## 4.14. *Bridge Position*

The position of the bridge must be related to neck length. That determines where the player expects to put the left-hand fingers. There are now standard values for the ratio of the neck length to the distance from the bridge to the top of the body: one standard ratio for violins and violas, and a different one for cellos and basses (see Chapter 12). In fact a modern full-sized violin is expected to have specific lengths for those distances; the lengths may vary by a few millimetres on older violins, but the ratio must be correct. On the larger instruments, neck length and therefore bridge position appear to reflect the maker's choice. A scientist would be happier with some rationale for relating the bridge to the overall dimensions of the body, accepting that it is virtually impossible to test whether there is a 'best' position for a bridge on a given front; the variation between good instruments indicates that there is a fair degree of freedom. Some makers have an attractive belief that the bridge should be at the 'point of balance' of the front; if that means where an isolated front without bass bar would balance on a point, the bridge would divide the front roughly into equal areas above and below it. Such a rule of thumb has practical value for violas. A viola front is not simply a magnified violin front; it is significantly broader across the lower half. This brings the point of balance closer to the saddle and enables the instrument to have a larger area and greater string length without being proportionally longer from the player's neck to the nut. The overall weight and balance of any instrument which can be supported entirely by gripping with the chin is a factor in player choice, perhaps especially with violas.

## 4.15. *The f-Holes*

The bridge position is said to be 'half way along the *f*s'. Since it should be fixed in relation to neck length, it might be more rational to say that the middle of the *f*s are opposite the bridge, presuming that such strangely shaped holes have a middle; it is equally meaningless to say that the bridge is in the middle of the oddly shaped island between the *f*s. There is much variation between well-behaved instruments. But the top of the bridge should be opposite the inner nicks on the *f*-holes because their sole purpose is to mark where the maker determined the bridge should be. If bridges have been properly cut and fitted and instruments well maintained, one should *not* be able to locate a bridge by the scratches on the varnish, but unfortunately all too often one can.

As to positioning the *f*-holes, one of probably many rules of thumb relates the lower circles of the holes to the curve of the purfling approaching the lower corners—but neither corners nor *f*-holes are standardized. One must assume from the way in which the position and shape of the *f*-holes of classical instruments have been measured and recorded in the greatest detail that such things were thought significant, but they vary enormously in every way, and there can be only one conclusion: that acoustically there is nothing critical about their shape or position. A story has been circulated that a well-known cellist has taken a knife to his very valuable cello and enlarged its *f*-holes; if true, it would make infinitely less difference to the noise he makes than to the value of the instrument. The one thing science has determined is that the ideal area for each hole, for the volume of a violin to behave as a Helmholtz resonator, is 5.5 sq. cm (but the ideal shape for that purpose is a simple ellipse!).

## 4.16. *Design and Acoustics*

Some people find the traditional violin shape attractive to look at. Some enthuse over particular versions of this shape in a manner which the uninitiated find as meaningless as the views of punters looking at the runners before a horse-race. Stringed instruments can vary in shape, whereas the shapes of wind and brass are determined by physics. There have been innumerable demonstrations that circles, golden means, and similar visual yardsticks approximate to one or other classical shape. These exercises might suggest something to a psychologist for the appeal of the shape; so far as one can see they have not the slightest acoustical relevance. There have been romantic comparisons with the symmetry of animals. Leaving aside that very few animals which appear to be symmetrical are as precisely so as connoisseurs expect violins to be, the insides of animals where the important works are, are totally asymmetric, just as violins have to be. One may also question whether a group of relatively uneducated skilled woodworkers did anything other than evolve a device on good structural principles which made an attractive sound. If the reader wants something to occupy a wet afternoon, start with all the practical constraints imposed on a stringed instrument held under the chin and bowed; the violin virtually designs itself, bass bar and post excepted. A guitar-shaped body with no projecting edges or corners is equally satisfactory for supporting an arched front. Instruments were and are made guitar-shaped instead of with C-bouts, and without corners. One of America's distinguished violinists, Joshua Bell, has performed on a guitar-shaped violin made by Stradivarius, and there are other fine instruments of that form, including one superb old double bass, played by a professional in one orchestra of which I was a member. The air space inside all members of the family is guitar-shaped, and there is nothing acoustically significant, let alone magical, about that shape either. A guitar-shaped body is adequately strong provided the ribs are a single piece of wood from top block to bottom block on either side. It is only because the waist ribs are made as separate pieces that there have to be corner blocks. It is arguable which form of the instrument is easier to make.

The extraordinarily shaped *f*-hole is a thing of beauty (which once cut is there for ever, joy or not), but a remarkably high proportion of artists from the sixteenth century to the present day have been dyslexic about the *f*s, making one wonder whether artist and craftsman look at beauty in quite the same way. Altogether one has to conclude that **there is no evidence that any particular or specific shape or detail of the box has any special acoustical significance other than the arching of the front.** Within practical and sensible limits, the family tolerate variation in almost every particular, and there are, annoyingly perhaps, some instruments which appear to break every rule in the book and still work well. There are also one or two modern experimental designs with, for example, the left shoulder reduced. There is no evidence that any variants have improved performance, and most attempted modifications seem to work in the other direction. Paraphrasing Cremer's statement, if there is no specification there cannot be a scientific design—nor can anyone claim to have the perfect model, because every piece of wood is different.

## 4.17. *Purfling*

Purfling is a thin sandwich of veneers glued into a narrow groove cut around the edge of both front and back of an instrument. At some point in the past a theory was advanced, and this has been repeated in books, that purfling increases, or is primarily responsible for, flexibility at the edges of the plates, and someone has even produced the idea that 'playing in' (see Chapter 9.16) occurs because the glue in the purfling groove cracks and makes the front more flexible. This has also been extended to the remarkable idea that the fronts of old instruments are more flexible because the glue holding the purfling has broken up. The main requirement of the back is rigidity, and it would not be purfled if that increased its flexibility. More of the edge of the front is parallel with the grain than across it, and those regions are flexible enough without adding to it. If the purpose of purfling was flexibility, it is surprising that tradition has placed it over the linings rather than further in from the edge. One may be sure too that long ago, makers and players would have perceived some difference in the behaviour of fine instruments which are not purfled at all and, certainly, of the many instruments which are double-purfled: which have a second filled groove inside the normal one. Instead, many makers rather frown on the practice. And if the glue was so poor that the vibration of playing cracked it in the purfling groove, spectacular disaster would overtake the instrument long before playing in was completed. If glue anywhere gives way, the symptom is obvious before most people find it: the instrument buzzes like a bee. Purfling has one simple function; if the edge of front or back receives a blow and is cracked, there is a good chance that the crack will not run beyond the purfling and into the plate.

### 4.18. *Humidity*

Equilibrating violins to different air humidities can change their behaviour, and the possibility that the water content of wood affects the sound has been a source of speculation. If a violin is set up in the cool atmosphere of a good craftsman's shop, at a sensible humidity of around 60 per cent, and it is then exposed to dry air—especially conditions in a centrally heated-concert hall in winter—the gap between fingerboard and strings decreases, sometimes by so much that the instrument cannot be played. When a cellular material such as wood is dried, it may shrink in one dimension, but expand in another; the body of a violin changes shape in a complex fashion. By the time the irate soloist has taken the instrument back to the luthier, it will probably have returned to its original shape. Any modification of the wood's elasticity or damping would have a trivial effect, in comparison with the changes in an instrument's behaviour when it alters shape. Humidifying devices placed in an instrument can help, but they need frequent replenishing. The ideal home for a violin is replete with tropical plants; it made good sense for the orchestra to be resident in the Palm Court.

## 4.19. *The Biggest Stress on the Box*

Because of all the other interests in the violin body, it is often over-looked that the biggest single force on the instrument is produced by string tension from saddle to nut: over 25 kgm on a violin today and perhaps up to 200 kgm (nearly a quarter of a ton) on a metal-strung double bass. One of the most impressive things (to an engineer) about the Stradivarius *Messiah* is that a line from nut to saddle is precisely in the plane of the edges of the front, and so the force of the strings is applied where the system is stiffest and most capable of resisting it. Actually this is testimony to the luthier who put in the longer neck and changed the neck angle in the nineteenth century. String tension will tend to bow the long arch of the front upwards, but that will only hap-pen if the top and bottom blocks tilt, which would stretch the back. The back is hardwood and very strong. Changes on a microscopic scale do occur when an instrument is first strung, sufficient to affect the fit of the soundpost, which almost always needs adjustment after a few weeks. Whatever other views we may have about the traditional form of the members of the violin family, we must admit that they are fine exam-ples of good structural design, or they would not have survived; during their evolution there must have been many that were not—and did not.

# 5

# Resonance and Response

◆ ◆ ◆ ❖ ◆ ◆ ◆

## 5.1. *Introduction*

The reader with an eye for elegant English may feel that the word 'vibrate' has been used *ad nauseam,* and the author should have rung the changes with 'oscillate', 'reverberate', or 'resonate'. One problem of scientific writing is that each of these words has a specific meaning, and the right one must be used in a given context. 'Resonate' is misused more frequently than it is used correctly in ordinary speech; resonance so intrigues physicists that it seems sometimes to prevent them from seeing the wood for the trees.

Throughout the previous chapters it has been tacitly assumed that the form of the vibration generated by the strings is transmitted by the bridge to the body, and that the body vibrates in that form. That is not what happens, but it would have been confusing to have introduced what does, earlier in our discussions. The wave forms generated by bowing are the basis of the body's vibration and of the sound, but in a nutshell, the string generates a wave form and makes it available to the body via the bridge. The body decides how much of the vibration it will take. That is what we now have to discuss.

## 5.2. *Resonance and Damping*

Resonance is the way in which something vibrates naturally. An object does not vibrate at all unless it is given some energy by striking it, shaking it, or other means. The object must be elastic. If it is deformed by something like a sharp tap, it not only recovers its shape, but overshoots, returns, and repeats the process, often many times. If a wineglass is tapped, the tap makes it ring, but the glass determines the frequency at which it vibrates. The sound dies away because the energy put in is used up but very little is turned into sound. Most of it is used to deform the material repeatedly.

To test for resonance, objects are often tapped because the blow lasts for a very short time, and does not then interfere with the vibration. When the plates of instruments are tested during making, they are held as lightly as possible between thumb and one finger so as not to damp the vibration any more than can be helped. Any process which absorbs the energy of a vibrating object is called **damping**; the term covers both applying something from the outside, and also the process of using up energy in changing shape while vibrating, which is called internal damping. Internal damping is enormously important. There is enough noise in the world as it is, but if most of the energy which caused something to resonate turned into sound, instead of being used up in changing shape, there would be long-lasting audible vibration from almost anything we touch. Internal damping is what causes most vibration to stop quite rapidly.

We must not confuse damping with stressing or constraining. Both of these change the way an object resonates, but do not necessarily cause damping. We allow a front or back to hang as freely as possible in order not to introduce stresses as well as not to damp it. A violin front freely suspended will produce a tap note around F. The note falls to about D when the *f*-holes are cut out because its shape has changed. It goes back to around F when it has its bass bar, but it vibrates somewhat differently to produce that F from the start. It will vibrate differently again when it is constrained by being glued to the rest of the box, and differently yet again when all the stresses produced by string tension are applied. None of these changes damp its vibrations; that happens within the wood.

## 5.3. *Many Resonances*

If a solid has a regular shape like a metal rod it will usually vibrate with one very clear resonance when tapped. A rectangular block of hardwood will produce an obvious pitch, with some noise in the background: the xylophone is an example. The noise comes from resonances of several different ways in which it vibrates: by expanding and contracting lengthways, across the width, and across the depth, and also by bending and twisting. The metal rod will also vibrate in many ways, but one resonance will usually produce such a loud sound that the others are difficult to hear. As a rule, the more complex the shape, the less one resonance will dominate and the more the other resonances will produce noise which confuses the sound. It is a little surprising that the isolated front or back of a violin does produce such an identifiable resonance pitch when tapped; the rest of the noise shows that there are many other weaker resonances there. (A brass cymbal has an enormous number of resonances without any of them dominating, so that it is pitchless, and that is not easy to achieve either.) If one taps the box of a violin, with plastic foam under the strings to prevent them from vibrating, we can hear that there are many resonances. We should not hear any identifiable pitch because none should dominate. If it sounded dead it would not be a worthwhile instrument, but equally, it should not continue to 'ring' for a long time; the resonances should be well damped.

## 5.4. *Testing for Resonance by Vibration*

An object will reveal its resonances when appropriately vibrated. Everyone has heard of a singer shattering a glass with a note to which the glass naturally resonated; the circumstances must be most unusual, or trumpet players would cause a lot of damage. We have all suffered the commoner situation, when playing or listening to music, in which some article in the room joins in with some of the sound. There is very little energy in sound in air. Everything in a room receives vibration at all the frequencies in every sound, and they will vibrate very very slightly at all of them, but when something is vibrated at a frequency of one of its resonances, it vibrates much more.

## 5.5. *Sharp and Broad Resonances*

The resonances of objects can be discovered by a device which produces pure tone vibration. If we vibrate a wineglass, starting with a low frequency, and gradually increase the rate, it will not begin to vibrate unusually until the frequency is a fraction of a semitone below its resonance frequency; it will vibrate violently at its resonance, and stop a fraction of a semitone above it. That is a sharp resonance. If we do the same thing with a somewhat irregular block of wood which produces a recognizable resonance pitch when tapped, we will find that it starts vibrating a little a few semitones below what we have called its tap note, and that its vibration increases to a maximum and then decreases for a few semitones above that before it ceases. That is a broad resonance. Over quite a wide band of frequencies the object vibrates resonantly, with a maximum in the middle of the band. One can hear a specific pitch from a broad resonance by tapping, because that is the frequency at which it naturally vibrates most.

## 5.6. *The Resonances of an Instrument*

When a violin is played its body resonates. Unlike a loudspeaker, where the objective is that it should not resonate at any frequency, but should vibrate exactly in all the complex wave forms which are applied to it, a violin produces sound only because the bridge makes the body resonate. It is essential that a violin body does resonate in many different ways, and the form of its resonance changes continuously with frequency across the whole range of sound frequencies it can produce adequately. It would produce very little sound unless it did.

## 5.7. *The Transfer of Vibration*

Before considering the behaviour of the whole instrument, there is a most important physical process controlling the transfer of vibration energy from string to body. Where there is stronger resonance the body vibrates more, and takes more energy from the string; where the resonance is less it vibrates less, and takes less energy from the string. If the body were made of marble it would not vibrate at all or take any energy. That is not a ridiculous thought, because a resonance-free body is ideal for an electric guitar, where one wants all the energy to remain in the strings, so that they continue to vibrate for a long time. **The amount of energy which passes from the string through the bridge to the body at any one frequency depends on how much the body is able to vibrate resonantly at that frequency**. The body determines how much energy at each frequency it will take from the bridge, and the bridge takes that energy at each frequency from the string.

However, the body normally also takes the energy at each harmonic frequency in proportion to the size of the harmonic in the string vibration. If this did not happen, the body would take most of the energy from a very lightly bowed string but a smaller proportion of that in a heavily bowed string at the same pitch, and the player would have no dynamic control. This is where damping is critical. As we shall see, the wood must mop up almost all the energy in each cycle of vibration, apart from the small amount turned into sound, and if it does not, there is trouble. **The sound produced at any one level of bowing contains**

**each string harmonic, its size adjusted by the body resonance at each frequency.** This raises a number of questions about mechanism, which we must address before we consider its implications for the actual sound produced.

If the bridge takes different amounts of energy from different component frequencies in the vibration of the string, what happens to the string's vibration? A vibration with changed components has a different tone. First, each time the string goes through its cycle, the bow restores the form of its vibration; otherwise, the string vibration would change progressively during the sustained part of a note and the sound would change.

Secondly, the body must not take more than a portion of the string's energy out of the string per cycle, or the bow will not maintain the dynamic. Cremer says that the body removes 10 per cent of the energy stored in the string during each cycle of vibration; others believe it is less. The rate of removal will depend on the individual instrument and the pitch at which measurements are made, for the overall rate will be the sum of the amounts taken by each resonance and each harmonic's size.

Thirdly, there are instruments which produce a small amount of sound for the work with the bow. That must mean that the body resonances are small. There are good instruments which require more work and good ones which speak easily, both of which can produce effective sound. Those which require more work have resonances which take a smaller amount of string energy relative to the amplitude of the string, and those which speak easily have resonances which take a larger amount of energy. The balance between bow work and resonance is important. It is easier for the player to control dynamic and to obtain a uniform pianissimo on one which needs more work. The instrument which speaks easily may produce a large volume of sound easily, but the player may have to exercise far more bow control, and must not push the instrument too far. An instrument must not be too resonant, or the string will not be able to meet the body's demand, and its oscillation will break down. Much depends on the player's natural bowing style. The explanation of the wolf tone phenomenon (see Section 11 below) depends on the principles set out in this paragraph.

## 5.8. *Resonance and Tone*

We can put all these factors together in a general statement about the sound output of instruments. A string produces a particular form of vibration when bowed in a particular way. The sound coming from an instrument has the form of that vibration modified by the resonance at the frequency of each of the harmonics. Therefore if the resonances corresponding with the harmonics of notes of different pitches are different, the comparative strengths of the harmonics in the sound produced will differ from note to note.

In theory the sizes of the component harmonics of a sound determine its tone, so that the tone could be different from pitch to pitch even if the bow produced the same wave form in the string at each pitch. We need to know how big the modifications are, so that we can consider whether hearing could detect the effect of such variations; it is evident from ordinary experience that any changes introduced by resonance are not sufficient to disguise the difference between the tone of bowing lightly at the fingerboard, of bowing normally, and of bowing close to the bridge.

## 5.9. *Assessing Body Resonance*

The earliest attempt to examine the resonances of instruments is recorded in the notebooks of the 1860s from which Helmholtz compiled *On the Sensations of Tone*. 'With the assistance of the violin-makers Messrs Hart, Hill and Withers' he tested the resonances of a number of instruments by using tuning-forks: a set of eighty forks, sounding from 240 to 560 Hz at intervals of four cycles. He found that an 'early Stradivari of 1696 and a Mazzini [presumably Maggini] of Brescia of 1630, neither particularly fine instruments', each had two very strong resonances which could be detected. On the other hand a 'Petrus Guarnerius of 1701 known to be genuine and Dr Huggins' Stradivarius of 1708 which had great equality of all four strings' showed resonance with every fork tried (see the Dover edition of Helmholtz's *On the Sensations of Tone*).

When electronic measuring became available, some indication of the variation in an instrument's resonance was obtained by an American physicist, F. A. Saunders, who was also a violinist. He measured the total sound output from strong bowing and found that it varied from semitone to semitone right across a violin's range. These values show the response of an instrument to bowing, and we shall call the information the **response curve** of an instrument (Fig. 5.1). It is often called a 'loudness' curve, but loudness is a sensation in the brain and, as the next chapter explains, one cannot equate physical measurements with

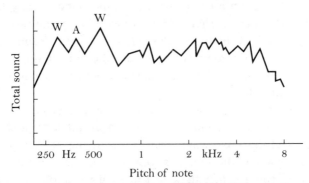

Fig. 5.1. A typical response curve of a well-made violin, showing the variation in total sound from strong bowing at successive semitones. Between two marks on the scale the sound level doubles. The two peaks W coincide with the 'wood' resonances; peak A is at air resonance.

sensations. Saunders was able to make response measurements on several named violins by classical makers, and on some fine instruments made in the first half of the twentieth century. His pioneering investigations produced valuable physical information, and his method is still used. An enlightened aspect of Saunders's work was to test a 'poor' instrument. Helmholtz too was interested in instruments which did not behave well. Perhaps if physicists had subsequently put more effort into examining poor instruments and if possible discovering reasons why they are poor, rather than, at least in some cases, believing that the object of research was to tell skilled makers what to do, our understanding of instruments might have advanced more rapidly.

More recently, physicists have tested violins by applying a pure tone vibration to the top of the bridge and measuring the amount of energy taken by the instrument from the vibrating source. This gives what we can call the **resonance curve** of an instrument (Fig. 5.2). The method gives a detailed picture of the resonances: that is, how much energy they take. But most of the energy is used up by the damping, in bending the wood, so that while it eliminates the unknown factors of player and bow, it does not give the sound output of a normally played instrument. The Saunders method gives typical strong sound output but does not dissect it into individual frequencies. A third method also applies pure tone vibration to the bridge and measures the sound at successive frequencies by placing a microphone in front of the instrument. It gives the most detailed picture of the relationship between a standard bridge vibration and the sound produced at each frequency for one particular

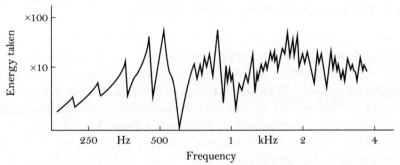

FIG. 5.2. A typical resonance curve of a well-made violin, showing the energy taken from a pure tone generator applied to the bridge at various frequencies. Each peak is a different resonance.

violin (and an extremely complex picture it proves to be). The picture obtained by any method includes the behaviour due to the tensions of the strings used, the particular bridge, and the particular sound-post setting.

Figure 5.1 is a typical response curve of a good violin. What violin this came from is not of any special interest because all good violins produce response curves, each of which is very irregular, like the one drawn, *but none of them are alike.* It is assumed that a peak on this curve indicates the maximum of a resonance at the fundamental of the note played, which is presumed to contribute most to the overall sound measured, though a coincidence of some higher harmonics on resonances may produce a peak. But resonance curves confirm that the first three peaks lying between the fundamental of the bottom string and about 600 Hz do represent resonance peaks. These three resonances occur at more or less the same frequencies in all the orthodox instruments which have been examined. Resonance curves reveal a far greater number of resonances than there are peaks of response, but likewise show continuously varying irregularity right across each instrument's range and also demonstrate that no two instruments are alike. The resonances determine the range. A good violin has resonances up to about 8 kHz (about four octaves above treble-staff C). Above that, a violin does not produce significant sound even though string vibration in the highest register may contain frequencies up to 30 kHz or more. Violas resonate up to around 7 kHz. Cellos have resonances up to about 5 kHz (roughly three octaves above violin open E); the limit of effective bass resonance is about an octave lower than the cello's.

## 5.10. *The Limitations of Physical Measurements*

To what extent do tests using pure tone vibrations to obtain resonance curves, or other information about instruments, represent what happens when an instrument is bowed? We have the same problem as with holography pictures. When the string is generating sixteen or more frequencies simultaneously, are the various resonances able to behave independently, or do they interfere with each other? This is not being destructive for its own sake. Resonance curves and holographs are the only information of this kind we have.

The resonance curve of a real violin has been applied to the theoretical vibration of an ideal bowed string to see what irregularity it produces in the harmonics, and it is the same sort of picture as one gets by harmonic analysis of a real sound from an expertly bowed note, of which there are a few examples in Chapter 6.12. The conclusion is that any one instrument has irregular resonances right across its range, so the relative strengths of the harmonics even from ideal string vibration will differ from note to note; if every instrument has irregular resonances different from every other instrument, then the strengths of the harmonics in notes of the same pitch played on any two instruments will also be different. The harmonics determine the tone we hear. And on top of this, a real bowed string has some continuous irregularity in its vibrations. This is not a situation which appeals to an exact science, as physicists sometimes call their subject; biologists meet this sort of thing every day, and Chapter 6 provides some biological solutions to it. In view of all this complexity, one may perhaps be excused for quoting from a recent serious book on bowed instruments the remark that 'the violin amplifies the sound of the strings perfectly'. Leaving aside that the device does not operate on sound and the howler about amplifying, that is more or less how an electric violin with a solid body works, and those who have heard one will know how perfect it is.

In fact, there is yet another process involved in the transfer of vibration from string to sound production, one which modifies the size of the harmonics and invalidates the assumption that what is measured in a resonance curve is the energy used up in vibrating the wood plus that producing the sound. The resonances of an instrument are more irregular and varying than those measurements show, and it would be very difficult to play an instrument if the resonances were totally in control. A mechanism was evolved empirically, almost miraculously one feels, to 'tame' the resonances. It will be easier to understand this if we deal first with the curious phenomenon of the wolf tone and its cure.

## 5.11. *The Wolf Tone*

The wolf tone is an anomalous sound produced by some instruments at just one pitch. This disagreeable sound is very often produced by cellos, usually around F to F♯ on the G string, rarely as low as D♯; it occurs just as strongly at the same pitch played on the C string too. A weaker version of it sometimes occurs on violas at a corresponding pitch an octave higher than on cellos, but it is unusual on violins. As a number of authors have said, there are more different explanations for this than for any other aspect of the behaviour of bowed instruments, though often they do not then produce one themselves, but dismiss the subject with comments such as the following. 'Wolf notes occur in badly made instruments'; the truth is the reverse. 'Makers should design violins so that they fall between notes'; an interesting idea if instructions then followed on how to achieve this, but since violins rarely have wolf notes, perhaps the author had little chance to apply his cure. 'The note only occurs on instruments with too high tension strings'; a grain of truth, for the tone can sometimes be lessened by using lower-tension strings, but this is not the cause. The extensive explanation in Arthur H. Benade's *Fundamentals of Musical Acoustics* (1976) might cause some people with a modest competence in physics to flounder.

The form of the wolf tone sound can be seen on an oscilloscope screen. A wave with the fundamental rate of vibration swells and dies, a wave with second harmonic rate appears, whereupon the fundamental reappears, swells, and dies again, and this repeats continually about five or six times a second. One can usually hear the octave pitch briefly, and the interval of a pitch and its octave is the most consonant of all, but the sound is not in the least like an octave tremolo. It suggests violent beating between two vibrations differing by about five cycles in frequency, but there is no suggestion of this in the wave form.

The wolf tone arises from three things. At the fundamental of its pitch there is a large body resonance. It is a very sharp resonance; if, for example, it falls on F, there is almost no wolfing on the E or F♯ either side of it. The resonance is insufficiently damped, so that the front does not dissipate most of the energy which it obtains per cycle into the wood, and it therefore would not stop vibrating almost immediately if the stimulating frequency stopped.

When the note is started, the wolf resonance takes energy from the string at the fundamental frequency. The bow is able to replace the energy being removed. Because of lack of damping, the vibration of the body increases rapidly, and takes more and more energy at the fundamental frequency out of the string. The body is now vibrating strongly *of its own accord.* The bow can no longer supply energy to the fundamental frequency of the string at the rate at which it is demanded by the wolf resonance, so that that frequency rapidly decreases in the string's vibration and disappears; the normal form of string vibration breaks down. The wolf resonance is therefore deprived of a supply of energy; it dissipates its stored energy into what damping there is, and its vibration decreases. The body has been taking modest energy from second and other harmonics and radiating sound with those frequencies all the time this has been happening, so one may briefly hear the octave pitch of the second harmonic when the wolf resonance becomes very small. But when it does, the bow can obtain control of the string again and start a normal form of vibration. This contains the fundamental, and the wolf resonance starts taking energy and building up again; this repeats every fifth of a second or so.

That the output end of a mechanical system can exercise control over the input end to this extent is not a concept with which everyone is familiar. An analogy is provided by a bicycle. If the gearing is too high, the legs move too slowly to put in very much energy. If the gearing is too low, the legs fly round and again little energy is transferred. With the right gearing, a lot of energy can be put into the wheels. But once energy has been put into the wheels, they can run for a time while the pedals are turned slowly, putting no energy in, and the machine slows down until the pedals catch up. It is the output end: the wheels, that control the gears and pedals, not the legs: the input end. (Any reader familiar with electronic circuitry will have realized after reading a few paragraphs of this chapter that the system can be explained relatively simply using the principle of impedance and admittance and a couple of analogue circuit diagrams.)

## 5.12. *Taming a Wolf*

If the wolf resonance is not very big, a skilled player may be able to to 'play it out', meaning, to control the string with the bow and make it vibrate normally, but this is not easy to do. The problem is that any increase in the string's amplitude feeds the wolf, and the amplitude has to be further increased. One ends up like Peter, trying to catch the wolf by the tail.

Four methods of eliminating the wolf tone can be used. A weight can be attached to the front at an arbitrarily determined place: effective but decidedly inelegant. A spring with a metal bar which resonates at wolf frequency can be placed inside the cello between front and back. Both cures are readily explained: they absorb energy from the front at the wolf frequency and prevent the resonance from building up. A traditional remedy which sometimes works is to use a heavier tailpiece. The simplest practical cure is to put a small brass sleeve filled with soft rubber on the tail of the C string between bridge and tailpiece, and 'tune' it—move it until a position is found at which the wolf disappears. Benade says the tail should be tuned to a slightly different frequency from the wolf; Cremer says it should be tuned to the wolf frequency. But what are we tuning? The tail of the C string, one sixth the length of the open C, has a resonant pitch of about *two* octaves and a fifth above that C, and roughly an octave above the wolf tone. That is the pitch we hear when the fundamental of the wolf momentarily dies, and not the wolf frequency we want to reduce.

When an instrument is played normally, the bridge vibrates all four tails and the tailpiece. A vibration-sensing probe shows that the whole system is vibrating at the many frequencies of whatever note is bowed. We are not concerned with the resonances which the four tails have, just because they are stretched strings, whether any one of them has a sleeve on it or not. The brass sleeve does two things: it gives the whole system of tailpiece and tails a specific sharp resonance, and it tunes that resonance to the fundamental of the wolf tone by its position along the tail. A probe shows that when the sleeve is in the tuned position and the wolf note is bowed, the tails and tailpiece execute a quite large sine wave at the wolf fundamental (together with the normal amount of vibration due to the other harmonics of the string). That sine wave is the tailpiece system resonance. The same resonance and resulting cure can be obtained if the sleeve is put on the G tail; but it works best on the C tail because the bridge, rocking about the soundpost foot, is vibrating through the largest amplitude at the C tail groove, whether the wolf note is bowed on the C or G string. All this appears to favour Cremer's proposal.

The brass sleeve produces the same end effect as the weight or the tuned spring system: it removes energy at the frequency causing the wolf, but by taking it from the top of the bridge, it deprives the wolf resonance of a supply of energy at a rate which would allow it to build up. It is withdrawing that energy from the *whole transfer system*. The energy is mopped up in the heavy tailpiece, not in the rubber in the sleeve. The rubber is there because you cannot put a piece of metal on a vibrating string without some soft padding or it will buzz, and if you screw it directly to the string, the string will be damaged.

The wolf is predominantly a cello phenomenon, in part because of the greater amount of energy which can be contained in the large heavy front, in part because the large bridge ratio facilitates energy transfer from string to body. It seems more often to be a phenomenon of large cellos, which can wolf at D♯ or even D, and may require a heavy sleeve to suppress them: another mark against large instruments. When a wolf has been eliminated there is no discernable difference between the tone of that note and the tone of pitches one semitone either side of it. This is discussed in the next chapter.

## 5.13. *The Stability of String Vibration*

Wolves are savage on steel-strung instruments because the high-tension and rigid metal strings stiffen the whole tailpiece system; they also stiffen the tailgut, which itself must be adequately flexible and not of solid wire. They can appear if a well-behaved respectably strung cello is restrung with steel. Let that be a warning! But the underlying lesson is that the body of an instrument must not be so resonant at any frequency, in relation to its damping, that it interferes with the stability of the string's vibration. An instrument must have resonances; it speaks easily if its resonances are large at all frequencies, but at what point does a valuable resonance become a wolf? Does this put a significant limit on sound production?

What the wolf phenomenon shows is that the body must not remove too much energy from the *fundamental* frequency of a string. The second harmonic in the sound can be two or three times that of the fundamental, and the corresponding resonance can be removing large amounts of string energy at that frequency; that is typical of the lowest notes of all four instruments, but the string vibration remains stable. The pitch heard is that of fundamental frequency, more or less whatever size the fundamental is in the sound (see Chapter 6.14). It could therefore be that the more energy which can be taken from any of the *other* harmonics, the stronger the sound will be, and the easier it will be to elicit the sound. Ideally, we want a body with many strong resonances, but with the apparent contradiction that we do not want a wolf whenever one of these strong resonances coincides with a fundamental at any pitch which is played throughout the whole range of an instrument. How can such a thing be achieved?

## 5.14. *The Essential Tailpiece Function*

The tailpiece and string tails together act like a generalized modest wolf-suppressor at all frequencies. The system is vibrated at all the frequencies of any string which is bowed, and absorbs that vibration in the tailpiece. It will remove energy from the transmitted harmonics in proportion to their sizes, and since the fundamental is always the largest harmonic in the *string's* vibration, that is reduced most. The tailpiece cannot discriminate between frequencies, but by removing more energy from the fundamental, whatever the pitch, it helps to prevent any normal body resonance from breaking down the string's mode of vibration, and may be regarded as a device which makes the behaviour of the instrument more even. How important is it?

My first inadvertent experiments with this mechanism some forty years ago happened when I made a lightweight metal frame as a substitute tailpiece, so as to maintain bridge pressure and prevent a soundpost from falling over in a double bass while I modified its real tailpiece. With the light frame in place, several notes were really difficult to control with the bow. The responsiveness across the playing range was very uneven. I packed large amounts of Plasticine onto the frame, and when the instrument began to behave properly, the composite tailpiece was reasonably close in weight and weight-distribution to the original. Since it is unlikely that our ancestors would have evolved the tailpiece in this rapid empirical fashion, nor did they have bicycles to help them understand the principles of energy transfer, one continues to marvel at the achievements of blind trial and error, even if it was to escape from a pack of wolves.

The behaviour of the tailpiece system means of course that measurements of the energy removed at each frequency from the top of the bridge, to compile a resonance curve, will include the energy removed by the tailpiece. The resonance curve will suggest that the body resonances are larger and more variable than they actually are, and that they produce more variation in the sound than they do.

The pitches of the string tails do not appear to enter into the process. The ability of the tailpiece system to vibrate freely is increased by passing the tails over the tailpiece fret, and if there were no fret they would probably buzz. Heron-Allen's book says that the tails should also be parallel; Chanot was right, for the the system will be less stiff if they can be. The difficulty is that players expect the strings to be in standard positions on the bridge, but tailpieces are usually bought in with the holes for the strings already drilled; for example, good German-made violin and viola tailpieces have string holes almost identically spaced, and if they produce parallel strings on violins they cannot do so on violas.

Louis Spohr, who died in 1859 and is notable for having advanced the technique of violin playing, invented a tailpiece with independent movable frets, so that the tails could be tuned individually. He was honest enough to say that he did not know what it achieved. One is inclined to agree.

### 5.15. *The Identified Resonances*

The three response peaks originally discovered by Saunders in all good violins (see Section 9 above), and subsequently shown to correspond to three larger resonances at roughly similar frequencies, have been the subject of theory, belief, and experiment. Further investigation has shown that three resonances in violas, cellos, and basses have a similar origin to those found in violins. The other peaks and resonances in all instruments do appear to be quite random.

### 5.16. *The Air Resonance*

The peak marked A in Fig. 5.1 coincides with the resonance of the air in the body. It can be identified by filling the body with gas of a different density from air, such as carbon dioxide, which shifts the frequency. The space inside a violin is complex, and there are several small resonances, but the significant one can be heard by blowing across an *f*-hole. This resonance is broad and less definite if the inside of the body is not well finished. Although the ideal area of a violin *f*-hole is about 5.5 sq. cm, the frequency of the air resonance is hardly changed by varying *f*-hole size or shape within reason. The resonant frequency of a chamber containing air is determined by the number of holes in it. The ocarina works on this basis and is the only 'musical' instrument which does. If you seal one *f*-hole of a violin with masking tape (don't, unless you are sure that the tape will not remove some varnish when you remove it) and then blow across the other hole, the pitch will be about four or five semitones lower than that with two open holes. There is one difference between air resonance and the behaviour of the air at other frequencies. At air resonance, air is puffed in and out of the *f*-holes whatever is happening to the wood. At all times, air is puffed in and out of the *f*-holes on a smaller scale because the box expands and contracts, but when the box expands and pushes on the air around it, air is sucked in through the *f*-holes and vice versa, so that this slightly reduces sound production.

## 5.17. *The Wood Resonances*

The other two peaks in the low-frequency part of the violin's response curve, marked W in Fig. 5.1, coincide with what are called the wood resonances, though of course all the resonances involve wood. The frequencies of these resonances were found to be related to the body length of normal instruments of the family; they go down in frequency more or less directly as the length of the body increases. Blocks of rosewood in xylophones have resonances related to their dimensions, and it is not surprising that similarly shaped and stressed boxes should do so.

## 5.18. *The Identified Resonances in Lower Instruments*

The sizes of the four members of the family are not in proportion to the pitches to which they are tuned. If they were, a viola would be one and a half times as long as a violin, and a cello would be twice the length of such a viola. A viola of that size would have wood resonances similarly placed with respect to the pitch of its strings as they are positioned in a violin in relation to its string pitches. But such a viola would have an air volume over three times as big as a violin's. In other words, the three resonances do not move together with size. Table 2 shows roughly the lengths the instruments would have to be in order to position their wood resonances to correspond in frequency with those of a violin. It also shows their actual volumes and those they would need to have to make the frequency of the air resonance correspond in pitch for each of them. The air resonances of the conventional instruments do correspond roughly to the violin's, but the wood resonances are all considerably higher in the range of the three lower instruments.

Considerable importance has been attributed to these resonances in relation to the sound of the instruments. Certainly, if a harmonic

TABLE 2

Comparative Lengths and Body Volumes of the Four Instruments

|  | Violin | Viola | Cello | D bass |
|---|---|---|---|---|
| Body length in inches (mm) | 14 (355) | 16 (407) | 29 (735) | 43 (1090) |
| Length needed to make wood resonances correspond with a violin | 14 (355) | 21 (538) | 42 (1065) | 68 (1725) |
| Ratio of actual body volume to volume of a violin | 1 | 1.5 | 17 | 58 |
| Ratio needed to make air resonance correspond with a violin | 1 | 1.5 | 17.5 | 68 |

corresponds to a large resonance, it will have a larger amplitude in the *sound*; if it falls in a low-resonance region it will be smaller. But it has been claimed that because all three resonances occur towards the bottom of the violin's range they enrich the *tone* of the violin's lower register, and because the wood resonances are higher in the viola's range, they are responsible for the 'weakness' of low viola. They are said to affect in that way the tone of all three lower members of the family. They do. When these instruments are played by musicians, they have the opposite effect, as we shall see in the following chapter. But whatever effect they have, their position will not be significantly changed by making any long, broad, or high-ribbed viola which can be played in the conventional position. The limitation on string vibration is bow input, and if the front of a viola is made larger, the amount of bow energy is spread over a larger area of wood and produces a proportionally smaller vibration; the same total sound is produced. One cannot find a single reason for struggling to play a large viola if a 16 inch (407 mm) instrument is comfortable to play. The characteristic differences between violin and viola tone are almost entirely determined by things other than size and resonances (See Chapter 6.27).

To move the wood resonances of a cello to correspond with those of a violin, the body would have to be about the size of a double bass. For similar reasons, there is no point in playing a big cello if a 'lady's size' is more comfortable; small cellos can produce wonderful sound and

sound volume. In the double bass, all these resonances lie higher in relation to its range; in its lower notes, the third harmonic, measured by
Fourier analysis of the sound, can be twice the size of the fundamental
and second harmonic (see Chapter 6.12). There is nothing to be gained
from giant-sized basses, but it is an amusing thought that whatever
Vuillaume had in mind when he made his celebrated octo-bass with
levers to stop the strings, its wood resonances would have enhanced the
fundamental of its bottom strings—but only if it had been tuned like a
normal bass, and not an octave lower as he tuned it.

## 5.19. *The Saunders–Hutchins Experiment*

On the assumption that the three identifiable resonances did play a significant part in the tone and perhaps the sound output of the four conventional instruments, Saunders, together later with other physicists,
worked out ways in which to alter instrument structure to move the
frequencies of the wood resonances, and to change the air resonance by
box volume and the number of holes in it. To these designs, the skilled
luthier Carleen Hutchins made a set of eight violin-like instruments,
each with the three resonances in similar positions in their ranges. They
range from a 'violin' an octave above the conventional instrument down
to a bass at low C, so that they provide a complete series in fifths and
octaves. It is said that they produce very similar tone, especially where
they overlap, and that their sounds blend very closely with each other,
and so lack the characteristics which lend individuality to the four members of the conventional family. This, as we shall see in Chapter 6, is
not surprising. One or two of them are not very suitable in size for
human proportions, and apparently the ultimate bass was almost too
delicate to manipulate. But they confirmed that one could move three
of the resonances about—at the expense of other properties and a huge
amount of skilled workmanship.

A distinguished acoustician's praise for these instruments extended to
saying that the one tuned to the notes of the normal viola could 'carve
up a string quartet'. We know some excellent viola players who could
carve up a string octet on a conventional instrument if they wanted to,
one of them when playing a small viola which was the first instrument
made by a 70-year-old amateur. Fortunately most viola players do not
so indulge, though it has been heard in professional quartet playing. We
can excuse Tertis for thinking a viola should be large and have deep
ribs. He lived before adequate scientific knowledge was available, and

every violaist owes him a great debt for finding Cinderella's slipper. But the addiction of some modern players to large instruments can only be attributed to player psychology.

## 5.20. *Bridge Resonance*

Bridges resonate within the audible frequency range of instruments. A violin bridge has resonances around 3 kHz and 6 kHz. The cello bridge has one at about 2.1 kHz and one around 3 kHz. The lower-frequency ones of both bridges take the form of the top rocking from side to side about the waist. At its higher resonance, the violin bridge vibrates from top to bottom; the higher cello one sways the whole bridge from side to side on its legs. The lower of the violin bridge resonances, and both the cello ones, can boost the sound output in what appears to be a valuable frequency range in a solo instrument (see Chapters 6 and 7). And like so many other things which science is now revealing about the traditional orthodox instrument, a bridge cut by a skilled luthier does have its resonances in those regions.

## 5.21. *Sound and Identifiable Resonances*

Saunders and others believed that large resonances in the low range of instruments produced rich tone because of a strong fundamental or second harmonic. The idea that sound with a large fundamental produces any particular tone sensation does not fit with some simple examples. Flute sound has a large fundamental and second harmonic and few others. It has a very clear sound rather than a rich one; the bottom octave is weak, needing light accompaniment. When a mute is put on a violin bridge (see Chapter 3.16), the sound is reduced to fundamental and second harmonic with a little third and fourth. The muted string produces a very weak thin sound. In normal playing, the tailpiece reduces the fundamental. And when it is properly played, the low range of the viola is a rich sound. We must look at the relationship between physical sound spectra and hearing before accepting any simplistic conclusions connecting tone with resonances and harmonics.

## 5.22. *Old and New Instruments*

Despite their limitations, physically measured response and resonance characteristics provide about the only non-subjective way of comparing instruments. Otherwise comparison is based on playing and listening. Assuming that instruments can be identically set up and have identical strings, the sound then includes the expertness of bowing, and transients which are of exceptional importance in perceived sound; both player and listener hear more than the sustained pitch component of the sound displayed by physical analysis. There is no doubt either that foreknowledge of the maker and age of an instrument can affect the judgement of both player and listener, and there is a long-standing belief that old instruments, particularly those made by well-known names of the Classical period, have better 'tone' than others. But it is not a tall story that an entire audience were convinced they were hearing the sound of Kreisler's Stradivarius until he threw the trade fiddle away and produced the real thing.

Nothing to support any such beliefs has emerged from scientific measurements made under identical conditions on a number of famous classical instruments and on well-made instruments of the nineteenth and twentieth centuries. Every well-made instrument has an irregular randomly varying response across its range. The air and wood resonances occur in more or less the same places, with varying degrees of size. But the response and resonance curves of each instrument are different. There is not a single resonance feature which is shared by old instruments and is not found in new ones. Every old instrument differs from every other old instrument by as much as it differs from every new instrument and by as much as new ones differ amongst themselves. Nor is there greater likeness between instruments made by the same maker, or to the same pattern, or, with modern instruments, from the same trees.

We can compare those findings with the results of properly conducted 'blind' tests when old and new instruments are named and played to sophisticated audiences, and they are then asked to identify them by the sound when played in a random order out of sight. The earliest aural test appears to have been in 1817 before an audience selected by the French National Academy. Similar tests were conducted by Savart in 1832 and Fry in 1904 (see A. Fry, *The Varnishes of the Italian Violin Makers and their Influence*, listed in Further Reading), since when a number of such trials with several instruments of all ages have been conducted. They have all produced results which one would expect from pure chance. We have carried out similar tests with violins and with violas, made by teachers and by amateurs in my wife's classes, with exactly the same results, though the professional performers say that all the instruments are quite different to play. An audience who heard a concert played entirely on Stradivarius instruments were surprised when told at the end of the performance, because they had heard nothing unusual. A test was broadcast on BBC Radio 3 in which a Stradivarius, a Guarnerius, a nineteenth-century French violin, and a modern one a year old were played by a distinguished violinist, to two equally famous violinists and to probably the world's greatest authority on the identification of violins. The two judging violinists were even allowed to play the four instruments before they were played out of sight. No one identified the instruments correctly by sound, and the man who went home like a cat with two tails was the modern maker because two of the experts had said his violin was the Stradivarius.

The conclusion is that **there appear to be no characterizing differences between the perceived sound from well-made orthodox instruments of any age when played by a skilled player**, and there is nothing which can be discerned in physical measurements which reveals any specific difference between new and old instruments. So does the irregularity of the sizes of the harmonics, caused by the resonances, dominate hearing's assessment of violin tone? Or, as long as an instrument is adequately resonant throughout its range, does it matter to hearing what size the harmonics are? We must attempt to resolve this in the following chapter.

### 5.23. *Tone and Age*

The more remarkable myth is that old violins have better tone because tone improves with age. This is hilariously irrational in one sense. How does anyone know what the tone of an instrument was like a hundred years ago? We do have a vague idea of what an instrument's tone would have been like two hundred years ago through the resurgence of the baroque violin for 'authentic' performances; the tone would have been nothing like that of old instruments which have since been modernized. It is over fifty years since the first response curves of violins were measured, with no doubt the best electronic equipment of the time, but it would be virtually impossible to reconstitute the equipment of that period to make a fair comparison. The resurrection of old gramophone records by modern computerized methods may be miraculous, but the original records were themselves not exactly high-fidelity recordings, and above all, what was recorded was a player's playing.

More seriously, what changes are possible? The air volume does not change. If old instruments had bigger resonances, those would be seen at once when comparing response and resonance curves with new instruments. Players often say that some old instruments speak easily; they have greater *responsiveness,* but responsiveness is not tone. Before we discuss that, there are a few important asides. One rarely if ever hears an instrument by a well-known maker of the Classical period being played by anyone other than a fine player. And valuable old instruments will have been expertly set up with strings, bridge, and soundpost positioning to obtain the best performance *by the judgement of human hearing.* Setting up can change the tone of an instrument considerably, but it does not change what the maker made. Even the resonances of the box are not absolute; they depend on how it is stressed.

It has been suggested that the response curve of an instrument is its fingerprint, and could be used to identify it. Tested in precisely the same way as a previous measurement was made, and set up precisely as it previously was, it might be corroborative evidence. But for identification of the maker, one might as well with today's forensic techniques search it for Stradivarius DNA: after all, it is said that one of his instruments bears his thumbprint in the varnish—or is it the print of the technician who varnished the instruments in his workshop? There are very few people in the world who can identify instruments with absolute authority, and so far as ordinary mortals are concerned, a violin is what authority says it is. Exactly the same thing applies to identifying a beetle.

## 5.24. *Testing and Playing*

We may not be able to distinguish well-made instruments, whatever their age and provenance, by listening to them expertly played, but there are significant differences between them; they are not at all alike to skilled players. Playing is an extremely complex process. When an experienced player tries an instrument, he is concerned with how it reacts to his bowing. He hears the sound which is produced and, particularly with a violin or viola, does so from a very peculiar position in relation to the instrument. His bowing incorporates his reaction and continuous adjustment, conscious or otherwise, to everything about the sound he hears as a result of how he is using the bow and what he feels physically, as well as through hearing while playing the instrument—that is (or should be) an important part of playing. In scientific terms, he uses feedback: he uses properties of the output of a system to modify the input. The standard method of eliminating the individual characteristics which every electronic amplifier would otherwise impose on the music and speech fed into it in electrical form is by feedback: comparing the output with the input and modifying the input accordingly, so as to produce uniform behaviour. If a player does detect any differences from note to note, he will bow to reduce this—not necessarily consciously. An example is provided by a violin with one rather large resonance which can be detected by tapping it with the strings damped. In normal playing this is 'played out', just as a mild wolf note may be. When the instrument is pushed to the limits in a fortissimo rapid passage, and the box is vibrating violently, the large resonance can be excited and its pitch can also sometimes be heard. The player is no longer entirely controlling the behaviour of the violin.

The listener hears the player's interpretation of the instrument. Playing gives an experienced player some indication of what the device is like as a player's instrument, more about what it is like as an instrument for him, and that will include the extent to which its behaviour compares with an instrument he is used to playing. Physical tests will not tell what an instrument would be like for a player, let alone for a particular player. Players differ more than instruments. And players' psychology differs more than either.

### 5.25. *Responsiveness*

Typically, then, an experienced player is concerned with the whole behaviour of an instrument and its reaction to his bowing, for which the usual word is an instrument's **responsiveness**. The sound he hears is vital, because that is what he monitors, but stripped of myth and foreknowledge, instruments that are well strung and set up all produce the unique kind of sound we identify with them—sound, *not* tone. A well-made violin sounds like a violin, but only when a player causes it to sound like a violin. Responsiveness is concerned with how an instrument reacts to all aspects of bowing. It includes the facility with which the player can produce a controlled sustained pianissimo or fortissimo on every part of the instrument's range, but it is concerned just as importantly with transient response: how immediately the instrument speaks, the rapidity with which it responds to every subtle nuance of bowing for very rapid passages, sforzandos, spiccato bowing, and so on. The sensation which the listener receives is judged on sound resulting from such interactions, but what is usually attributed to the box should far more be attributed to the player, inseparable as the two are.

Resonance is essential, but clarity and rapidity of response are particularly associated with adequate internal damping in the wood (as well as in the strings), because damping ensures that the instrument does not continue to vibrate with one set of frequencies in their respective sizes when the bowed string is producing different frequencies and different dynamic. This must extend to ensuring that the instrument responds to the continuous minute variations of string vibration as well as to larger ones; the wood must not average them out. At present there appears to be insufficient knowledge of the structural properties of wood to understand damping in detail. The long fibres of cellulose along the grain are the main elements responsible for its elasticity. The hard lignin polymer around the fibre is mainly responsible for its rigidity. These materials are interspersed with hemicellulose. All three elements will damp: that is, they will absorb energy when they are deformed and recover.

Experienced players are usually much less concerned with an instrument's 'tone' than with its behaviour. Some say that old instruments are more responsive. Do any of the things producing damping change in long-term ageing? The properties of a three-hundred-year-old spruce front could be measured, but we need a time machine to find out what it was like three centuries ago. One has to be particularly cautious about any experiment which endeavours to speed up ageing or tries to deduce the possible effect of an infinity of small vibrations over centuries by subjecting wood to larger ones over a shorter period of time. A fundamental dictum of biology is that for time there is no substitute. A remarkable recent suggestion is that violins were not meant to be played under the environmental conditions of modern concerts and studios and that this degrades the structure of the wood so that they 'wear out'—a proposal unlikely to commend itself to performers on prized instruments by the great classical makers! One could as well venture that they were not meant to be played with longer necks, higher bridges, and modern bows, or that they were meant to be kept in damp houses, transported in stagecoaches, and exposed to the smoke of candles and the fumes of wood and coal fires.

Every proposal, every experiment which tries to relate some property of the box with what is heard begs the fundamental scientific question posed at the end of Chapter 1. It presumes that the box determines the magic, and that is a belief. To be sure, every maker and every owner of an expensive instrument would like to think it was true, but it is no more scientific than teachers telling pupils that they will never be able to produce good sound unless they have an antique instrument, and that can ruin any learner's confidence. There is more than a grain of truth in the saying that the real test is to be able to produce good sound from a cigar box. Certainly, if a player thinks an instrument does what he wants, it will be easier to play. It is understandable that at the limit of technique of the finest concert performer, the detailed responsiveness of the instrument with which the player is totally familiar is inextricably linked with confidence. Every French horn has one difficult note; if four players try the same horn they will all find the difficult note—but nine times out of ten, each will find a different one. If the relationship between player and instrument is as personal as that with an apparently simpler physical device, even though it is notoriously difficult to play, what should one expect of as complex an object as a violin?

We may be certain that responsiveness is not simply ease of speaking. It appears to be recognized amongst the most advanced players that the Guarnerius-pattern instrument requires more work than the Stradivarius-pattern one. It is therefore interesting that David, Heifetz, Joachim, Kreisler, Paganini, Perlman, Ricci, Spohr, Stern, Szeryng, Vieuxtemps, and Ysaÿe, amongst others, all preferred playing a Guarnerius. There are people who say they can detect a richer tone from a Guarnerius; it has even been said that one can 'dig into it', whereas a Stradivarius can be 'pushed too far'. Certainly the shape of the Guarnerius front suggests that it is stiffer. But one has no hope of detecting any such differences by listening unless an instrument is played by a fine performer, and experienced listeners and players can often identify some of the great soloists by their playing when they have no idea of the particular instrument being played, so large is the contribution of the player to the sound.

## 5.26. *The Production of Sound*

The final stage of the violin mechanism is the production of sound in air, and apart from air resonance producing sound through the ƒ-holes, the sound is produced by the surface of the instrument, primarily by the front. Any part which vibrates produces some sound, and at various times people have 'discovered' that the back, the ribs, the neck, the scroll, the open unplayed strings also vibrate. It would be astonishing if they didn't. There are at least two deaf string players in professional orchestras who can presumably only work by direct physically felt vibration. (And the first man to say 'Only two?' gets seven days playing minimalist music!) But how much do the various parts contribute significantly to the sound radiated? Huggins, who carried out so many experiments on his Stradivarius, used a lightweight deal rod and the sense of touch of one finger to probe the extent of vibration of various parts of the instrument when played, and showed in 1883 that the point of minimum vibration on both front and back was over the soundpost, and that the front vibrated very much more than any other part.

The whole instrument does bend and twist when played, but on a very small scale, and the amount of movement of all other parts, except strings and bridge, is very tiny compared with the movement of the front. Suppose that everything apart from the front of the instrument contributed as much as 10 per cent of the total sound emitted, which is probably generous. A 10 per cent increase in sound vibration does not mean that a listener perceives sound to be 10 per cent louder than without it. It is on the margin of the ear's capacity to detect such a difference in amplitude (see Chapter 6). It makes remarkably little difference to what a listener hears if part of the back of a violin or viola is damped by a shoulder pad, and much of the back of a cello or bass is always damped by the player's body.

The actual production of sound in the air is the simplest part of the whole mechanism, for it is a faithful transcription of the form and extent of the vibration of all the parts of the instrument according to their areas, assuming for this purpose that the air inside the body is a part of the instrument. Having followed the story this far, we hope the reader will not be dissuaded from continuing if we say that the physical laws which apply to the violin are reasonably straightforward, and it is the violin which is complicated; our hearing, on the other hand, works according to rather strange laws. But whereas most of us have to accept what the physicist says happens to an instrument, when we discuss hearing its sound, it is our hearing, rather than the oscilloscope, that is the ultimate arbiter.

# 6

# Hearing String Sound

♦ ♦ ♦ ❖ ♦ ♦ ♦

## 6.1. *Physical Sound and Sensation*

The previous chapters have outlined discoveries about the mechanism
of bowed instruments, and how that produces the sounds in the air; for
much of this we are indebted to a small number of skilled investigators
working during the past fifty years. We now have to try to relate those
sounds to the sensations we hear. At least one thing is helpful in this.
Important aspects of instrument mechanism have been described in
terms of pure tone vibrations, and what we have called their sustained
pitched sounds are most easily appreciated as sets of pure tone harmonics. Some of the most useful knowledge we have of hearing has also
been obtained by exploring with pure tones.

Knowledge of the ear's mechanism is quite extensive, but we know
much less about hearing: the perception of sound by the higher levels
of the brain. Ears detect what they can of the sound as it goes past
them; the brain can only perceive what the ears send to it. Listening to
music or any other sound is much more complex than simply experi-
encing a sensation as the sound is actually received. The sensation at
any instant must be related to what has preceded it. When we hear a
violin solo, our attention is concerned with a synthesis of many things,
such as pitch and intonation, dynamic, phrasing, and rhythm. Every element of the music involves a perspective in time. We may think of pitch
physically as the frequency of the fundamental, but pitch only has meaning in the context of where it occurs in the music. In typical listening
circumstances, our attention often only goes consciously to one of the
components when it does not meet expectation. We might regard pitch,
dynamic, rhythm, and phrasing as relatively straightforward because
they are indicated by the written music; in truth, it is their subtle
manipulation that comprises performance.

In contrast, tone is much less tangible, and because the word is used in so many different ways by musicians, we limit it to the first scientific definition put forward, by Helmholtz (see Chapter 2.2): the sensation produced by the harmonics. A synthesized sound with harmonics matching those of the sustained part of a violin's note, has the tone of that note. It does not resemble the sound of a live-bowed string with the same harmonics, and so we shall use the term **timbre** for the difference we *perceive* between the two. It is not necessarily directly shown by the physical differences we can see between pictures of synthesized and real string sound. Amplitude does not directly equate with loudness. Indeed, as we shall see, we may describe pitch by the frequency of the fundamental; the sensation of pitch is far more than that. All these things are due to the way in which sound is processed by our hearing.

## 6.2. *The Nature of Hearing*

Our senses were naturally selected for the survival of our ancestors in the circumstances in which they lived. This happened a very long time ago. We can see only the colours of light which will pass through water: this was the light available to our marine ancestors. Some creatures can see ultraviolet, which is absorbed by water. Our sound-detecting system was evolved for the needs of an animal, and there is nothing to suggest that the ear's machinery differs at all from that of mankind a hundred thousand years ago when we were living very like any other animal; indeed, the machinery closely resembles that of several other animals. Sound is processed so as to emphasize things most useful to each animal. Making any sound meaningful, as in speech or music, happens entirely in the brain, but the ear system we have inherited from our ancestors has had a profound effect on what the brain has selected as music and as musically attractive sound. The word 'ear' is often used by musicians as a synonym for hearing, but we must distinguish the detecting device: the ear, from the interpreter producing sensation: hearing, which occurs in the brain.

Sound enters the part of the ear we can see. From that moment it is modified; then it vibrates minute bones which change it again *before* it reaches a remarkable device which reads what it can of the modified vibrations. This device (in the cochlea, a snail-shaped spiral hole in bone) is a coding machine; it produces streams of electrical impulses in thousands of nerves which convey information about the vibration to the brain. It has, perhaps, a little in common with a computer. The paths along which the impulses travel in the brain are very complex. Different aspects of the sound with which we are concerned in music, such as its pitch, its rhythm, and the relationship between the sound coming into either ear, may be dealt with in different parts of the brain, about which we know almost nothing in detail. The brain receives a complex code of impulses from the ears, and they create the sensation. We must not think of this as sending the brain a representation of what we draw on paper as a wave form, or a set of harmonics. Also, our attention may go to particular aspects of the sensation, but other features are being noted at a subconscious level; we usually realize this if they are absent from a sound. Our automatic concern with some characteristics is a part of our ancestry; it is also linked with the ephemeral nature of sound. Sounds have to be sensed as they happen and change. We can decide for how long and in what order we look at things. Hearing is rather more like watching a film; both require some element of memory, short-term or longer-term, to obtain information about what is happening.

### 6.3. *The Range of Hearing*

Some approximate frequencies for reference are:

Fundamental (open string): double bass low C = 31 Hz; cello C = 62 Hz; viola C = 125 Hz; violin A = 440 Hz.
Fundamental of C, 2 leger lines above treble staff = 1 kHz; C, 6 leger lines above treble staff = 2 kHz.
The sixteenth harmonic of middle C is 4 kHz.

We can hear pure tones as low as 16 Hz—an octave below double bass low C—and up to three or four octaves above treble staff, though that depends both on our age and on the levels of noise to which we have been exposed in our lives. But we do not hear pure tones of different pitch at all equally. We are far more sensitive in the two octaves above treble staff (about 1 to 4 kHz) than to low and to very high frequencies (Fig. 6.1). The harmonics of notes are distributed over ranges where our hearing has very different sensitivities. For example, the fundamentals of notes below about violin open A are signalled less strongly than any of their higher harmonics. This affects our perception of loudness and tone. The dynamic scale we have used so far assumes that each three-fold increase in the amplitude of sound vibration roughly doubles the loudness (see Chapter 1.4). It is a reasonable rule for sound above the

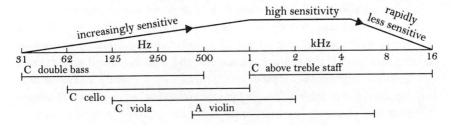

FIG. 6.1. The sensitivity of hearing at different frequencies. Below, the spans of the first 16 harmonics of various notes (whichever instrument plays them).

treble staff. The lower the pitch, the less well it represents how the perceived loudness corresponds to a sound's amplitude.

## 6.4. *How Many Harmonics Matter?*

A strongly bowed string can produce twenty or more harmonics. The sound in the air may contain as many. How many do we hear? In Section 2 above we said that hearing reads *what it can* of the incoming sound, for a good reason. The brain can only create sensation from the information it receives. The coding machine can read and send quite good information about some harmonics, but it may send a poor account of some, and nothing about others. This is vital if we are to understand tone. It will also simplify discussion if we do not have to consider two dozen harmonics.

The mechanism of coding vibration is complex. The description given in this chapter is a simplified account of a very complicated system, but we are able to concentrate to a large extent on a specialized aspect of its functioning: how we hear pitched sound. The principles of sensing vibration are not too difficult to understand. When vibration reaches the coding device in the cochlea, it causes a long narrow resonant membrane to vibrate. If the membrane were uniform like a string, it would resonate at just one frequency. The ear's membrane has continuously changing properties from one end to the other. It is stiff at one end and floppy at the other, and it is wider at one end than at the other. When it is exposed to a pure tone vibration, only the bit of the membrane which is resonant at that frequency vibrates. As a result, a high frequency vibrates a small area towards one end, a low frequency towards the other end; each different frequency in a sound vibrates a specific small area of the membrane.

There are thousands of vibration detectors all along the membrane; they are the ends of nerves which sense vibration and fire impulses to the brain. We sense the loudness of a pure tone by coding how much its area vibrates. If the vibration is larger, the area vibrates more; it does not increase in area. We sense its frequency by a complex code representing the rate at which the area is vibrating. If the frequency changes, the area moves along the membrane.

A sound containing several frequencies is therefore 'spread out in frequency order' on the membrane. The spacing of the frequency-responding areas is important and musically fascinating. We can show the complete harmonic series of string sound in two ways. They can be spaced equally (as in Fig. 2.1) because each pure tone differs from the one below by the same amount: 100, 200, 300, and 400 Hz all differ by 100. Or they can be spaced as they are on a musical scale, with equal distances between octaves, that is, equal distances between 100, 200, 400, and 800 Hz (Fig. 6.2; compare Fig. 2.2), and that is quite close to the way in which pure tones are distributed along the coding machine's membrane; successively higher harmonics are closer together.

1          2          4          8          16

FIG. 6.2. Harmonics of most notes are distributed on the ear's coding device with octaves (harmonics 1, 2, 4, 8, 16) equally spaced.

The way in which the spacing limits what harmonics can be signalled is revealed by a simple test. If one ear receives two similarly loud pure tones differing by a semitone, neither can be discerned; the sensation is a 'rough' noise. If the pitch of the higher tone is slowly raised, there comes a point where both tones can just be distinguished, and as the difference increases, the tones become clearer while the noise decreases, until both tones are heard clearly and there is no roughness. If those tones are two harmonics, what can be heard depends on how close their areas are on the coding machine's membrane. The roughness is generated in the receiving ear; play one tone into the left ear and the other into the right, and both are always clearly heard, however close they are in frequency.

The lowest members of the harmonic series comprising the sound of

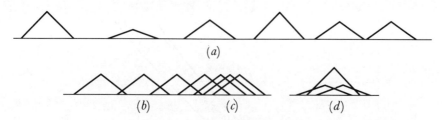

FIG. 6.3. The distribution of harmonics (schematic representation). Each pure tone vibrates its specific area of the coding device, whatever its amplitude. Except for very low frequencies, the first six harmonics occupy separate areas (*a*). The higher the harmonics, the more they overlap. If overlap is slight (*b*), they are signalled with some roughness. If the overlap is greater (*c*), they mask each other and generate only roughness. A large harmonic (*d*) may be signalled if those on either side are small.

the violin family are widely spaced on a musical scale (Fig. 6.2), and for most notes, the first few harmonics do occupy separate areas on the membrane (Fig. 6.3*a*). But because the areas occupied by the harmonics get closer together as one goes up through the series, they soon begin to overlap (*b*). The bits of membrane where areas overlap are no longer vibrating at a single frequency; those parts signal that they are being vibrated, but this only produces the sensation of roughness. Something of the frequency of the rest of each area is signalled indistinctly. Higher up the series they overlap more (*c*); they mask each other's frequencies entirely, and produce only roughness. Readers who wish to go into the detail of this will find an explanation in Fig. 6.4, and the next paragraph, but the essentials are summarized in the paragraphs which follow.

Fig. 6.4 shows what happens for any sound made up of *equal amplitude* harmonics, though the boundaries where overlap begins and where total roughness occurs are not as sharply defined as the diagram might suggest. As an example, violin open G has a pitch of about 200 Hz, so the difference between each pair of harmonics is 200 Hz. If we follow the 200 Hz pitch line, the 6th harmonic (1.2 kHz) is within the **clear** zone; the 10th harmonic is just on the edge of **total roughness**. The first six harmonics are coded clearly; harmonics 7–10 **overlap** and are heard progressively less clearly with increasing roughness. From harmonic 10 upwards all that the harmonics contribute to the sensation is roughness. For other pitches, the numbers mark the position of the harmonics nearest to the boundaries of the three zones.

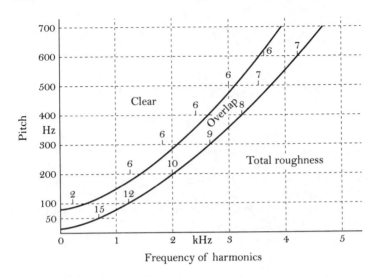

F IG. 6.4. The clarity of perceived harmonics (see text).

Generalizing, we can divide the signalling of string sound harmonics into three groups: clear, overlapping and indistinct, and totally rough. What is signalled does depend on the pitch of the note; nothing about hearing behaves quite uniformly. If all the harmonics were of roughly equal vibration, and whichever instrument is played, notes of pitch of about viola G (200 Hz) up to about the top of the treble staff (600 Hz) have 6 clear harmonics, and overlap begins at the 7th harmonic. But the higher the pitch within this range, the fewer the number of harmonics in the indistinct band. Viola C has 6 progressively less distinct harmonics. At middle C total roughness occurs at the 10th harmonic. At violin A it happens at about the 8th harmonic, and at C above the treble staff there are 5 clear harmonics and no indistinct ones; the rest just generate roughness. Our hearing behaves differently for notes of pitch below the bass staff. The membrane is not long enough to separate the frequency areas and has a broader resonance. Only the first two harmonics of open cello G (100 Hz) are clear, but tones can be discerned indistinctly up to the 12th harmonic. At cello C (62 Hz) and below, which includes all the lower range of the double bass, all the harmonics overlap, but they are partially signalled right up to the 15th, four octaves above a fundamental.

Since bowed strings produce a complete series of harmonics, all the areas of the overlapping harmonics, except for the first of them, overlap on both sides (Fig. 6.3*b*). The clarity of what is signalled to the brain from any such higher harmonic therefore depends both on the size of its own vibration and on the sizes of the harmonics on either side of it. The resonance of an instrument varies with frequency, and for each bowed note, how much will be signalled of each harmonic which overlaps, will depend on its amplitude in that note. Although something can be signalled by a very large amplitude harmonic in the total-roughness region, with very small ones either side of it (Fig. 6.3*d*), it is most unlikely that that will ever happen with bowed string sound.

Since sounds are difficult to describe, what is meant by roughness is best illustrated by real sound. The double bass is traditionally described as gruff; over most of its range it produces a buzzing pitchless background with its notes, and, to a lesser extent, so does low cello sound. That is roughness. There will also be a very small amount of pitchless hiss from bow friction. The extent to which we perceive roughness decreases as pitch rises on all instruments; the buzz becomes hiss in high double bass notes, but it can be heard as hiss up to pitches of at least violin A with strong bowing. It is a distinctive characteristic of lower bowed string sound. There is no sign of the noise in a picture of the sound on an oscilloscope screen, or in Fourier analysis of the sound. It occurs entirely in the ear, and though no doubt people have tried, there is no way of making a bass or cello without it! Roughness is less in the sound of strings lightly bowed at 1/5 length, because, as we saw in Chapter 2, the higher harmonics which occur in the region where roughness is generated, are much smaller. Whether roughness is akin to beating between sounds with slightly different frequencies is a source of argument.

## 6.5. *What Contributes to String Tone?*

Is it surprising that most of the tone sensation is really generated by only six or so harmonics, double bass and low cello apart? It will simplify our discussion of the very uneven loudness response of the ear to different frequencies if the number of effective harmonics is limited in this way. We can show that this is true using an an electronic synthesizer (see Section 16 below), and we can limit discussion of string *tone*, as defined in Section 1 above, to 16 harmonics for bass notes, 12 for the middle range, and 8 or fewer in the high range; timbre is a different matter.

Roughness and the limit on sensing harmonics is a general phenomenon of hearing any sound producing overlapping harmonics. The sawtooth wave sound (Fig. 2.10d) produces powerful roughness at low pitches. It is present to some extent in low bassoon sound, and very evident from the bass saxophone. Saxophones produce a complete series of harmonics; though superficially like clarinets, they have a conical tube. Clarinets have a parallel tube and primarily produce the odd numbered harmonics, 1, 3, 5, 7, and so on. Although clarinet sound contains very small harmonics in between these, the main harmonics are spaced twice as widely as those of string sound, and overlap does not begin until about twice as high a frequency as with string harmonics. Even the lowest clarinet notes do not have any roughness (except in the hands of the inimitable Acker Bilk, but he did not produce a normal harmonic analysis).

There is of course a $64,000 question. If a full orchestra plays *ff*, why do we not hear only roughness? One answer is that if a score is well laid out as described in any good text on orchestration, the enormously powerful harmonics of the brass dominate all the other vibrations present. Another answer is that in some modern music we do.

## 6.6. *The Loudness of Harmonics*

There are three obvious questions about the loudness of bowed strings. First, how does our peculiar dynamic scale of hearing affect playing? There seems to be a larger dynamic range on the violin than on the bass; the margin between playing softly and loudly on a bass is much smaller than on the higher instruments. Cello and bass have much bigger fronts than violins and violas. They have higher bridges. They do produce much larger sound vibrations. Secondly, why don't they swamp a violin? Obviously, because hearing is much more sensitive to higher-pitched sounds. Thirdly, if that is so and tone is created by the *perceived* level of the harmonics, should we not adjust the sizes of the harmonics as measured in the air, according to how loudly each is heard, to get a better idea of what contributes to tone? How tone is affected by where a set of harmonics lies in our hearing range, is demonstrated by speeding up or slowing down a tape recording of music. By doubling the speed at which the tape runs, we move all the sound up an octave. The frequency of every harmonic is doubled; the harmonics keep the same size relationship to one another. But all the lower frequencies are moved into regions where hearing is more sensitive to them, and the highest ones may be moved up to the region where we become less sensitive again. The tone changes out of all recognition. Tone certainly depends on the relative loudnesses of the harmonics as sensed by hearing.

How and perhaps why such things happen may be most easily approached by considering how a sense of hearing evolved. It originated as an advantage to animals who could detect vibration in their environment. Animals have only one way of detecting that a part of them is being moved by touch or by vibration. The end of a nerve is positioned so that when the part moves, the end is stretched; stretching causes the nerve to fire an electrical pulse, which travels along the nerve into the brain. That tells the brain that movement has occurred. To detect sound, the element which stretches the nerve end has to resonate to the sound. Natural sound consists of a very large number of random frequencies. The system must resonate to that kind of sound; it could have many separate elements each resonating at a different frequency (an insect method) or, as we have, one element resonating to different frequencies in different places. It must have sensors: nerve ends, all along the membrane, wherever the vibration happens. This is a basic ear.

If the brain knew from which parts of the membrane the signals were coming, it might discern something about the frequency, though probably not with any great accuracy. Since a nerve end is repeatedly stretched by a vibration, more accurate information about the rate of vibration can be sent by relating the rate of the pulses to the rate of vibration. By sending information about frequency in this way, the brain is told the character of the sound, but it need not necessarily know where, along the membrane, the pulses originate.

A primitive ear would start as a crude device able to detect only large vibration. There are several ways in which it can be enabled to detect lower-level sound. The most obvious are to make the resonance of the membrane very sensitive, and to use an external funnel which collects a little more sound, like the ear-trumpet used before modern hearing-aids. The nerves could be made to fire at the slightest vibration. The question is why ears evolved to have such very different sensitivity at different sound frequencies, a phenomenon which so complicates understanding our perception of sound and tone. For us to hear a pure tone at all, at the fundamental of double bass low C (31 Hz) the sound must have about a thousand times the amplitude of one we can just hear an octave above the treble staff. And why did hearing develop our odd dynamic scale of loudness?

It depends on what kind of faint noise is valuable to an animal. Some need to detect footsteps—low-frequency sound; this is not helped by hearing a lot of high frequencies at the same time. Tiny high-pitched sound from mice, without loud low sound, is valuable to cats. The range which had most survival value for mankind was 1–5 kHz; otherwise we would be most sensitive in a different range; that it happens to be entirely above the treble staff was not a factor which entered into our evolution.

Two things make our hearing sensitivity peak in the 1–5 kHz range. First, the sound is modified before it gets to the coding machine. The tube between the outer ear and the eardrum, on which the sound pressure operates, contains air, and the air resonates. Wind instruments work because the air in them resonates; their resonances are very sharp so that they can produce specific pitches. The ear's tube has two very broad resonances which have been measured by placing a tiny microphone by the eardrum and comparing the level of sound there with the sound received by an identical microphone just outside the ear. Fig. 6.5 shows how the amplitudes of pure tones are changed between the two

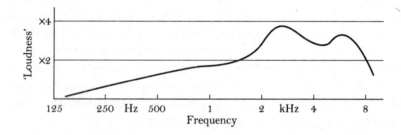

FIG. 6.5. The resonance of the tube between the outer ear and eardrum; at the eardrum, sound at around 3 kHz has ten times the amplitude that it has outside the ear.

microphone positions. The diagram uses the dynamic scale, so that at about 2.5 kHz—about two octaves above violin open E—the sound vibrating the drum has ten times the amplitude of the external sound (equivalent to making it four times as loud) but there is little change in the fundamentals of notes in the bass staff or in sounds of very high frequencies. A musical sound has the amplitudes of all its harmonics changed in this way, even before it vibrates the coding machine.

The other sophistication is brought about by adjusting both the numbers and the sensitivities of the sensors (Fig. 6.6; compare Fig. 6.1). At the two ends of the membrane where low and high frequencies are

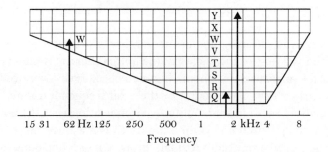

FIG. 6.6. The system sensing sound (schematic representation). In silence, the membrane of the coding device lies along the frequency scale. Each square represents perhaps 150–200 sensors, firing when membrane vibration reaches them. Suppose a pure tone vibrates one column width of membrane. Vibration at 2 kHz reaching level Q signals faint sound. It must reach level W at 62 Hz to signal faint sound. All the sensors at the top of each column signal very loud sound, when vibration reaches level Y. The more sensors in a column, the more levels of loudness that can be judged. Compare Figs. 6.1 and 6.7.

detected, there are fewer sensors, and they will only fire if stretched by larger vibration. We can detect only larger-amplitude sounds there. Along the 1–5 kHz part of the membrane there are many sensors. Some signal a minute vibration, and they fire with all bigger vibrations. The rest are graded in sensitivity so that the larger the vibration, the more sensors signal. The sensation of loudness will partly be indicated by the number of streams of impulses going to the brain from an area, but it may also be caused by the particular nerves which are firing. The density of sensors and their graded sensitivities increase continuously from the low-frequency end to the peak-sensitivity region and then rapidly decrease to the highest-frequency end.

A moderate-amplitude pure tone of 2 kHz fires many sensors. The same-amplitude sound at 200 Hz fires fewer. All these nerves are also conveying some information about the frequency at their positions by their rates of firing; loudness and pitch are therefore aspects of a *single sensation* produced by one set of impulses. But this does not necessarily mean that any one nerve is sending impulses at the actual vibration rate (see Section 13 below). In addition to all this there is an involuntary mechanism by which, to an extent, the overall volume of loud sound may be turned down before it gets to the coding device.

6.7. *The Reason for our Dynamic Scale*

The resonances of the ear tube are fixed. Our dynamic sense is determined by the grading of the sensors; it is quite different from any physical amplitude-measuring system. To detect danger, we needed an ability to sense a very faint sound in the vital frequency range, and to detect a small increase in its amplitude: an indication that the source of noise might be approaching. With a louder sound we needed to sense a small increase in *its* amplitude. A small increase in a loud sound is many times greater than a small increase in a faint one. A tiny increase in a loud sound is meaningless. We use this property in string music; subtle changes which are effective at low dynamic would go unnoticed in loud passages.

The grading of the sensors provides the dynamic scale we have used. It only holds reasonably well for sounds from about violin open A upwards, regardless of which of the family actually plays. But since, as we shall shortly see, the fundamental is of no special importance in most bowed sound, it is reasonably true for a violin's entire range. The amplitude of the sound in the air is broadly speaking proportional to that of the bowed string. So, in principle, starting with a very low-dynamic violin note, we need about three times the string amplitude for hearing to sense that the sound is twice as loud; ten times for twice as loud again. Suppose we say that doubling loudness is advancing one dynamic marking, that is, changing from *pp* to *p* is increasing the string vibration by three times. It is ten times from *pp* to *mp*, 30 times to *mf*, 100 times to *f*, and 300 times to *ff*. Does a player use a three-hundredfold range of string vibration? A range of three-hundredfold in string amplitude from bowing a string mechanically at 1/10 length has been directly measured, so it is possible.

We do not really play a violin like that. The maximum range of dynamic is obtained by using light bowing at 1/5 string length and heavy bowing nearer the bridge. Nor is the dynamic scale we use when playing music quite as steep as that (see Chapter 7.4). But the principle is correct, and it has important implications, especially for orchestral playing. A violinist must add more vibration for the last step in dynamic than for the first four steps put together. That is why conductors shout, 'Don't start the crescendo too soon!'—to amateur orchestras.

## 6.8. *Loudness and Harmonics*

We need now to look at some of the detailed information which has been gathered, about the relationship between pure tone amplitude, frequency, and perceived loudness. Some altruistic people (or long-suffering students of acousticians and audiologists) have listened to thousands of pure tones of different amplitudes and frequencies. They have judged when one pure tone is twice as loud as another of the same frequency, and indeed three and four times as loud. They have judged when two sounds of different frequencies have the same loudness. People with normal hearing reach surprisingly good agreement about these values. Some of the results are shown in the famous Fletcher–Munsen diagrams (Fig. 6.7). Don't be put off by the picture. The explanation of how our hearing works should help to understand it.

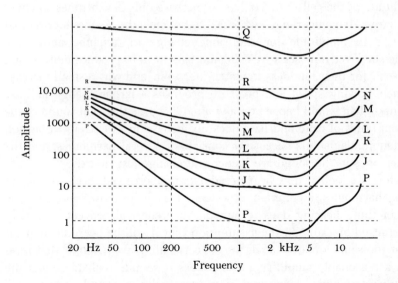

FIG. 6.7. The loudness of pure tones. Sound is judged equally loud along each curve, at the given amplitudes and frequencies (see text; after Fletcher and Munsen).

Start with the vertical line for a pure tone of 1 kHz—C above the treble staff. The loudness of a pure tone of this frequency doubles from one curve of the graph to the next: from J to K or from M to N. There are many graded sensors here which give our typical dynamic scale. Along each curve, pure tones have equal loudness. So if we follow the curve L, we see that a sound with an amplitude of 100 on the scale, has the same loudness from about 500 Hz to 2 kHz. This loudness is produced by only 80 amplitude units at 3 kHz, but at 6 kHz the amplitude must be more than 500 units. In the other direction along curve L, when we get down to 62 Hz (the fundamental of cello open C) the amplitude must be over 2,000 units to have the same loudness. There are fewer sensors here, and they are only fired by much larger vibrations.

From about 500 Hz upwards all the curves J to N are roughly parallel to each other. This means that the steps in our judgement of loudness—our comparative dynamic scale—hold for any frequency in this range, whatever the actual loudness levels of the pure tones. Things are very different at low frequencies, where the curves are close together. A cello C fundamental of 62 Hz must have an amplitude of about 1000 to have loudness J, but when its amplitude is increased to about 7000 it will have reached loudness N. If curve J to curve N represents $p$ to $ff$, the amplitude of the cello's 62 Hz has to increase only seven times to cover this large dynamic range, whereas there must be a one-hundredfold increase in amplitude for the same change in dynamic above the treble staff. We now see why cello and bass have to produce more sound in the air for their loudness to match the violin, and why a small increase in their bowing speed and pressure produces a larger change in their loudness than would happen on a violin. Of course the total sound of the bottom notes of cello and bass does not behave in as extreme a fashion as their fundamentals because it consists of several harmonics, and the higher ones in the sound are louder and change less quickly.

Before we look at how hearing adjusts the perceived levels of a set of string harmonics, a common experience may help us to appreciate the sort of thing hearing does to sound. An orchestral concert is usually transmitted by radio on the assumption that it will be heard at home at about the same loudness as in the concert-hall. If we listen at that level with a reasonable amplifier and speakers it sounds realistic. Turn the amplifier's volume down and it reduces all the sound—every harmonic—in the same proportion. To make the music more realistic at this general lower level, we have to turn up the bass control and increase the relative size of all the lower harmonics. Because hearing is so much more sensitive in its higher-frequency range, when we listen to a sound of many frequencies at a relatively low level, like the sound of a solo stringed instrument, the higher frequencies are stronger than the low ones in the sensation, and the lower the total sound level, the greater this differential is.

There is an obvious problem with the cello and bass at low loudness. Curve P of Fig. 6.7 gives the amplitudes of the smallest pure tone vibration that an average person with normal hearing can just hear. Any harmonic in a sound whose amplitude does not reach that line cannot be heard. What happens to the lowest harmonics of double bass notes? The answer is simple; until they reach an amplitude of about 500 on that scale, we can't hear them. That certainly happens at low levels of sound in musical terms. I hope it will be more intriguing than worrying that when a cello plays open C *pp* we can't hear the fundamental and that when the bass plays very quietly on its bottom string we probably can't hear the second harmonic either. Of course we can hear the *pitch* of these notes. There would be no point in butchering the scrolls of fine basses and attaching a chimera of trombone tubing and clarinet keys if one couldn't perceive low C. All will be explained in due course.

Should you think that hearing operates in a very odd way, it was not evolved to sense notes of constant pitch. There was no reason for man to be able to discern musical pitch until he became interested in it (see Section 13 below). That is very important in understanding the origin of instrument sound. It is no coincidence that a violin happens to produce very little sound above 8 kHz; our hearing ability is as poor at 8 kHz as it is at the fundamental of double bass low C. Would we have developed different instruments if we were cats? They can hear for a further octave or so above us, but cannot hear the low notes we can. It is the curious way in which we hear pitched sound that selected the characteristics of the violin family.

## 6.9. *Adjusting a Set of Harmonics*

Can we devise something from the way in which our hearing perceives the loudness of pure tones to give a more realistic picture of how the levels of the harmonics in a bowed string note are presented to the brain? We can only look at this in principle, but it is a very important principle, which we can test by our experience of listening to the four members of the family. What we want is a characteristic rather like Fig. 6.5, which showed the way the resonance of the ear tube changes the levels of the sound between the outside world and the eardrum. And in fact the curves K and L in Fig. 6.7 are not unlike that of Fig. 6.5 turned upside down. That should not surprise. The sensors are detecting sound which has already been modified by the resonances of the ear tube. If we had only one row of sensors, all of identical sensitivity, along the ear membrane, that would produce one curve for Fig. 6.7, and it would be very like Fig. 6.5 upside down; in fact the sensors have used the 2 kHz resonance of the tube much more than the higher one. A few further observations about total sound levels will show that it is reasonable to use a curve like L turned upside down, for the *principle* of adjusting the loudness of string harmonics.

The curves of Fig. 6.7 represent the loudness of single pure tones. The loudness sensation we obtain is due to the total number of sensors firing. Curve Q is the level at which one pure tone, vibrating one area, causes pain. The combined sounds of a heavy metal pop group may be only a little way below that, but they are firing nerves right along the membrane. The level of their individual harmonics (if that isn't too polite a term for them), combining to create their loudness, must be well below curve Q. Curve R may represent the level of loudness of a full orchestral tutti *ff.* The individual harmonics of that sound will be well below curve R. So it is not at all unreasonable to put the level of the individual harmonics making up the overall loudness of a solo stringed instrument, playing at moderate dynamic level, down at about curve L or even lower.

## 6.10. *Perceived Harmonic Balance*

We will use the pattern of harmonics of an ideal string bowed towards the bridge to illustrate the *principle* of how they are presented to hearing; we can then discuss how bowing at the fingerboard, and the irregularity produced by body resonance, would be affected. In Fig. 6.8 we have drawn a curve for the enhancement of the frequencies; it is based on the form of curve L in the Fletcher–Munsen diagram (Fig. 6.7). We can demonstrate the *comparative* levels of the harmonics, as signalled to the brain, by combining the size of the string harmonics with this hearing-enhancement curve. It is very convenient that we are using dynamic scales for both curve and harmonics. Each line representing the amplitude of a harmonic as it occurs in the sound, can be added to the hearing curve. (We are using logarithmic scales.) The new height gives the *relative* perceived loudness of each harmonic. The diagram uses a musical scale for frequency; octaves are equally spaced.

Fig. 6.8 demonstrates the effect on three bowed notes. The number of harmonics shown for each note are those which are signalled before they are in the total-roughness zone (see Section 4 above). A low-pitched note such as cello open C has fifteen sensed harmonics; they are

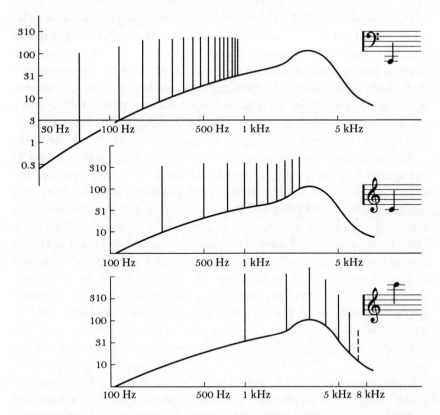

F IG. 6.8. The principle of how the ear adjusts the relative levels of the harmonics of three strongly bowed notes when signalling them to the brain, is
shown by adding the harmonics of the sound to a curve of the ear's sensitivity. Only the clear and partially signalled harmonics are shown (see text).

progressively made to sound louder. Not only are the higher harmonics louder, but there are many more of them in the top octave, tilting
the overall balance strongly in that direction. Next we take an inter-
mediate-pitched note, middle C, from which nine or ten harmonics are
clearly or partially signalled. The first few harmonics are on the rising
part of the curve and progressively enhanced. The rest are in the peak
region of greatest increase in loudness. Finally we have a high-pitched
note: C above the treble staff has only five clear harmonics. The first
three are very strongly presented to the brain. The fourth and fifth
are reduced. The sixth is much reduced as well as being in the total-
roughness band. Above that it does not matter whether they are
reduced or lost to roughness; we can't hear them.

This picture applies whichever instrument plays the note. The enhancement curve goes below the baseline in the cello C diagram. We have met this before. If a harmonic put on the curve is not big enough to cross the baseline it will not be heard at all. And if the frequencies of the high harmonics are higher than the resonance of an instrument, they will not contribute to what we hear. We can now visualize more realistically how the harmonics of the instruments generate tone. Everything concerned with timbre is superimposed on this framework.

We can do some simple sums (all the answers are in Tables 3 and 4) and apply the principle of Fig. 6.8 to all the instruments. All the harmonics up to C above the treble staff (1000 Hz) are progressively enhanced. Divide 1000 Hz by the frequency of the fundamental of a note, and that gives the number of harmonics *progressively* enhanced. The strongly enhanced harmonics are between 1 and 5 kHz. Divide 5000 Hz by the fundamental's frequency to give the highest harmonic in this strong band. Any harmonic above 5000 Hz is progressively weaker in the sensation. Any harmonic above an instrument's resonance disappears, and also all harmonics in the total-roughness band. Table 3 shows how the harmonics are represented to hearing for the open bottom string and the open top string of each of the four members of the family.

In discussing tone in Chapter 3 we saw that when a mute is applied to the bridge of an instrument, the sound has very few harmonics, and muted sound has thin tone. We also know (Chapter 2.9) that notes lightly bowed at 1/5 string length have weaker high harmonics than notes bowed at 1/10 string length, and that the latter have a richer sound than the former. Table 3 provides a body of information about the number and comparative strengths of the perceived harmonics in sound from strings similarly bowed towards the bridge. We can use Table 3 to test a proposal that the *richness* of bowed string tone is greater when a larger number of harmonics are present, and when the higher harmonics of the sound are more strongly represented by the ear to hearing.

The bass and cello have a large number of strong higher harmonics and are rich in tone throughout the range of Table 3. The viola has only slightly fewer strong higher harmonics up to the A string and is characteristically rich. The violin, on the other hand, begins to lose higher harmonics when it gets to its top string; the sound there is clear but less rich. This matches our hearing's impression of the various instruments. The significant test, however, is what happens when we ascend

TABLE 3

The Harmonics Available to Hearing from Normal Bowing at Various Pitches

| Open string | Frequency of fundamental (Hz) | Harmonics available * | Progressively enhanced harmonics (−1 kHz) | Strong harmonics (1–5 kHz) | Weak harmonics (5 kHz−) |
|---|---|---|---|---|---|
| Bass low C | 31 | 1–16 | 1–16 | — | — |
| Cello C | 62 | 1–15 | 1–15 | — | — |
| Viola C | 125 | 1–11 | 1–8 | 9–11 | — |
| Violin G | 200 | 1–10 | 1–6 | 7–10 | — |
| Bass G | 100 | 1–10 | 1–10 | — | — |
| Cello A | 220 | 1–10 | 1–5 | 6–10 | — |
| Viola A | 440 | 1–9 | 1–3 | 4–9 | — |
| Violin E | 660 | 1–7 | 1–2 | 3–6 | 7 |

* The harmonics below the total-roughness region.

the top strings of the instruments, where several limitations come into play (Table 4).

As a player ascends a violin E string, the harmonics are strong but decrease in numbers until at octave E only harmonics 1–3 are in the strong band; harmonics 4–5 are weak. The sound, as our hearing

TABLE 4

The Harmonics Available to Hearing from Normal Bowing at Various Pitches

| Octave of top string | Frequency (Hz) | Limit of instrument resonance (kHz) | Harmonics available * | Progressively enhanced harmonics (−1 kHz) | Strong harmonics (1–5 kHz) | Weak harmonics (5 kHz−) |
|---|---|---|---|---|---|---|
| Bass G | 200 | 2.5 | 1–10 | 1–5 | 6–10 | — |
| Cello A | 440 | 5 | 1–8 | 1–2 | 3–8 | — |
| Viola A | 880 | 7 | 1–6 | 1 | 2–5 | 6 |
| Violin E | 1320 | 8 | 1–5 | — | 1–3 | 4–5 |

* The harmonics below the total-roughness region.

perceives, becomes increasingly 'pure' and, in the instrument's highest range, approaches the pure tone itself, which has the least tone character of any sound. The viola's open A has nine enhanced or strong harmonics, but these are reduced to five at octave A on the top string. The sound becomes less rich, but the high notes are richer than those of the violin.

The cello presents a quite different picture. It produces nine strongly sensed harmonics on its open A, and when it reaches octave A on the top string it still has eight harmonics within the enhanced or full sensitivity range of hearing; hence the wonderful 'reedy' richness of high notes on a cello gut A string, beloved of every composer. The bass still has ten effective harmonics at the octave of its top string, and is as rich as the cello when playing an octave lower than the cello. As soon as it tries to compete with the cello at cello top-string pitch, its harmonics disappear and the sound is thin and poor. Remarkable technical feats are now performed on the highest range of the bass, but Prokofiev knew precisely what he wanted in the *Lieutenant Kijé* Suite in order to make the music as much of a joke as the undoubtedly fact-based story he was portraying.

Neither table is exact to one harmonic; people's ears differ. But the highest harmonic which is available to hearing when the octave of the top string of both cello and bass is played, is close to the limit of effective resonance of these instruments. With the viola and violin, it is hearing which curtails the high harmonics. In other words, nothing can be achieved by attempting to push the upper limit of the resonances higher. Is this fortuitous? It is unlikely that the early makers discovered such limits by experiment, however they may have expressed their results. In their baroque form, instruments were not normally originally played in high positions, and using an out-curved bow they could not be strongly bowed. Perhaps it was the fairy godmother who gave them a new bass bar and bridge when they underwent their transformation.

## 6.11. *Conclusions: Tonal Richness*

The progressive enhancement of the harmonics by hearing applies to any set of harmonics that the bow generates. For all notes within the two staves, the distribution and number of enhanced and strong harmonics are such that stronger bowing at 1/10 string length or nearer the bridge makes sound richer but also increases the roughness. Bowed towards the fingerboard, the string produces weaker higher harmonics, and the balance is tilted towards the lower ones (see Chapter 2.9). The tone is less rich but clearer, and it cannot be enriched by strong bowing there. For notes well above the treble staff there is no richness because we do not hear enough harmonics strongly enough, and in fact bowing in different positions on high violin E notes only affects dynamic.

From the bottom of the bass staff downwards, there is always distinct roughness. It increases with dynamic and with bowing towards the bridge. Whether strongly bowed notes from the cello and bass in this range are 'rich but muddy' is a matter of opinion. The roughness decreases with bowing near the fingerboard and bowing lightly, but is always present. This is part of the difficulty of tuning low strings. Far from meaning that the pitch does not matter, it is vital for the intonation of an ensemble that bass instruments are in tune. Since the sound can be more clearly sensed the more lightly any string is bowed, we have a reason for the recommended practice of bowing lightly when tuning. The frequent problem bassists and cellists meet is that in the general cacophony which is called 'tuning' by many amateur orchestras, the lower string players cannot hear their instruments properly even when very strongly bowed, and so they tune by *armonici* two octaves above pitch, which are not exact octaves on any strings, but it is dangerous advice to suggest to people that they should tune by *armonici* and make them 2 per cent flat!

## 6.12. *The Harmonics of Real Strings*

The idealized patterns of the harmonics (Fig. 2.11) are made somewhat irregular by the resonances of the box (see Chapter 5.9). A few examples of the harmonics of real string sounds are given in Fig. 6.9. They are typical of those in a number of publications. If they are compared with Fig. 2.11 (bearing in mind that in Fig. 6.9 they are distributed on a musical scale), we see that the irregularity introduced is not enormous; the dashed line shows that they broadly follow the trend of harmonics in a theoretical picture. There are some other interesting things about these real harmonics which we can discuss later, but all we need note now is the degree of irregularity which is typical of real bowed string sound: that it will be different, but of a similar kind, at each different pitch, and that the listener does not detect the differences in tone across reasonable intervals played on one string. All we detect is the general balance of higher to lower harmonics. Why are we unable to

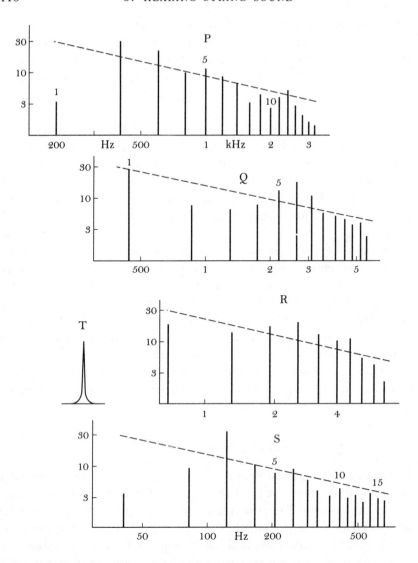

FIG. 6.9. The sound of real instruments. The relative amplitudes of the harmonics of open strings bowed at 1/10 string length: P. violin G; Q. violin A; R. violin E; S. double bass low E. Jan Kaznowski's Homulka (1850), with strong 'projection' harmonics around 2 kHz. My German double bass (1900). Dashed line: the amplitude levels of a sawtooth wave; T. the shape of a harmonic as drawn by the analyser (see text).

sense anything more specific about what, according to Helmholtz, was the cause of the sensation of tone? We can only understand this if we examine the sensation of pitch.

### 6.13. *The Origin of Musical Pitch*

In a paper in *Psychology of Music* in 1977 (see Further Reading), I pointed out that sound of constant frequency hardly occurs in the natural terrestrial environment, and that very little natural sound has constant amplitude either. Natural sound is continuously transient. It is no coincidence that almost all language consists entirely of transients, and the generation of sounds of sufficiently constant frequency to have identifiable pitch is an invention late in the history of man. Once such sounds could be produced by any method—blowing, plucking, bowing—changes were made empirically, to produce sounds which hearing found more attractive. We now know that what was progressively selected was sound in which the harmonics approximate to whole-number multiples of a fundamental. This selection was very advanced by the time Helmholtz showed that harmonic components existed. I argued that if man does something not advantageous to survival, and without knowing why, there must be other reasons, and that selecting this attractive sound resulted from a coincidence in the way hearing behaves. A transient, consisting of many continuously changing frequencies, sweeps over the coding machine and sends a correspondingly changing array of signals to the brain. If a sound has fixed pitch it is continuously vibrating the same areas in the same way.

The area of the coding device vibrated by one pure tone causes many sensors to fire. The signals in the individual auditory nerves to the brain suggest that the nerve ends are sending pulses related to the vibration, but not with every peak of the wave. For example, one nerve may pulse, miss two peaks, pulse, miss four, pulse, miss three: it pulses on the third, then the fifth, then the fourth cycle. Only a few nerves behaving in that way would allow the brain to observe that, *taken together*, they have a common pulse rate at vibration frequency (Fig. 6.10). A pure tone will create pulse patterns like that in anything between fifty and several hundred nerves, depending on amplitude. The harmonics of pitched sound produce a series of areas, vibrating at simple multiples of the fundamental rate. The nerves from each area will pulse like the pure tone example. The brain could observe in the mass of input that half the pulses of the second harmonic's input match the rate of the

FIG. 6.10. Nerve pulses and pitch. In lines 1–5, the pulses correspond with the 2nd, 3rd, 4th, 5th, or 6th cycle of a pure tone since the previous pulse. If the brain observes these together in five nerves, there is at least one pulse at every cycle, as shown in the bottom line. In reality, some hundreds of nerves may be firing like this.

fundamental, a third of the pulses of the third harmonic's input match, and so on. Compared with any natural sound, this is a special sensation for the hearing brain; a very large number of impulse trains match and go on matching. If the brain does not know where the impulses come from, and has to operate on the total package of rates, *the identity of the individual harmonics is lost.*

If we apply that idea to the paradox of pitch, pitch matches the frequency of the fundamental, and it may seem obvious that the fundamental should produce the pitch. But why should hearing assign pitch to the lowest frequency regardless of the higher and often more strongly signalled frequencies in the sound? Because what the brain can observe to be common in the large array of impulses is the pitch rate. That distinguishes musically attractive sound. Its input creates a single sensation, which has an identifiable property: pitch, and has a single characteristic: tone, which contains more and more reinforcing signals the stronger are the contributing harmonics. We can test this, using an electronic synthesizer, in a way particularly helpful for understanding some of the problems about string sound we have already met. We can listen to a set of pure tones with frequencies in the ratios $2:3:4:5:6 :7:8$—a 'note without a fundamental'—or even a sound with ratios $3: 4:5:6:7:8$—'with no second harmonic either'. In both cases we hear a perfectly good pitch, called virtual pitch, at the frequency that the missing fundamental would have.

Hearing is more complex than this simplified outline. But if you are tempted to pursue the subject in typical acoustics and audiology texts, you will probably find that the mechanism is described in terms of 'tuned nerves'. Mammalian receptor nerves cannot be tuned; the membrane is. Such an approach misses the key point that hearing's reaction to the artefact of pitched sound is an accident, and that there is no

reason why ability to perceive it should have been selected for any natural purposes.

### 6.14. *The Fundamental in String Sound*

*Pitch is the single sensation of the pulse rate that the harmonics have in com-
mon.* This answers several questions. The fundamentals of cello open C
and of low notes on the bass can have such small amplitudes that they
are below audibility, but we hear the virtual pitch. Fig. 6.9 shows that
the fundamental of bass low E is very small, and the second harmonic
has half the amplitude of the third, because of the small low-frequency
resonances of the instrument. The fundamental of violin G is small for
the same reason. But the strings vibrate in their fundamental mode. If
they did not, they would not generate the series of harmonics which
create the pitch. So there is no point in trying to move the resonances
of the instruments towards the bottom of their ranges by making larger
ones; make human-sized ones with good resonances for the other harmonics and hearing will do the rest. There is historical evidence suggesting that the cello has decreased in size from some of the earliest
versions, and certainly the bass has.

Strong higher harmonics, because of both their amplitude and their
enhancement by the ear, can make a strong contribution to pitch as well
as to richness, which is why it is a nonsense to say that low viola sound
is weak. This also is why some string sound which we perceive as being
of pitch frequency, can be well heard at a distance (see Chapter 7.7).
There is no observable difference between a cured wolf pitch note,
which has its fundamental substantially reduced, and the semitones
either side of it with large fundamentals, because the fundamental
makes little contribution, and when an octave-pitched sound momentarily appears in the wolf tone, the string must be vibrating in its octave
mode, for if only the fundamental vibration had disappeared, we would
hear the virtual pitch generated by the rest of the harmonics; the string
vibrates for a fraction of time like the bowed octave *armonico* (see
Chapter 2.13).

In the double stop fifth, the bridge amalgamates the vibrations of the
two strings, producing a single sensation in which the low harmonics
overlap on the coding device and, for example, the fundamentals of the
two vibrating strings generate a pitch rate which is an octave below the
fundamental of the lower note—the sub-octave. This results in a rough
sound in which the sub-octave may be discerned.

### 6.15. *Tone and the Identification of Sounds*

One source of confusion over tone stems from Helmholtz; he said that we identify what kind of instruments are played because they have different tone, and the only difference he could find between their sounds was that they had different harmonics, so the harmonics determined the tone. We can readily identify oboe from clarinet from violin when they are played, and their harmonics are very different from one another. But if we record on magnetic tape, notes of similar pitch from those instruments, played as evenly as players can manage, and then we remove the first quarter-second of each note, it is not at all easy to identify what instrument produced the sound, though we are aware that they are different. An instrumental note starts with a transient: and that is what we use to identify it. Helmholtz did not know that starting transients existed. So either we have to say that the starting transient embodies the tone, or, as we have done from the beginning, we adopt the Helmholtz definition and say that the sustained part of the note creates the tone. The starting transient tells us that a violin is being played, but, as we discuss in Section 6.20 below, it does not provide us with any information about what violin it is, because the way in which the sound changes is entirely determined by how the individual player bows the beginning of the note. The only part of the sound which contains any characteristics we can attribute to the box is the sustained part, because that is where variation due to box resonance is observable—if it can be observed.

What the sustained part of a note can convey is actually very limited. We look at a diagram of the amplitudes of the harmonics; they appear to be nice discrete elements, and so the first six are, on the coding device. Information scientists may say they are not surprised that tone should be signalled by so few elements as six harmonics, but tone is signalled by hundreds of elements, the pulsing nerve cells, whose combined signals create a single sensation. If we have difficulty in identifying totally different *kinds* of instrument by that sensation, what chance have we of identifying individual violins? There is another way of testing these conclusions.

### 6.16. *Testing by Synthesis*

We can use an electronic synthesizer to explore what we can and cannot detect in sustained sound. We can imitate any set of harmonics, such as those in Fig. 6.9, and create the tone by sounding together pure tones of those frequencies and amplitudes. We adjust the synthesizer to generate the chosen set of, say, the first eight harmonics before we listen to it. Then we listen, turn off the sound, set the pure tones to new values, and listen again. We are quite incapable of perceiving that a change has taken place after any one of the harmonics has been halved in amplitude. We can obtain the sizes of the harmonics of real notes bowed at 1/10 string length on two quite different violins; to the eye they may differ appreciably in their departures from a sawtooth wave's harmonics. If we create sounds of the same pitch with such harmonics, using synthesis, and compare them with a short silence in between, we cannot distinguish them. This is comparing the *tone* of sounds of different instruments at the same pitch, independent of a player's contribution. We cannot remember the tone of a violin bowed normally, after even a short time.

However, we can readily perceive differences in sounds in which the overall *balance* between the sizes of the higher and lower harmonics differs. And there is an obvious difference in the fullness or richness of sounds with harmonics 1–4 and those with harmonics 1–8. But if there are seven harmonics, it makes remarkably little difference to add the eighth, ninth, and further harmonics. This appears to confirm our conclusions about how we sense the sounds, and about our inability to identify violins by sound described in Chapter 5.

But change the amplitude of a harmonic *while we are listening,* and we perceive that something is changing. We may believe that the tone has changed, but if we compare the original with the changed sound, with silence between them, there is no audible difference. Our sensitivity to change while it is happening, even in the middle of an array of other signals, is very great.

Such constant-pitch sounds with the tone—the harmonic content— of a bowed string, do not produce sensations like those of a real instrument. We have defined the difference as **timbre** and, physically speaking, there is one significant difference between the two kinds of sound.

## 6.17. *The Nature of Timbre*

In the real sound, the harmonics of what we call the constant part of the note are changing continuously when a string is expertly bowed. The reason for describing in Chapter 2 some of the various departures of the bowed string's vibration from simple theory is that these produce an essential characteristic of the sound. This is the natural irregularity of a string bowed uniformly; it is quite different from the irregularity of inexpert bowing, which we readily perceive.

A very skilled violinist, trying to maintain as constant pitch as possible on a stopped note, produces sound whose pitch varies irregularly over about 1/10 semitone; the variation in normal expert playing will be somewhat greater (see Chapter 2.18). The irregularity shows in the Fourier analysis of the sound. It is conventional to draw the harmonics as in Fig. 6.9, but that is a stylized picture. The analyser looks at a sample of many cycles of recorded sound and accumulates the exact frequencies and amplitudes of the pure tones present in each cycle. If we analyse the sound produced by eight pure tone generators, we get eight vertical lines. The form of the spike produced by a violin harmonic is shown in Fig. 6.9T, and indicates the variation in the harmonic about its maximum frequency and amplitude.

What variation in a pure tone can we detect? There are values obtained in a similar way to the Fletcher–Munsen data, which give the smallest difference in the frequency of a pure tone that people can detect at different frequencies and different amplitudes. The values are for two pure tones presented with a short interval between them. What we would really like to know is hearing's critical ability to detect gliding change—continuous changing frequency—but it is not possible to quantify that exactly; attempts to test this suggest, perhaps not surprisingly, that detection depends on the rate of change. We can detect without difficulty a rapid gliding change of frequency which is too small to sense as a change when heard in separated steps. From middle C upwards we can discriminate between two separately presented pure tones 1/10 semitone apart; above the treble staff we can discriminate 1/20 semitone for about two octaves. For a gliding change we can probably halve these figures. If the *pitch* of a bowed string changed by 1/10 semitone: if all the harmonics moved together in one direction, we would certainly detect it. Normal vibrato is an excursion of only about 1/6 semitone and is very easily perceived. But what if each of the harmonics is varying randomly in pitch and, to an extent, independently of each other? We are aware that, together with the tone, there is a continuous change occurring. We cannot discern specifically what is happening, but our particular sensitivity to change makes us aware of this major difference between real bowed string sound, and synthesized sound of truly constant frequencies. Such variation appears to be the prime cause of *timbre*. Frequency change causes the area vibrated to move along the coding membrane; new sensors are brought into the vibration on one side, and sensors stop firing on the other, quite apart from any variation in firing rates of the sensors. This suggests that the main source of the sensation will be the lower harmonics on separate areas rather than those which overlap.

The attractiveness of continuous small random irregularity in the sense of timbre is a fascinating aspect of musical sound, and it is not unique to the violin family. There is a commercial range of metal flutes made with such computerized precision that they appear perfect. They are extremely easy to play—and they are all characterless. There also exist flutes which have been put together by hand, with little imperfections here and there inside the tube, which are more difficult to play but make a sound with wonderful timbre. There is an Arab tradition of leaving a small imperfection in every carpet because only Allah can make things which are perfect. It is a riddle only Allah can solve that to be perfect to our hearing, an instrument must be imperfect and behave irregularly.

## 6.18. *What Pitch is String Pitch?*

Pitch is what we hear. If the pitch is compiled from the contributions of all the harmonics to the pulse rate of fundamental frequency, and they are continuously changing, then what is a violinist's A = 440 Hz? It is the centre point of the pulse rates fed to the brain, which at any one instant may be spread over at least 438.5–441.5 Hz, and maybe 438–42 Hz. We have to be pernickety about when we use 'pitch' and when we use 'frequency'; we can speak of the pitch of a pure tone, but not the frequency of a note. So how accurately can we tune a bowed A if we can't hear it to better than a tenth of a semitone? Tuning to the mean of a slightly confused sound is not easy. We should bow the string lightly at the fingerboard because the timbre is less pronounced than that of a string bowed strongly towards the bridge.

It should not, however, be thought that we all have such perfect coding machines in our ears, that if the harmonics in a sound were constant in frequency and amplitude, and exact multiples of a fundamental, we could all tune sounds perfectly by pitch: by the pulse rates going to the brain. The evidence from animals with ears very like our own suggests that when one pure tone is received, the pulse rates of the counting system show a variation too. Recordings of impulses in auditory nerves when a *pure tone* is heard, reveal a degree of variation in the pulse rates not dissimilar to the variation in the frequencies of the harmonics of real string sound. When we play, we make the pitches by our hearing. There is comfort in the thought that the listener can't hear pitch any more accurately than the player (though there are occasions when one wishes the player could). When we need to tune things exactly we must use beats: pulses created in the ear which are at the rate of the difference in frequency between two sounds only a very few cycles apart. There is a point related to all this: that we can hear beats between a bowed string and a pure tone very close to its fundamental frequency— very readily with a cello. We do not normally hear beats between the sounds of two cellos producing stopped notes of very slightly different pitches, presumably because neither has sufficiently constant frequency to create them; for the pleasure of players and audience in ensemble performance, thank Heaven we don't!

### 6.19. *Harmonicity*

The term **harmonicity** is used to describe the extent to which the harmonics of an actual musical sound approach exact whole-number multiples of the fundamental frequency. I do not know whether it was coined by string makers, but they use it to describe this characteristic of strings of different materials and tensions, and that aspect is discussed in Chapter 11. In the evolution of musical instruments, the modifications and adjustments that were introduced improved their harmonicity—as judged entirely by what hearing found attractive. This had reached an advanced stage by the time that Helmholtz discovered harmonics. But it must not be taken to imply that exactness of the harmonic ratios produces the most attractive sound. It is informative to see what hearing did select as tone and harmonicity during this evolution, when people had no idea of what they were selecting in physical terms, but that is very different from prescribing what people should like. It was *some* people's hearing which selected the tone, timbre, and harmonicity of bowed string sound, and people differ considerably in their sensitivity to harmonicity. A lack of harmonicity is demonstrated by many primitive instruments using pipes and reeds, such as shawms, chalumeaus, racketts, and cornetts—all too painfully to some ears. The most important developments for stringed instruments were the production of strings uniform in property throughout their length, and the reduction of stiffness.

The more the harmonics depart from exact multiples of the funda-mental, the more their contributions to pitch depart, and the wider becomes the band of rates which provide the sensation of pitch. Now add the continuous variation of the timbre factor. The sensation pro-duced by a bowed steel or steel cored string which some people find so disagreeable may perhaps be best described as having an excessive timbre effect and a widening of the pitch sensation, to the extent that one is unhappy as to its accuracy. We know that people with normal hearing are very similar in their ability to discriminate such things as loudness and frequency in tests. On those grounds we might assume that what the ears send to the brain would be very similar. How people react to that input when listening to the sounds of musical instruments varies enormously, and must relate to a higher level of mental activity than the perception of the sound itself.

## 6.20. *Transience*

Transience is changing sound, which is perceived in a different way from constant pitch sound. Our ability to recognize transient sound is remarkable. The frequencies are entirely different when high- and low-pitched voices say the same sentences. The changing pattern is very similar. So great is our memory of the detail of transient sound that most of us can recognize dozens of individual voices, from radio, amongst friends and family, and on the telephone (which only transmits sound up to 4 kHz).

The starting transient of a properly bowed note has harmonics with the frequencies of those of the steady sound which follows; it has the pitch of the note, and its frequencies have good or poor harmonicity according to that of the string. It is the amplitudes of the harmonics that are continuously changing, and they are quite different from the amplitudes which establish the steady tone. The starting transient *is* the process of bringing the amplitudes to steady values, and it is determined by how the string is bowed; the transients are some of the things by which an individual player can be recognized. There is always addi-tional noise in starting transients—noise which is not unwanted sound, but essential to identification. Pizzicato and spiccato sound contain noise which we use in recognizing them as such, as well as frequencies which provide pitch. We may sense pitch frequencies in the starting transient which are not available in the sustained sound because they overlap and are masked.

The rate of change in transient sound can be very fast, and we have to assume that the response of the coding machine—how readily it vibrates to an incoming sound—is very rapid, and that it must also be very heavily damped. Another point which demonstrates the peculiarity of a constant sound arises from this. We can hear sound of extremely short duration. If we are presented with a constant-pitched sound, we can hear that there is sound before we can say that it has pitch (not what pitch it is). In a way that is not surprising; to say that a sound has pitch, we need to hear enough to know that successive vibrations are at roughly the same rate. As I know from my experiments on this, the results need careful interpretation because if any sound starts from silence, or indeed stops, that does constitute a transient (a matter of particular interest to a certain John Cage). At higher frequencies, we need roughly the same length of sound (between 12 and 15 msec) to hear that there is pitch; it is about seven cycles of a pure tone of A = 440, and the higher the frequency, the more cycles we need. But at lower frequencies, it looks very much as though we need about three and a half cycles of sound, which would be the minimum number of cycles for counters to ascertain that a wave is behaving regularly. This seems to suggest that even when a note contains several frequencies, the time taken to discern the pitch depends on the fundamental's rate of vibration. The presence of timbre may make the task more difficult.

Recordings of violin sound reveal that it takes about 40 msec for a stationary violin string, uniformly normally bowed, to establish its stable form of vibration, and up to half a second for light bowing at the fingerboard (see Chapter 2.12). That is the duration of the starting transient. A skilled player can considerably reduce the starting transient time of a lightly bowed note by an initial kick, but this creates a bigger transient. Putting these values together with those in the previous paragraph, the violinist should be able to recognize the pitch within the starting transient time; if it is not satisfactory, it takes less than 10 msec for instruction to go from the brain to the finger to do something about it and to correct it during the transient. Things are not so simple for low cello and for bass, because it takes longer to establish the vibration, and for the lowest notes, it may take a tenth of a second for hearing to establish the pitch. Whether that gives a bassist an excuse for playing behind the beat, depends on how much the conductor knows about these things; the beat is established by the noise, not the pitch. Thus, pizzicato produces a huge initial transient with an immediate percussive effect, in which rhythmic exactness is essential; the pitch follows. From listening to pizzicato we can hear that pitch is determined during the period when the amplitudes of the harmonics are changing very rapidly, and we do not detect a change as the sound dies. That certainly does not happen with most orchestras' tubular bell, which prolongs the agony even on the rare occasions when its fundamental is within striking distance of pitch appropriate to the music.

We have to conclude that we are no more capable of detecting anything specific to a *particular* instrument from bowed transients than we are from the sustained part of the note. The transients depend entirely on what the player does with the bow.

### 6.21. *Vibrato and Portamento*

Vibrato carried out by rocking the finger is a change in pitch. (There can also be amplitude vibrato, which some acousticians incorrectly call tremolo; this is considered in Section 22 below.) All the harmonics move simultaneously in the same direction, and the effect is integrated in the pitch sensation. It should be equally distributed either side of the required pitch. One wishes that every singer could be given a framed copy of the entry in the late Professor Greenish's splendid little dictionary of musical terms: 'vibrato: a slight oscillation of the finger on a stringed instrument; also, singing in an unsteady tremulous manner'. People differ considerably in their awareness of and liking for vibrato, and so do players. It is often said that it should not exceed 1/6 semitone (a 1 per cent change in pitch), but the extent to which it is effective and detected depends on hearing's ability to perceive change at different frequencies, and that ability increases, the higher the frequency and the greater the number of harmonics contributing to the pitch. Even if a rocked finger could produce a 1 per cent change on the bottom string of a bass, taking into account also the overlap of the harmonics, vibrato is not effective. In the treble staff, a 1 per cent change in a harmonic traverses two or three times the minimum detectable change in pitch. Modest vibrato in the high range of the violin, where a small number of harmonics contribute, is attractive. In high cello sound, large numbers of strong harmonics change; great restraint is needed, and excessive vibrato makes us realize why the sirens on emergency vehicles are so obtrusive on our hearing. But watch a player with excellent intonation. The vibrato on a note is often not started until after he has established the pitch; the reason should be obvious.

The violin family more easily produce portamento than any other instruments except the pedal steel guitar and trombone. Few musical devices are more subject to taste and context. Exactly the same thing is perceived when a player corrects intonation by sliding the finger (sometimes called 'playing under the note'), as when a jazz or folk fiddler does so for intentional effect. In some music it is offensive, in some exciting. Is this just taste, or are we subconsciously aware that the fiddlers usually have superb intonation, for the whole of what they do is based on continuous monitoring and feedback between ear and hand? The art of portamento culminates with Grappelli. Some classically trained violinists can 'do a Grappelli'—some rather obviously cannot. There is, however, an optimistic suggestion in Piston's *Orchestration* that 'a glissando is executed by sliding the finger along the string and we hear the successive semitones'—from an orchestra? An individual may be able to pick out the semitones by flying spiccato; sixteen violinists attempting to do this (sometimes called 'tremble-o') synchronously would be likely to produce a rather different effect.

## 6.22. *Loudness Variation*

It is obvious without any measurement that a beginner's irregular bow speed and pressure cause a string's amplitude, and consequent loudness, to vary. The important issue is the nature of the difference between the bowing of a moderate player and that of an expert. A sustained note has pitch, tone, timbre, and dynamic level, and the only one of these which is directly under bow control is dynamic level, for all the others are inherent properties of the string. The usual description of the expert's sound is 'good tone', but that is just the common synonym for a nice sound. Analysis of the sound shows that with expert bowing, the variation in amplitude is very small once steady pitch has been established, and that moderate players produce significantly greater overall variation.

In terms of simple statistics we appear to be much more sensitive to changing frequency than to changing amplitude. Using pure tones, an average person can detect a frequency change of about 1 per cent but just sense a 30 per cent change in amplitude. But we are detecting different things in different ways. From lowest to highest dynamic, violin string vibration increases by at least a hundred times. At the lower end of the dynamic range, one needs very little change in pressure or speed to produce a 30 per cent change in amplitude. The Fletcher–Munsen diagram (Fig. 6.7) suggests that there is some self-compensation for lower-instrument pitches; the rate at which loudness increases with amplitude is greater, but the amount of energy the bow has to contribute in order to increase the amplitude of a heavy system is also greater. For all instruments, it is much more difficult to produce quality sustained pianissimo than forte because hearing is sensitive to the percentage change of the amplitude. Bow control is paramount to producing quality stringed sound, and a consideration of the complex system of control required of the bowing arm explains why it is so immensely difficult to imitate mechanically.

Hearing does not appear to appreciate rapidly fluctuating *overall* loudness in sustained pitch such as we hear in less-good bowing. It is not obvious from our knowledge of the hearing mechanism why this should be so, and it may relate to higher levels of perception. Electronically generated sound adds support to this view. There are forms of vibrato generated by keyboards which are tolerable, and other forms which some people find very unattractive. It is sometimes difficult to assess the difference by listening, but after examining the vibrations on an oscilloscope, one concludes that a regular pitch vibrato in the sound seems to be acceptable to most people, while amplitude vibrato is less attractive, and when it occurs with metronomic regularity at around five or six times a second, some people are very unhappy. This may be related to a quite different phenomenon. Our brains can be peculiarly affected by regular variation in light or sound level at rates between about 5 and 12 times a second. If we hear a pure tone of 16 Hz we obtain a continuous sensation. If we hear what is actually a pure tone of 12 Hz or less, we hear twelve or fewer separate pulses a second, and this may induce an odd sensation. It is safe to test this at very low amplitudes using good quality headphones under carefully controlled conditions, *but under no circumstances should it ever be attempted using a powerful amplifier and speakers; it could do serious damage to a listener.*

## 6.23. 'Ambient Timbre'

There is an old saying that it does not matter what violin you play in the open air; an instrument sounds different in an enclosed space when we are receiving reflected sound. All instruments sound dead when played in a room completely lined with sound-absorbing surfaces, and the bowed string is particularly affected. We could dismiss this phenomenon by saying that we have created unnatural circumstances, but it deserves closer consideration.

If you plug one ear and listen to a pure tone in an ordinary room, its loudness will vary as you move your head and as you walk around. In some places the reflections will be adding to the sound, in others they will be reducing it (Fig. 6.11). If you keep your head still and change

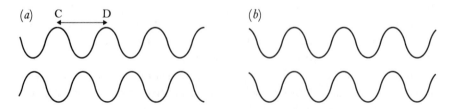

FIG. 6.11. If the direct and reflected waves of a harmonic arrive at one ear as at *a*, they reduce each other; if as at *b*, the loudness is increased. The perceived level depends on the distance each wave travels in relation to its wavelength C–D (see text).

the frequency, the loudness will change; the distribution of places where the sound is louder and softer changes. For a pure tone of 1 kHz, if the distances travelled by a direct and a reflected sound differ by 16.5 cm, the two will cancel. If the path differs by 33 cm (or any multiple of 33 cm) they will reinforce each other; they cancel at any path difference which is 16.5 cm longer than one at which they reinforce each other. The distances for reinforcing or cancelling are different for every har- monic in an instrument's sound, and the higher the harmonic, the smaller the path differences which produce changes. Sound reaches the two ears over different distances, so that the ears are differently affected. The instrument producing the sound may also be moving about (more so with some players than others). This phenomenon happens in a room, but it does not happen in the open air unless there are reflecting surfaces.

Two facts arise from this. One is that there are small random amplitude changes in individual harmonics. The other is that any harmonic in reflected sound which has travelled a distance which would cause reinforcement, must have originated as a different cycle from the one which is being directly received from the source. If the frequency of each harmonic is varying slightly from cycle to cycle, this will increase the overall perceived variation in the sustained sound. We could call this **ambient timbre**. The effect of reflected sound on frequency is absent from constant-frequency synthesized sound of several harmonics when heard via speakers in a room, but if amplitude vibrato is added, the sensation some people obtain is even less attractive than when it is heard through headphones without it.

Ambient timbre occurs in recorded sound if engineers mix sound from several microphones. Some timbre is created by the room in which a recording is played, particularly by 'stereo' sound. It may appear 'better than the real thing', but it will not be the real thing. The nearest recording to a live performance is obtained from two microphones in a dummy head, where the ears are. The story goes that the engineers who first thought of this used a model head of the elderly Beethoven. But a recording made in this way, heard through headphones, will be much closer to the experience of listening in the studio or auditorium.

### 6.24. *General Conclusions*

In expertly bowed string sound, hearing observes pitch, timbre, harmonicity, and loudness from a single compounded sensation. All these elements and the transients are entirely determined by the string and the player. Roughness is manufactured by hearing. Tone is the only element containing characteristics of the resonating box, and tone is a crude sense incapable of producing differences which hearing can characterize or remember. String tone has general attributes: thinness from few harmonics, clarity from weak higher harmonics, and richness from the balance between higher and lower harmonics. Some of those attributes are determined by how and where the string is bowed. But the balance can also be affected by other parts of the mechanism, and we can apply these conclusions to two much-discussed phenomena, by simple tests which some readers may be able to carry out themselves.

### 6.25. *The Tone of Individual Strings*

Notes of different pitch on the same string, played with similar bowing, produce no change of tone until stiffness enters into string vibration in high positions, but there is a difference between two notes of the same pitch played on different strings. To skilled players and experienced listeners, each string has an individual sound. If it *was* literally true that the box resonances take from the bridge, and the bridge from the string, energy proportional to the size of the box resonance at each frequency (see Chapter 5.7), then when the same pitched note is played on two different strings at similar bowing dynamic and bowing position, the

vibrations of the strings should be very nearly the same, while the resonances are the same, so the notes ought to sound the same, but they
do not. The one consistent difference between adjacent strings on an
instrument is that they are in different positions on the bridge.

In Chapter 3 we saw that the vibration of a bottom string produces
twice as much force on the bass bar bridge foot as on the soundpost
bridge foot. Bowing a top string disposes its vibration forces the other
way round, with twice as much force on the soundpost foot as on the
bass bar foot. From one string to the next, there is an increase of about
30 per cent on one foot and a decrease of about 30 per cent on the other
foot. The total vibration force produced on the bridge is more or less
the same for all strings equally bowed. A 30 per cent increase or
decrease in amplitude makes a change in loudness on the margin of
what an average person can perceive. Argument along these lines leads
to the conclusion that the position of each string on the bridge is of relatively little significance. That certainly is not true.

Replace the G string of a normally strung violin by an E string identical with its existing E, tune it to E, and play the instrument. Then,
instead, put two identical G strings, tuned to G, in the outside positions
on the violin. In both cases there is a small change in the balance of
string tension across the arch and in the pressure on the soundpost,
compared with a normally strung instrument, but on both modified
instruments there is a normal string in the normal position whose
sound can be compared with that of the identical string in the abnormal position.

When violins restrung in these ways are played, the tone of notes
from the E in the G position is not perceptibly different from that of
the E in the normal position on the bridge, but the volume of sound a
professional player can produce from the abnormally sited E is far
smaller than that from the E in its normal position. The tone ought not
to differ; E strings produce few harmonics we can hear. But the amount
of energy the resonances of the instrument can extract at the frequencies of those harmonics is very much less, a change solely brought about
by reducing the force at the soundpost foot to just one-half, despite doubling the force available to the body's resonances at the bass bar foot.
As judged by player and listeners, taking account of how hearing
assesses loudness, the total vibration of the front is reduced by far more
than half, although the total force available to the bridge is the same.

On the other hand, the sound obtained from bowing a G string put
in the E position is quite abnormal. It may be compared to a recording

of a normal violin's bottom register strongly bowed, but played through an amplifier with the bass tone control turned right down and the treble control up. It is recognizably the sound of a bowed string, but it has a completely different tonal balance, and is quite different from any sound one gets from any normal instrument of the family. The sound can be heard easily at 30 metres. Judged by hearing, the lower harmonics have been reduced very substantially for a decrease in input force of only a half at the bass bar foot, but very strong higher harmonics are produced by doubling the force at the soundpost side. The G string in its normal position on this instrument produces normal sound.

## 6.26. *The Importance of the Bridge Ratio*

That simple experiment indicates that the ability of the different box resonances to extract energy from the bridge depends dramatically on the level of vibration force at the particular bridge foot. In general terms, if a complex object resonates at a particular frequency, some places, called antinodes, vibrate strongly, while other places, called nodes, are virtually stationary; a resonance will be excited far more by applying vibration to an object at antinodal regions than at nodes. The box resonances at lower frequencies are primarily excited by the vibration of the bass bar foot, and the resonances at higher frequencies are primarily excited by the vibration of the soundpost foot. If we look at this in a simplistic way it is not surprising; we would expect the larger more flexible area of the bass bar side to vibrate at the lower frequencies and the stiffer soundpost side to vibrate at the higher frequencies. But if we take a sophisticated scientific view, if we want a quantitative measure of the modification of a string's harmonics by the resonances, we need to have four resonance curves, each obtained by applying a standard pure tone vibration at the position of one of the strings on the bridge and, furthermore, applied in the plane in which each string is bowed.

Which ever way one chooses to look at it, the effect of the bridge ratio is greater than is suggested simply by bridge dimensions and bowing angle. The asymmetry of the bridge and box plays a large part in determining the balance between the higher and lower harmonics in the sound of each string. It is hardly necessary to add that if the sound from an instrument were determined only 'by the resonances' there would be little point in a composer writing sul G (play all the notes on the G string).

Skilled playing is an interaction of the player with the sound he produces; he bows with expectation and adjusts by the actual sound he hears. The excellent professional who played the restrung violins described above was completely thrown at first by having a string in the wrong place, and needed some time before he found appropriate bowing for the abnormally placed strings. The bridge ratio is a significant factor in responsiveness—the relationship between player and instrument. It emphasizes again the important role of the bridge.

### 6.27. *The Tone of the Viola*

Even experienced hearing can sometimes find it difficult to distinguish high solo viola from similarly pitched cello, when both are expertly played. The harmonics each produce are similarly modified by hearing. But the puzzle to most people is why a viola does not sound like a violin—which it sometimes does, for there are violinists who can make one sound disappointingly like a violin, because they do not bow it appropriately.

We can apply our conclusions about what controls the sound produced by a bowed instrument in a series of simple tests. Start with a normal violin, remove the E string, and move the other three strings across; add a C string so that it is strung as a viola. Bowed like a viola, the instrument's sound has marked characteristics of a viola. The bridge ratio has tilted the balance of the harmonics of all three violin strings towards the higher frequencies; the A, for example, now has richer tone than an A in the violin position on the bridge, and that is very characteristic of viola A. Next, suppose that a small viola is 16 per cent longer than a violin; it does not follow that the significant factors in sound production are changed by just 16 per cent. The bridge is larger in each of its three dimensions; a normal viola bridge is over 50 per cent heavier than a violin bridge, and stiffness increases by much more than 16 per cent for a 16 per cent increase in each dimension. If a violin-size viola bridge is put on our restrung violin (it will be only 25 per cent heavier than a violin bridge because it will be of violin height), the viola-like sound is increased. Add a half-gram weight towards the top of the bridge, and even more viola sound is apparent. Add a heavier tailpiece. (We found that ebony violin tailpieces averaged about 12 gm, and a metal violin tailpiece by a brand-leader was 27 gm.) The converted violin now sounds very like a viola—when played by a good violaist.

Violas always require more work than violins; the converted violin does not need quite as much because its transformation is not complete. A 14 inch (355 mm) violin's front, thinned to a tap note of F, with *f*-holes and bass bar, weighs about 80 gm. A 16 inch (407 mm) viola's front, thinned to tap note C, with *f*-holes and bass bar, weighs around 125 gm. Combined with a heavier stiffer bridge, a heavier front requires more bow work, producing stronger higher harmonics. All these differences between violin and viola have some effect on the sound produced, but by far the most important ones are the bridge ratio, which alters the tonal balance, emphasizing the higher harmonics of each string compared with the same-pitched string on a violin, and the way in which it is played. So has the viola a weak low range because there are poor resonances down there? A violinist bows the C string and says 'this thing has a poor bottom end'. A violaist knows that if he bows the bottom string strongly, that produces strong higher harmonics and he produces a wonderfully rich sound. The only thing specifically attributable to the viola box itself is the weight of the front. All this supports the conclusion in Chapter 5.8, based on different considerations, that the size of a viola makes no difference to its sound.

## 6.28. *The Characteristics of the Four Instruments*

The generality which appears from our discussions is that the four members of the violin family differ in the factors which determine the balance of the harmonics in their sound, and even if the discerning ear can on occasions be mistaken, in general they do each have their own characteristic sound. If one designs instruments of different sizes to be as similar as possible, as in the Saunders–Hutchins experiment (see Chapter 5.16), it is not so surprising that they are said to sound very alike over the ranges where they overlap. But one is tempted to question whether generation after generation of the great composers would have devoted some of their finest creative work to the string quartet if the instruments had been much more alike in sound.

Because such a large part of the sensation hearing obtains from a member of the violin family, other than through bowing, appears to be determined by the strings, the bridge, and the soundpost, **setting up**— the selection, addition and adjustment of all the components put on the bare instrument—is very skilled and important, but this is judged by hearing, and it is no good to tell the customer that all the readings on the dials or the print-out are correct, if he doesn't like the sound and responsiveness when he tries playing it.

An orthodox well-made instrument will have three identifiable resonances determined by its dimensions; it will have many other resonances too. They are inherent characteristics of such a stressed structure. It is no surprise that a poor instrument should have its two wood peaks at unusual frequencies; if it departs that much from orthodoxy in construction it is likely to have many other properties which differ from good ones. It does not help skilled makers to be told the properties of all good instruments—they make them. It does not really help to tell the maker of a poor instrument that it has atypical resonances; there are simpler ways of discovering its behaviour.

We know today that large numbers of overlapping resonances, without excessive peaks and troughs, are obtained from a suitably arched front of a wooden box if it is constrained and vibrated asymmetrically. We know the box should not have a very large sharp resonance anywhere, and that symmetry favours specific modes of vibration and small numbers of large resonances. We also now know that it would *not* be satisfactory if instruments were uniformly resonant across their range; it is because they lack resonance at the very bottom of their ranges that good violaists, cellists, and bassists bow more strongly there and produce their rich sounds by evoking high harmonics. We know that the boxes are tolerant of a degree of variation: far greater than is acceptable for woodwind and brass instruments, where the exact shape of the air space is critical, but the material of which they are made is less so. Indeed, there is enough variation amongst effective instruments to justify the belief that the detailed shape has been determined more by eye than ear. Yet instruments made by the same superb craftsman with the same shape in every respect have different resonances, even if they are made of wood from the same trees.

So instruments can be made to a pattern, but they cannot be designed to have a behaviour. One might be able to design for a small number of specific sharp resonances by considering each piece of spruce, but one certainly cannot design for irregularity; it is not a specification. That agrees with Cremer's statement that a violin cannot be designed by the methods of aircraft engineers. Of course everything we have discovered is based on modern concepts. The evolvers had no idea of what they were selecting in terms of physical properties, and when one sees the false assumptions which can arise from considering only the physical characteristics of the box and of the sound, we may be thankful that they did select by the only important criterion: the desirable sensations produced when played. Wind instruments were evolved and tonal music

was and is composed in exactly the same way: to produce desirable sensations. Hearing decides everything worth having; all we are now
beginning to do is to discover reasons—by studying hearing.

### 6.29. *Black Boxes*

A 'black box' is jargon for anything which has an input and an output,
and the user doesn't understand what goes on in between (and sometimes, what the output actually means). To the evolvers of the violin
family, that description fitted instruments excellently; it is hoped that
this book will make them a little less black to present-day makers and
players. The term is electronics slang, and there are now commercial
pressures on violin and bow makers to buy electronic black boxes and
measure the elasticity of wood, the resonances of bridges, and so on. In
the light of our discussion, when someone produces a physical specification for the perfect violin, which would have to be made using black
boxes, it will be interesting to know how few players will like the product. There are no black boxes which sense wood in the way a skilled
craftsman does. To pretend that instruments are better because black
boxes have been used is simply inventing new fairy-tales to replace the
traditional ones we now know to be nonsense. If apprentice makers
start using black boxes they will never develop the natural skills which
makers must have. The prices of many black boxes bear no relation to
their contents. Makers must buy and maintain machines and high-
quality tools and invest in wood. They are hard-pressed to pay the
mortgage on the prices people are prepared to give for the limited output they can achieve in a year. They do not have time to use black boxes
they cannot afford, almost certainly cannot understand—and do not
need; that has been amply demonstrated by the black boxes used in
research. The more serious matter is that players do not want them to
be used. They do not want a standardized violin!

### 6.30. *Modern Developments*

There are many good things about electronic keyboards. They have stable pitch in exact equal temperament and acclimatize young musicians'
hearing to it, which a piano does not do. The reproduction of starting
transients of some instruments is not unrealistic, and percussive instruments can be reproduced quite effectively. But even when sampling (the
recorded sound of real instruments) is used, electronic keyboards fail to

imitate bowed strings. So much of what we identify with the bowed string depends on the huge variety of transients it can produce. The silicon chip can achieve astonishing things, but in typical keyboards its success is also its downfall. Stable frequency is constant frequency. Regular frequency variation is possible but rarely used, random variation is not easy, and it would be very difficult to generate irregular independent variation of harmonics. The regular amplitude vibrato inflicted on so many of these instruments is the easiest of things to produce, and to many people it is what makes the sound very unattractive. The reaction to typical keyboard sounds was excellently summarized by my colleague Dennis Unwin: once you have observed the pitch and tone of such a constant-content note, hearing is bored.

A solo violin has a small voice, and though skilled composition can use it entirely satisfactorily with full orchestra, there are those who seek the easier way out of amplifying its sound (before the invention of the microphone the only people who could sing to audiences had voices— *sic transit gloria mundi*). There is no place on a violin where the vibration corresponds to the sound produced. The mechanism behaves differently if the body is a solid block or a frame. There is nothing against generating a sound by using the vibration of any particular bit of an instrument, if one likes that kind of sound. Far more extraordinary noises appeal to some people. But the only way to amplify a violin so that it sounds like a violin is to use a microphone at an adequate distance away from it. That is not a simple matter; it is obvious from a comparison of live and recorded performances that some sound engineers can produce a disagreeable version of violin sound which does no service to fine players. Amplifying live violin sound to an audience requires the discipline of keeping the instrument still, at a fixed distance from the microphone. To watch Grappelli perform with a microphone is a lesson in itself.

## 6.31. *Subjective Hearing*

We now appear justified in having called the bowed sound following the starting transient a constant pitched sound, though it is not constant-frequency sound. Because of the way in which we hear it, it has no properties which enable us to memorize it and recognize it again. We need sound to have specific changing patterns to do that. It is not surprising therefore that it is subjective, and that people believe some of the long-established myths associated with the wooden box. Indeed, it is said that if one records the starting 'chough' of flute notes and puts them in front of the sustained part of violin notes, listeners will say it is a flute playing. Perhaps that is the ultimate example of how powerful is suggestion to hearing. Many of us can recognize the changes produced by a set of strings with different harmonicity. Players sense strings of different tension, and we may detect this because they then play differently. We can probably sense the effect of moving a soundpost slightly, but if we are honest, any such change appears to be greatest immediately after we have just made it, and the impression can wear off. There are even players who move soundposts slightly during a concert interval, not only believing that the change will be appreciated by the audience but, in an extraordinarily anthropomorphic way, thinking that instruments like it! It is as well that instruments do not have their response curves attached to them. Because once a player sees a resonance peak he will convince himself that it does something to the tone, and if he believes it he will hear it. It is a remarkable triumph of mind over hearing.

There appears to be no property of any significance to hearing that one can measure scientifically on an isolated well-made violin. Can anything significant be measured when the instruments are actually played? What do people who set themselves up as judges of *tone* in competitions believe they are selecting? After the 1975 instrument exhibition of the Scandinavian Violin Makers Association, the actual sounds of the eight violins judged by a panel of professional violinists to be of 'excellent tonal quality', and those of the seven judged to be poorest, were subjected to a special method of analysis producing long-term average spectra. This gives the average intensity of the sound in a succession of narrow bands of frequency across an instrument's range, and may be considered a more sophisticated form of the response curve (see Chapter 5.9). It is at least an analysis of real sound. The results showed that the output of the two sets of instruments was remarkably alike, the only possibly significant difference being that the 'good' instruments *lacked* some resonance in the region of the octave of the E string. The modest conclusion of two experienced acoustical physicists was that this cast doubt on the value of this method for predicting tonal quality. An equally valid conclusion is that it casts doubt on the ability of judges to distinguish anything about instruments by listening to them being played. It is possible that judges can detect something of how instruments respond to the particular playing style of the individual chosen to perform on them, and it is quite likely that if, on the next day, the instruments were played by another person with an entirely different

style of bowing, they would be placed in a quite different order. The following week those judges might be classing twenty graduating violinists, and commenting on *their* tone. Which tone? The players' or their
instruments'? The most sensible conclusion is that it is just as forlorn
a hope for physicists to believe they will find some method, however
sophisticated, of categorizing the sensation from an expertly played
violin by analysing the sound as it is for judges to believe that they can
classify boxes by listening to a skilled performer playing them. The
search for the philosopher's stone was abandoned some years ago.

In competitions for craftsmanship, experts can judge only the external appearances and that tells one very little about how an instrument
is likely to behave. They would discover far more by looking at the
parts and their fit during assembly. Medicine is making much slower
progress towards the elixir of life than advertisers of cosmetic preparations.

### 6.32. *The Individuality of Instruments*

Nothing that we have discovered or deduced implies that instruments
are alike. The box has an important role in how the player feels he must
apply his bowing to produce the sound he wants. Its resonance and
internal damping are obviously significant in its responsiveness, coupled
with the kind of strings, bridge, and soundpost setting. Orthodox well-
made instruments behave very differently to players, and the more
experienced the player, the more the differences are apparent to them.
The challenge—and it is a very big one—is to discover what the differences are between players, what the differences in responsiveness are
between instruments, and how they interact with one another. One will
need some quite remarkable black boxes to discover those things, and
even if that is achieved, it does not follow that one will be able to tailor an instrument to a player.

### 6.33. *Helmholtz and* The Sensations of Tone

One cannot underestimate the importance of Helmholtz's discovery that
what human hearing selected as musical instrument sound comprised
harmonics with frequencies which are approximately simple whole-
number multiples of the frequency of the fundamental. Actually,
Helmholtz's most important discovery, which occupies a very large part
of *The Sensations of Tone*, followed from this one. It was that those same

simply related whole numbers underlay the scales and modes and harmony upon which the entire structure of both primitive and conventional (confusingly called 'tonal') music was developed. To put this in context, it was not until 1833 that Savart showed pitch to be a frequency, and not until 1870 that Helmholtz discovered the harmonics. Much wonderful music had been written by 1870 using the properties of 'tonality' inherent in the mechanism of human hearing, without knowledge of any kind whatsoever about the underlying physiological mechanisms which are accidental but natural properties of hearing. Schoenberg, born in 1874, initiated one of the great illogicalities ever introduced into an art form. One cannot create atonality with a 'tonal' system of pitches. One cannot tell normal hearing to abandon that which is inherent.

With the methods at his disposal, Helmholtz could only discover very limited things about musical sound. He made an incorrect deduction (that we identify sound by tone); every scientist has done that at some time. The real influence his work has had on generations of scientists arises from the underlying assumption that the *physical* description of a musical sound is a direct representation of the sensation heard; and that has led to so many misconceptions. Helmholtz also put forward a theory of hearing which sent physiology along the wrong track for seventy years. It has been said that the true measure of a scientist's greatness is the extent to which his theories eventually hold up the progress of science. Helmholtz's ideas about instrument sounds were so compelling that scientists—even those with some musical ability—have been reluctant to believe their own senses when they offered alternative evidence. Perhaps it will console musicians and makers that scientists can be subjective too.

# 7

# Under the Ear and Far Away

◆◆◆❖◆◆◆

## 7.1. *Playing and Listening*

We have to learn to play, but we must also learn to listen, and there are odd beliefs about listening, apart from those about 'tone'. Experienced players may judge an instrument almost entirely by exploring its responsiveness to bowing, but they usually ask for the opinion of listeners and often like to listen while others play it. Performers believe that some instruments 'project' better than others, meaning that some can be heard well in an auditorium, and there are also explanations for some odd ideas that audiences have about hearing solo instruments.

## 7.2. *The Distribution of Sound from a Source*

Since sound is a succession of compressions and expansions which travel through a material, each layer of material pushing and then pulling on the layer in front of it, it may seem that a vibrating plate should produce sound in a beam, and when very close to an instrument, the sound is stronger directly in front of it. But air can move in any direction and always goes from a region of higher pressure to one where pressure is lower. Directly in front of the plate, the air has no option; it is compressed and expanded as the sound wave passes through it. At the edges of this beam, pressure is normal and compressed air moves into it. Likewise air is sucked back from the sides as well as from the front in the rarefaction part of the wave. The beam gets broader very rapidly, moving into normal air wherever it is available (Fig. 7.1). As soon as sound spreads in this way and is moving in a new direction, it too has a boundary with normal-pressure air into which it can spread. Spreading always happens at the boundary between vibrating and nor-

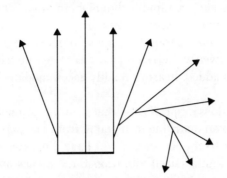

FIG. 7.1. Distribution of sound from a vibrating surface (see text).

mal air and causes the sound to travel sideways and then in the opposite direction to the frontal beam; in this way sound is radiated in all
directions, and since it travels at about 330 metres a second in air, its
distribution around an instrument is very rapid.

The convex shape of an instrument's front makes little difference to
spreading, but because the pressure and rarefaction is spread over a
larger and larger area as it moves out, the amount the air moves—the
amplitude of the sound—is soon very much smaller than it is directly
over the vibrating surface. If we measure the sound amplitude at various distances from a small vibrating source in the open air (Fig. 7.2),

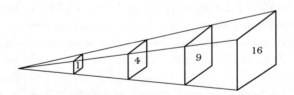

FIG. 7.2. The sound from a small source is spread over increasingly large areas;
the amplitude of the vibration correspondingly decreases.

the vibration at two metres is a quarter of that at one metre; at three
metres it is a ninth, and one sixteenth at four metres (an inverse square
law). That looks as though you don't have to be very far away before
you won't hear anything, and if you have listened to playing in the open
with no hard surfaces around, there is a grain of truth in this, but our
hearing adapts remarkably to the total loudness of a sound (see Chapter
6). It was selected to sense sound in the open air, where it would

usually spread in such a rapidly diminishing way. The spreading law appears extreme when measurements are made close to the source. In an auditorium, the direct sound from a solo instrument has one-quarter the amplitude at twenty metres that it has at ten metres, and when the reflected sound is added, hearing readily accommodates such differences in overall level.

What the law does emphasize is that sound has much greater amplitude very close to an instrument. If sound from one part of a violin front travels six inches to the left ear, it will have a quarter of the amplitude of sound from a similar-sized vibration three inches away, and at such short distances spreading is also peculiar; it makes a big difference whether the ear, when close to an instrument, is directly in front or at the side of it. Different parts of the violin and viola front resonate at different frequencies, and their distances from the left ear are significant; if the vibrating areas change, the sensation may also change. The right ear is much further away, and partly in the shadow of the head. The difference between what is received by the two ears will vary. In this way a violinist can receive sound in such a way that he may hear differences from pitch to pitch which cannot be detected at any reasonable distance. The discussion in Chapter 6 about what we can detect refers to listening at at least a couple of metres from an instrument. The player is therefore controlling his playing according to what he hears, and not to what the listener receives. A session player often listens through headphones to the sound of the group to which he is contributing. It would be interesting to see how a skilled violinist would react if he played while wearing ear-sealing headphones reproducing the sound he was creating ten metres away, but at levels he would normally receive direct from his instrument. One suspects he would find playing confusing.

The sound has been measured around an *isolated* cello in a room with sound-absorbing surfaces when the bridge is vibrated by pure tones. Up to about E above middle C, the sound is roughly at the same level all round it at five metres and normal listening height; there are slight differences between higher frequencies at different places around it until the sound has travelled ten metres. This is an example of musically meaningless physics. Leaving aside whether pure tone vibrations represent complex resonance, and the omission of a large sound-absorbing object called a player, the research suggests that from place to place at five metres around a cello, the relative levels of the several harmonics in what is received will be slightly different. There is no prescription for what the comparative amplitudes in cello sound should be, even if we were capable of perceiving an effect from such small differences. A cello sounds like one everywhere around it.

The distribution of pure tones around an isolated violin is somewhat similar; the level of the high harmonics is less even, until the sound meter is further away from the instrument, but they may also be in the totally rough region of hearing and not be heard anyway. In real life, bodies and clothes are good sound absorbers, and sound absorbed near an instrument when it is at high pressure represents a loss. The discussion of whether the backs of instruments produce a few per cent of the total sound (see Chapter 5.26) is academic for cellos because almost all of it will be absorbed by the player's body. That is just as well because whatever sound might be produced by the back would be quite different from the sound produced by the front. Cellists are in a better position to hear themselves as others hear them than those who play the smaller instruments. In an orchestral cello section in Noah's ark formation, two by two, a lot of high-pressure sound is also absorbed by the backs of players in the desk ahead, but there is rarely difficulty in hearing cellos; conductors more often have to quell their enthusiasm.

## 7.3. *Subjective and Measured Loudness*

Something approaching an ostensible value for the perceived loudness of one real sound can be obtained by a complex calculation based on the actual amplitudes of each harmonic in the sound at the point of listening to it. But hearing continuously adapts to sound levels. We do not sense anything absolutely. We adapt to the level of light. Things only seem warmer or colder depending on what temperature was previously felt. Meters with a microphone may be used to measure what is called loudness, especially for noise in the environment, and they include various devices which try to match some of the characteristics of hearing. Can anything be made which takes account of the sound immediately previously heard, which is what our perception does? That is why we have discussed everything in terms of dynamic: comparative loudness, and not sound levels. But if reading this book tempts you to try any of the scientific literature on musical instruments or books on acoustics, many values are given which could suggest loudness, though very few of them do. A comparison of some published measurements with our experience verges on the ridiculous.

## 7.4. *Bel and the Dragon*

A commonly adopted unit for expressing physical sound level is the Bel; our hearing is unquestionably the dragon. A Bel was supposedly that increase in sound amplitude which doubles its 'physical loudness': an increase of about three times. There is no such thing as physical loudness; it only occurs in our brains. Perhaps it was a wicked fairy's joke that an increase in loudness which we can just detect is about one tenth of a Bel; this was irresistible to measurers. That is all the dreaded deciBel or dB means. One decibel would be an increase in sound which could just be detected—if all frequencies behaved similarly. On that assumption, 20 dB or 2 bels is twice as loud as 1 bel, and 30 dB or 3 bels is twice as loud as 2 bels. Here is a small selection of published figures for sound levels, expressed in dBs. Try to make some sense of them.

40 dB = *pp* = quiet office
60 dB = *mf* = busy office
80 dB = *ff* = heavy traffic
90 dB = *fff* = loud motor cycle at 5 metres

90 dB is the maximum exposure for one hour a day without hearing damage. The loudness of a strongly bowed good violin varies between 87 and 97 dB across its playing range: the bottom string of a good viola, 85–96 dB. Violin G (calculated) has five harmonics each in the range 70–80 dB; violin G (measured) has one harmonic of 28 dB and the remainder below 20 dB. In an auditorium during a concert, a soft solo violin measured 50 dB; the complete dynamic range of the orchestra was 60–85 dB.

The decibel scale is a relative one, but if Einstein had been given figures like that he would not have got very far with his Theory. Even if one put a microphone as close to a violin as a player's ear, are we to believe that he is in danger of hearing damage if he played loudly for an hour? Can a violin or a weak viola compete with heavy traffic, let alone a motor cycle? And how was a violin's harmonics recorded at below 30 dB, when 50 dB is a soft solo at the distance of a member of an audience? Never compare published figures. Values in decibels of sound containing several frequencies show only how much physically larger one sound was compared with another, when measured with the same particular sound meter under the same conditions. A good violin bowed strongly varied in physical sound amplitude over a range of three to one (97 − 87 = 10) as measured by that sound meter. Assuming that exactly the same conditions prevailed, the minimum sound from the viola was supposedly just two detectable units of loudness less than the violin. The measurements tell us very little about what we would hear, and nothing about how loud any one sound in one set of measurements would be in comparison with the sound in another set.

It is probable that in an auditorium the measured loudness of a full orchestra does only vary by about five times, and it may be five times whether you are at the front or back of the auditorium or even in the band, but five times what? It is relative to the general sound level heard at the time. Under particular circumstances the loudness of a solo violin in chamber music may vary over a range of five to one. But from $pp$ to $ff$ is not an increase of sixteen times under any conditions. When we hear music we are simply aware that the sound is soft or loud or getting louder or softer. We obtain the same impression of dynamic change whether we are in the front row or at the back of the hall, and when hearing a large orchestra, the comparative loudness of the various sections may not be as ideal in the front row as further away. One aside: a composer can specify tempo by a metronome value, and pitch by notes, but his dynamic markings are entirely in the hands of the performers and the ears of the listeners.

## 7.5. *Position in the Auditorium*

Concerts are held in a variety of buildings, often with some seating behind the orchestra, or behind pillars in churches. Extensive questioning of audiences about performances on solo instruments reveals a conviction which conflicts with sound measurements. Although most listeners are several metres from a soloist, and a lot of the sound arrives by reflection, they believe they hear better if they can see the soloist and indeed can 'see the strings' of the instrument. It is impossible to test this rigorously, though some related experiments are relevant. Blindfolded people at two metres can tell quite accurately which way the front of a cello is facing. At ten metres they may not even be able to point accurately to the cello. Is there more in this than meets the eye—or the ear—or both?

## 7.6. *The Directionality of Human Hearing*

There are two options available to an animal by which to detect sound moving past it. We detect pressure changes in the air. Sound can equally well be sensed by detecting that the air moves backwards and forwards. There are advantages in both methods. Some insects use minute bristles which are vibrated by air movement. The hairs can only move in one direction, and by turning until the hairs vibrate strongly, they can discover precisely where the sound comes from. Their system is made very sensitive by having hairs which resonate at particular frequencies. They are usually only interested in sound of one or two frequencies: those made by other members of their own species, whom they want to locate in the long grass for obvious reasons. If they had many hairs, corresponding to different frequencies, they would have discovered the basis of tone millions of years before Helmholtz did.

In whichever direction sound goes past our ears, the relative pressure changes are the same. This does not provide much help in discovering the direction of a source. The external funnels help a little; our hearing is most acute when a sound comes in at 45° to the head on either side (Fig. 7.3), but a source cannot send sound at 45° to both sides of the

FIG. 7.3. Maximum sound reception by a human ear occurs when the source is at 45° to the way the head is facing.

head, and most people straining to hear a faint sound instinctively turn the head at roughly that angle so that one ear points in the believed direction of the source: a case where one ear is better than two. Animals with rotating ears do better, but the main benefit they obtain is that they are less likely to reveal their position by moving ears than moving their head. The advantage of our pressure-operated hearing system is that it *does* hear sound coming from all around. When we were hunted by predators it had great survival value, and it still does, now that the predators have four wheels.

Our hearing is not really designed for pointing the head exactly in the direction of a soloist. Our sound 'radar' was meant to provide a rough direction, so that source location could be carried out by our eyes, and if sound is confused by room reflections it is much more difficult. But we are confused even more by this artefact of sustained pitched

F IG. 7.4. Locating direction. Suppose a sound arrives at the two ears with a time difference. (*a*) Hearing cannot tell from a pure tone whether P, arriving at one ear, corresponds with Q, or with R at the other ear, because they are identical. Sustained sound with reflections is similarly confusing. (*b*) Varying sound enables hearing to identify that X arrived at one ear before the same transient Y arrived at the other, and this helps to locate the direction of the source.

sound we have invented. Fig. 7.4 shows the essence of the problem. If we try to determine source direction by sensing the time difference between the same sound arriving at the two ears, we have to identify the detail of the sound exactly instant by instant. If sound is constantly changing, every minute detail of the sound wave is identifiable, and the system could sense the time gap between receipt by the one ear and then by the other. But if harmonics are pure tones, further confused by timbre and reflections, how does the system tell whether one peak is in front of or behind the other? Trying to locate the source of a pure tone in a hard-walled room is rather like finding a gas leak by smell. We have to rely on a mixture of loudness difference between the two ears and the time difference of arrival, and we are not very good at doing either. There can also be a disconcerting consequence which some readers may have experienced when hearing stereophonic recordings through headphones: the music can suddenly seem to be coming from behind us instead of from in front. Perhaps therefore we want to see the soloist because our brains feel we ought to be able to locate the sound source by hearing, and our ears cannot do so. There are of course other reasons for wanting to see the great virtuosi, such as impressing our grandchildren one day.

When there is a soloist with an orchestra, the situation is so foreign to natural hearing that one cannot expect the brain to do anything about direction. The illusion of television is that the sound normally appears to be coming from the moving mouth, but is broken whenever a film is badly dubbed from another language. Watching a live performance of a concerto has much in common with this.

## 7.7. *Projection*

Tests with audiences suggest that the audibility of a solo instrument at a distance depends on the strength of its resonances in the 1–3 kHz band. One physicist who discovered this expressed surprise, for sound of all frequencies spreads similarly, and high frequencies are absorbed by air slightly more than low ones. The explanation is physiological. We hear pitch. All the harmonics contribute to pitch, and those in the 1–3 kHz band are most strongly sensed, though as contributions to the pitch characteristic. A good instrument should have adequate resonances in that band (see Fig. 6.7), a combination of the natural resonance of a professionally cut bridge and a well-set soundpost in the box, which together produce strong frequency response across that band.

Some violins sound loud enough to the player, but do not project well. The Fletcher–Munsen curves (Fig. 6.7) and the simple experiment of adjusting volume and tone controls on an amplifier help to explain this. If the sound is loud—as it is to the player—his hearing is working with a 'loud' characteristic, and there is much less difference between the perceived effect of lower frequencies, and that of the 1–3 kHz band. In the auditorium the actual sound levels are very much smaller and hearing is operating on a much lower overall characteristic, where comparatively speaking it emphasizes the 1–3 kHz band, and the stronger the frequencies in that band are, the stronger the perceived sound will be. This is one instance in which a listener can judge a property of an instrument better than a player. Instruments which will accept strong bowing, normally do have excellent projection because this emphasizes higher harmonics. Such an instrument, which will hold its own in a concerto, may have to be carefully controlled in chamber music.

Hearing a steel-strung cello in a concerto is a rather different matter. Powerfully bowed, the higher harmonics will dominate in the sound. But they are heard so strongly for the same reason that we can hear a xylophone, and a bell, against the full orchestra, despite their small actual sound: their harmonics are not harmonious. After junior orchestra concerts, children often ask whether you heard them playing. Give an encouraging affirmative; don't add that the way to be heard above an orchestral section is to play out of tune. Brahms, Dvořák, and all the other great composers orchestrated for a gut-strung cello and expected the conductor to make the band accompany it. We owe them that, just as much as we do to observe the markings they put in the scores. The curse of the present age is that people think loudness is a substitute for quality, while those who have ruined their hearing by loudness can no longer sense subtleness in quality.

## 7.8. *Orchestral Sections*

The sensation obtained from a solo instrument depends on subtle variations in its sound. Much of this disappears in sectional sound. There is timbre from the continuous random changes in all the harmonics, but it is a much broader phenomenon. Unison in octaves from a string quartet, which is very rich in reinforced harmonics, is a very different sound from similar scoring for orchestral strings, which is simply robust. Hearing can distinguish the individuality of two players in unison; three good players in unison can produce 'sectional' sound, and above that number it is (or should be) impossible to distinguish the effort of an individual. The sound of an orchestral section is very different from that of one amplified violin.

In sectional sound, vibrato produces a band of pitches with a unique character. It is in effect an extended band of timbre, but its harmonicity depends on the strings used. Musically speaking, there are acceptable limits to the band-width. Those who have listened to successive grades of children's orchestras will know the sound of a very wide-band unison and how it converges on the acceptable as the unison becomes more so. Yet another common misuse of the word tone is involved. There is no real difference between the tone of the string sections of a good amateur orchestra and of a professional one. There are usually very big differences in such things as synchrony of rhythm and phrasing; in how many amateur orchestras does every player start a phrase with the bow on the string in the same position along it, or play with the same dynamic? Printed music is only a guide, and performance needs to depart just as subtly from regularity as pitch does from a physical scale. What listeners usually mean when they praise the tone of professional orchestral strings is the cohesiveness of the ensemble.

The more surprising thing is the way in which the loudness of the sound generated increases—or rather doesn't increase—with the number of instruments in unison. About ten players are required to double the apparent loudness of one instrument. Some of this phenomenon arises because the sound from one instrument may partly cancel that from another: the strings are not all in the 'stick' phase at the same time and all in the 'slip' phase together. Part of it arises through the way

hearing responds to loudness. Similarly, it requires about thirty performers to be three times as loud, and a hundred to reach four times—
hence the forces needed in a vocal chorus with a full orchestra. The
actual difference in loudness between sixteen first violins and twelve
seconds or violas in a full orchestra is small, bearing in mind their normal respective roles. The cello and bass sections are determined by their
use in supporting the harmony of full orchestra, and there are usually
fewer in a string orchestra.

## 7.9. *Two Fairy Stories*

Some cellists and bassists have a superstition that some of their sound
is transferred through the spike to the floor and radiated from there.
They prefer a wood to a stone floor; they believe that the wood 'resonates'. Leaving aside that a listener wants to hear the tone of an instrument and not that of a wooden platform, no more than one or two per
cent of these instruments' vibration can be conducted through the spike.
Measurements show that the sound at a distance is less when a cello or
bass is played on a wood surface than on a concrete one, because the
hard surface reflects sound better. But a secure wooden surface gives
players greater confidence. My bass has scored grooves in a number of
tiled cathedral floors, and there are several girls who will remember a
rehearsal on a school stage with a very steep rake, when my bass
removed the stool from under the cellist in front of me and left a (fortunately very lightweight) young lady sitting on the tailpiece.

Some cellists carry—at the highest professional levels, have carried
for them—a riser, a substantial wooden bridge with its top set at an
angle to the floor, into which the spike is placed, which at least puts
fewer abnormal stresses on a cello than an angled spike. Such a structure will reflect sound towards the player rather than into the auditorium. But it may convince the player that he is playing better—and as
a result he may.

## 7.10. *Domestic Testing*

Since an experienced player selects his own instrument because of how
it behaves for him, there is a certain danger about using that experience
to influence the selection of an instrument by another player. In advising the less advanced person, an experienced player should be able to
detect whether there are real shortcomings. One would like to think

that teachers would also inspect an instrument for such things as its structural condition, bridge, and strings (see Chapter 12), but teachers vary quite unbelievably in their interest in, and ability to observe, matters other than the sound and playability of an instrument.

If, for what it is worth, you want to judge the sound of an instrument, hear two or three different people play it in as large a room as possible and walk around the room. Remember that a part of the sensation is created by the room and most by the player. Ask the players for honest opinions about it. The one occasion when this is not possible is the first time a new instrument is strung in company. The situation is comparable with uncles and aunts admiring the latest addition to the family. Like a new arrival it may not behave at its best, but no one will tell the proud parent it sounds like a hurdy-gurdy.

# 8

# The Bow

♦ ♦ ♦ ❖ ♦ ♦ ♦

## 8.1. *Introduction*

The violin would not exist but for the discovery of bowing. People who do not play sometimes ask why the left hand was chosen to do the intricate things while the right hand just pushes a stick with some horsehair on it up and down. It may stem from the notion that the left hand is 'making the notes'; televised pictures of soloists enhance this view. Richard Wilson relates that when he was a viola student at the Guildhall School of Music, he had a poor instrument and despaired of producing a reasonable sound. William Primrose visited the School and, to illustrate something in a seminar, picked up this viola and played. None of them had ever heard such wonderful sound.

If you ask professional players to estimate the contributions of bowing and of their instrument to the sound they produced, they never rank bowing below 75 per cent, and some have even suggested 90 per cent. This is not exact science, but the message is clear. Bowing is of paramount importance for the violin family's sounds, and it is the bowed sound which has established the instruments' position in music for several centuries. It is far more difficult and complex than the left hand's work. It is therefore sensible for right-handed people to bow with the right arm, but the handedness of playing appears to have been this way round with plucked instruments from early times, when the role of neither hand could have been particularly demanding. If handedness was established for plucked instruments that way, it could follow that the hand that rocked the plectrum ruled the bow too. It might seem to be another of the fairy godmother's gifts that things started the 'right' way round; a possible reason of a quite different kind is suggested at the end of this chapter.

## 8.2. *How did a bow originate?*

A bowed stick as a means of tensioning a flexible element is one of man's earliest inventions, and the hunting bow is probably the origin of the stringed instrument; the same simple technology was used many centuries later to tension flexible material and rub it across a string. The violin became a possibility from that moment: a system producing sustained sound from a string. That more recent moment seems to be as shrouded in the mists of time as the earliest plucked string. There are scholarly treatises attempting to deduce by when this happened, such as that of Werner Bachmann, who suggests that bowing was a recent invention, possibly as late as the eighth or ninth century AD, but his book, *The Origins of Bowing* (London: Oxford University Press, 1969), offers nothing on the origin of the bow itself. The unknown inventor deserves to be listed with the Amati family. Unlike the rubbing wheel system in a hurdy-gurdy, the very concept of a bow controlling a string is improbable. The hurdy-gurdy may have been invented around the same time, and one may venture that once any method of producing sustained string sound was discovered, the impetus to find other ways of doing it was created.

The critical question is how hair became involved with musical instruments. It is said that a thousand years ago in the region now called Turkey, strings were made from plaited hair. If this brought horsehair into an instrument maker's hands, it could have led to a chance experiment. One can understand that once hair was found to work it was widely adopted. The bowing method offered so much more flexibility than a wheel mechanism that thereafter it never looked back. Indeed, until the revolutionary idea of Tourte in the late eighteenth century, it hardly looked forward either.

## 8.3. *The Out-Curved Bow*

The principle of the bow is simple. A ribbon of hair is held under tension by a bent stick. Early representations show the wood in an almost semicircular arc, with the weight of the stick a long way from the string—awkward to control and suitable only for simple music. By adding a frog and tip, an almost straight stick could be used, with which more sophisticated music could be played. But all out-curved bows have the same characteristic (Fig. 8.1). Pressure on the hair increases the tension between tip and frog; the stick curves more, and the ends move

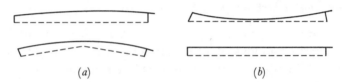

FIG. 8.1. Bow mechanisms. (a) When the out-curved baroque bow is pressed on a string, the ends move towards each other, and the hair moves towards the stick. (b) With the modern bow, tension straightens the stick by rotating the tip, and the hair moves away from the stick.

towards each other, which reduces the hair tension. When the string is at the middle of the bow the conditions are very different from those when it is at either end of the ribbon. The baroque bow has this out-curved form, and only relatively light bow pressures are possible.

## 8.4. *The In-Curved Bow*

The elegant principle of the in-curved bow, devised by Tourte, is that an increase in hair tension causes the bow stick to straighten and move the hair away from the stick (Fig. 8.1). The crux of the mechanism is the rotation of the tip of the bow. The tip does move slightly towards the frog when hair tension increases, but unlike the out-curved bow, the stick does not respond by curving in more. A baroque bow could have the same hair tension as an in-curved bow before playing, but its tension varies far more with pressure, and it is the relative constancy of tension of the in-curved system which makes it possible to use the elasticity of the hair in the range of modern bowing techniques, as well as to apply greater pressure. The skill of the bow maker lies in selecting wood, sensing its natural elasticity as it is thinned, and making the diameter of the stick appropriate for the mechanism. Different levels of pressure are used in playing the four members of the family, and the stick must be appropriately stiff for each. The innate skill of the bow maker is possibly greater than that of the violin maker; it is certainly rarer.

The tip of the bow is its Achilles heel. Hair tension applies a force in the worst possible way in relation to the grain of the wood. The shape and dimensions of the tip as well as the quality of the wood are extremely important, and an elegant design does not always go hand in hand with the best mechanical strength.

## 8.5. *Bow-stick Materials*

Snakewood (*Brosimum* species), a most attractive very heavy wood, was and still is used for the best baroque bows. For quality modern bows, pernambuco (*Caesalpinia echinata*) is almost exclusively used. It has great strength across the grain as well as with it. At what stage of shaping the stick it is bent, using heat, differs between bow makers, but once bent it is very stable. As with the ribs of instruments, the more beautiful the wood—which actually means, the more its structure changes from one part to the next—the greater the chance of it breaking; but you are forewarned with ribs because the potential problem can be seen. Pernambuco cannot be split, and it is difficult to see the structure of sawn material, but that structure determines the behaviour of the bow. Sticks do break during bending, and it is best to discover concealed flaws early in the making process; this may be the origin of the story that Tourte destroyed sticks which did not meet his expectation. The stick tapers from frog to tip for two purposes: to bring its centre of gravity towards the frog and to make it most flexible where the tip imposes rotation. The curvature introduced must match the graded flexibility along the length. But the stick must not be so flexible that under tension it bends or whips; it must remain straight along the centre line of the hair. Unless the ribbon hairs are parallel and at approximately the same tension, they will twist the stick. Rehairing is a very skilled and responsible task.

Low-priced mass-produced sticks are usually made of brazil wood (*Caesalpinia sappan*), which well-meaning conservationists confuse with pernambuco. It is doubtful whether all the skilled bow makers in the UK use five cubic metres of pernambuco a year between them. Pernambuco is a coastal wood which grows in maintained stands in Brazil. Brazil wood grows in the Far East, and was called brazil when it was imported into Europe for the red dye it contains, a long time before Europeans even discovered South America. The country Brazil was named after the wood when it was found that it contained trees which also produced the red dye. It would, to say the least, be surprising if makers of low-priced bows in the Far East imported wood from the other side of the world instead of using a local product. A piece of pernambuco from which a quality bow can be made costs much more than a complete brazil wood bow.

There are also synthetic sticks of, for example, fibreglass. In principle it should be possible to measure a few of the physical properties of a good wood stick and make something which approximates to it, but some of these products are promoted with pseudo-science that Dulcamara would envy, suggesting, for example, that Tourte created *the* perfect bow, that a bow stick radiates sound, and similar nonsense. Heretical as some may find the suggestion, Tourte's bows differ from one another, as all bows do, and a player's choice of a bow is even more individual than his choice of instrument, though often achieved with far less vacillation. It is not impossible for some synthetic stick to suit a particular player despite its appearance, for if a synthetic manages to imitate some of the physical properties of pernambuco, it is virtually impossible for it simultaneously to have the shape of a wooden one. On the other hand, according to those who have tried them, very good bow sticks can been made of thin tubular steel, which appears to have better properties than most synthetic materials.

## 8.6. *The Properties of Hair*

Hair, like horn, hoofs, and nails, is made of keratin. The discovery by the Nobel Laureate Linus Pauling that hair consists of immensely long molecules of protein, wound in spirals and linked together by simple bonds of sulphur, initiated our understanding of why structures made by animals and plants have special mechanical properties which in so many ways are superior to substances made by man-controlled chemical processes. Wood is one outstanding example; hair is another.

What do we require of the bowing ribbon? It must be elastic, very flexible, and absolutely uniform along its length; only that will ensure that as it is drawn across the string, the portion in contact is continuously replaced by an identical piece of material. It must also have a hard tough surface which will withstand continuous rubbing and abrasion. If you take such a specification to a fabricator he will say that you can't have one material which is all those things, because hard and tough cannot also be very elastic and flexible. Hair solves this problem by having an elastic core with an outer surface of separate tiny plates called scales. Would that their discoverer had called them something like squamulae or tegulae, because scales produces the wrong mental image. There is hair with the plates overlapping like tiles on a roof, with sharp edges so that it is like a saw blade in one direction but offers no resistance in the other. The last thing we want is a surface which catches the string on projections and then lets it go ping. When the bow grabs and when it lets go must be determined by the way in which the string wants to vibrate. Ideally this requires the surface of the hair to be uniform. The fortunate thing is that there *is* hair which is very long and does not have any significant difference in either direction along it—and it grows on a horse. The separate plates are hard and tough, but the core to which they are attached is very flexible. That is what the animal wants. One can see natural reasons why it should be flexible and have a hard outer surface; one cannot see reasons why it should also be so perfectly elastic provided it is not excessively stretched, but that is its other valuable property. Most of the spring in a bow comes from the hair; the stick must give sufficiently to ensure the hair is never stretched beyond its elastic limit. That is one of the major failings of some stiff synthetic sticks.

The surface of horsehair platelets is actually minutely corrugated. It is testimony to their resistance to abrasion that much of the corrugation is still there five years after the hair left the business end of the horse, which is the probable age of the oldest part of the hair on a newly haired bow. Bowing does wear the platelets, but as a rule bows need rehairing for other reasons. The hair accumulates dirt and grease; the playing properties can be much improved by careful washing once or twice in the hair's useful life. A very mild soap or detergent should be used with no more than tepid water. The frog should be released by removing the screw, and great care taken not to bend the hair through a sharp angle. *Do not allow any water whatsoever to make contact with the tip or frog.* Small wooden wedges hold the hair in place, and if they get wet and swell they may split the frog or tip. Hair should be rinsed through three or four changes of clean water to remove all traces of soap (which would not assist in retaining rosin) and allowed to dry, hanging under only the weight of the frog, before reassembling. Eventually hair absorbs greases which could only be removed by solvents such as carbon tetrachloride, and it must be replaced.

The production of bow hair is a very rare and unbelievably labour-intensive craft. First, hairs of the different lengths of the four instruments' bows are picked out. Then the white and black hairs are separated; ones of other colour are rejected, for bleached hair is not satisfactory. A simple test for chemically treated hair is to stretch a fibre. Natural hair extends by 10–20 per cent before it breaks; treated hair may be just as strong, but it doesn't stretch. It is apparently only a tradition that bass bows have black hair, since it can be as fine as hair of any colour; the coarser hair is grown by mares.

## 8.7. *How Rosin Works*

Rosin is a partially refined natural resin. Other materials have been tried, but rosin appears the best substance to obtain high friction between hair and string—an entirely false statement, as the following paragraphs show. There is no a priori reason why a substance with better properties than rosin could not be produced, but current demand and product cost are hardly technology forcing.

The chemical nature of rosin (such as we know it), and the reason for its adhesiveness to surfaces, is discussed in Chapter 10. It sticks reasonably well to clean hair, clean gut, and metals. When a player rosins the bow, the object is to coat the hair with a minutely thin *layer* of rosin. Solid particles of rosin break off; some stick to the hair, and some are trapped between the strands. Both fall off during playing and collect on the island below the bowing area. They should always be removed with a soft dry cloth after playing. Because rosin so readily fragments, the impression may be gained that the hair is coated with tiny rough particles which produce the bow/string interaction. This is incorrect. Bowing is not rasping; that is why the hurdy-gurdy sounds like filing a tin can.

Static frictional force is due to the affinity of one surface for another, and in the 'stick' phase of bowing, the surfaces are rosin on the hair, and rosin on the string. The static affinity of rosin for itself is high. Once the two surfaces are moving relative to one another in the 'slip' phase, rosin produces relatively low sliding friction. The value of rosin is the big differential between its sticking and sliding cohesion. Rather surprisingly, some double bass rosins incorporate hard wax; it has been suggested that this reduces frictional noise, but since almost all the gruffness is manufactured in the ear, it is rather a faint hope!

It has been argued that friction generates enough heat to melt the rosin. It may. Only sliding friction generates heat, and the 'slip' phase for most notes lasts for less than a thousandth of a second. It may not make any difference whether the string slides over solid or liquid rosin in that time, but the rosin on the next bit of hair must be solid to provide static friction, which does not generate heat. The temperature cannot reach a level which damages the hair, and if heat is significant, there should be a difference between bowing gut, which is a poor conductor of heat, and bowing a good conductor like aluminium or silver. Perhaps proponents of the melting theory should show that there is a difference, or explain why the material of the string does not appear to matter. It is one of those problems which intrigue academics.

Rosins have recently been introduced which contain visible particles of precious or other metals. A scientific explanation of how this affects the bowing mechanism is awaited with great interest.

## 8.8. *Hair Substitutes*

Synthetic substances such as polyamides (nylon-type polymers) have been tried as alternatives to hair. For reasons given in Chapters 9 and 10, few polymers have surfaces to which anything will adhere well, and this is one of the few attractive properties they have for clothing. They do not coat with rosin as hair does. In addition, most polymers are plastic; they are elastic but gradually elongate under tension, and in due course the bow 'runs out of screw'. Most polymers are not readily wetted by water, and do not elongate when they are. Thus they are not amenable to the traditional techniques used when rehairing bows. Should the day come when a substitute for horsehair has to be found, it does seem that it will have to be some other natural fibre.

## 8.9. *Accessory Parts of Bows*

The balance of a bow: the distribution of weight, is exceptionally important. The weight of the frog is significant, and lapping material round the stick at the frog end adds to this. Lapping has a double function, for it also provides a sweat-resistant surface which can be gripped. Yet again, natural substances such as leather and whalebone have better properties than synthetic materials. Silver and gold are corrosion-resistant and dense. For frogs, ebony is dense while ivory (which was used especially on the small frogs of baroque bows) and tortoiseshell are even more dense. None of these materials were chosen for ostentation. As well as their high density, they have excellent durability, are suitable for fashioning, and rarely react with a player's skin. It might encourage the support of conservation measures if donations were used for the development of adequate substitutes for banned materials. Tortoiseshell is turtle shell, which occurs only in flat plates, rarely more than 6 mm thick. Any thicker artefact, such as the frog of a bow, is made by compressing pieces of shell in boiling water, whereupon they coalesce. It can be repeatedly recycled. Fortunately, nacre: mother-of-pearl, which lines some mollusc shells and is traditionally used to decorate bows, is abundantly available, and the particularly beautiful paua from New Zealand is apparently even standing up to the mass production of cheap trinkets for tourists.

Every bow maker until well into the present century must have made or specified his own thread for the screw which tightens the hair. The threads come in every pitch imaginable. Unfortunately, bow-makers did not know that the outer third of a triangular-section thread contributes nothing to the strength of a screw, and that a rounded shape provides a more accurate fit.

## 8.10. *Handedness in Playing Instruments*

The left side of the brain controls the right side of the body, and vice versa. The brain is asymmetric in that some of the higher functions are located on one side and some on the other. In particular, rhythm appears to be sensed in the left hemisphere, while pitch is processed in the right one. Whether this could favour the manipulative determination of pitch by the left hand's fingering, and rhythm by the right hand by bow or plectrum, is an entertaining thought. What cannot be disputed is that a very high degree of co-ordination is required between the left and right limbs, just as bringing together the two elements of music—pitch and rhythm—requires great co-ordination between the hemispheres. This helps us to understand why many people have an excellent response to rhythm without a corresponding sense of pitch or, less frequently, good pitch sense without adequate rhythm—which can cause teachers just as much frustration.

# 9

# How Glue Works

◆◆◆❖◆◆◆

## 9.1. *Introduction*

Glue is as essential a component of instruments as wood, yet little is written about it. The glue always used is derived from the inedible parts of animals and is often called Scotch glue. It is found in ancient Egyptian furniture and, apart from a casein glue derived from milk, it was the only adhesive known to woodworkers, including the first violin makers. During the past fifty years synthetic chemistry has created a wide range of new adhesives, and there would be no reason for luthiers to continue using animal glue if any of the new products were better suited to the task. But animal glue has several properties which are of exceptional value both for instruments and in the making process, and which are not found in any other glue. This has nothing to do with tradition; one cannot foresee that any product is likely to replace it. In this chapter, 'glue' means this animal glue in water, unless qualified by a descriptive adjective.

A plausible explanation of how glue worked was put forward long ago. Wood has many little cavities, and it was thought that liquid glue ran into the holes and set, forming a multitude of tiny mechanical studs in sockets. The idea was supported by experience that with some materials a better joint can be obtained after filing or sandpapering the surface. That may be so, but it is not because the surface is made rough. The stud-and-socket theory became untenable when processes such as making fern-frosted glass were discovered in the nineteenth century. Glue will stick linen to plate glass so strongly that the cloth will rip out tiny glass splinters and produce a beautiful effect. Glass has no cavities, but it has to be scrupulously clean. A layer of grease, far too thin to see, prevents glue from sticking to glass, indicating that the nature of the surface is very important in adhesion.

## 9.2. *Adhesion and Cohesion*

In ordinary language we use **adhesion** when referring to sticking one thing to another, but the underlying idea, that two things are actually attracted to each other, is an important scientific concept. If you put droplets of very thin hot glue on a range of different surfaces such as clean glass, softwood, newspaper, yew, polythene, and wax, the liquid will immediately spread out on some of them, but on others it will stay as compact drops. You can make good joints between those materials on which the glue spreads and *wets* the surface of its own accord, but you cannot glue satisfactorily to the others. Nor will you get any better joint by clamping glue between two surfaces and forcing it to spread. Adhesion is the *natural* attraction between a liquid and a solid, or between two different solids, for there must be adhesion between a surface and glue after it has set.

But why does glue not spread of its own accord on some surfaces? We can understand this better by using drops of water, for water is a most important material in glue. Consider the edge of a drop of water

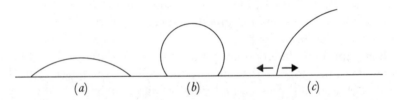

FIG. 9.1. Liquids on surfaces. (*a*) A water drop on a surface for which it has high adhesion spreads out. (*b*) If it has low adhesion for a surface, its cohesion makes it more spherical. (*c*) A 'tug of war' between adhesion and cohesion at the edge determines the shape of the drop.

on a surface (Fig. 9.1). If the surface has a strong attraction—a high adhesion—for water, the drop is pulled out. On a surface for which water has low adhesion, like wax, a drop pulls back into a ball even if you try to make it spread out. This shows that there is also a force attracting the water to itself. We call this **cohesion**: the attraction of the bits of any substance between themselves. At the edge of a droplet of any liquid on a surface there is a tug of war between adhesion trying to pull it out, cohesion pulling it back. The shape of the edge of a drop shows quite accurately the adhesion of a liquid for any surface.

Cohesion is a fundamental property. High cohesion between the components of a substance make it solid and give it shape. Liquids have lower cohesion than solids. They stay together but do not have a fixed shape. The smaller its cohesion, the more readily a liquid will evaporate, because there is less attraction to prevent bits of it from jumping out of the surface. Gases have no cohesion. A glue must have high adhesion to a surface both when it is liquid and when solid; it must also have high cohesion when it has set, or the glue itself will come apart.

When we say that the bits of a substance cohere, we mean the ultimate parts: the molecules. If you could subdivide a material repeatedly, you would reach a point where breaking its bits any more would destroy the nature of the substance, and those bits are its molecules. Every substance owes its individuality to the structure and composition of its molecules, which are different from those of any other substance. And there is a property as fundamental as the force of gravity, which produces the attraction between molecules: both their cohesion for one another and their adhesion to others, which varies greatly from one substance to another. This is the key to how glue works, and the ideas involved are also essential to an understanding of varnish. Fortunately, the main source of cohesive and adhesive forces arises from a simple principle.

## 9.3. *Polar Forces*

The world is made of atoms, combined into molecules. There are ninety-two different natural atoms but, remarkably, most substances which comprise living things are made of only four of them in a multitude of different combinations: hydrogen (H), carbon (C), nitrogen (N), and oxygen (O). In essence, every atom consists of a nucleus which has a positive electrical charge, surrounded by a 'shell' of electrons which has an equal balancing negative charge (Fig. 9.2). When atoms form

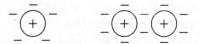

FIG. 9.2. An atom may be visualized as a core with positive charges, surrounded by a 'shell' with exactly balancing negative charges. When atoms combine to form molecules, they share their negative charges, making a strong chemical bond between them.

molecules their negative shells are shared. That forms very strong
bonds between them: chemical bonds. Overall, the positively and nega-
tively charged parts of the atoms in a molecule are still equal, but they
are not necessarily evenly distributed in space. That only happens if the
molecule has a symmetrical shape (Fig. 9.3). If the atoms are arranged

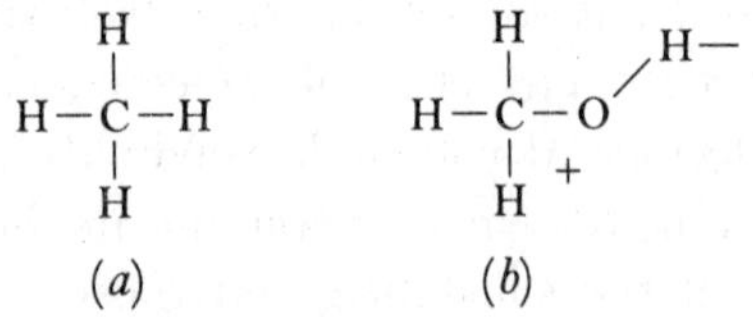

FIG. 9.3. Dipoles. If the atoms of a molecule are symmetrically distributed (*a*),
the electrical charges are evenly distributed. If the shape of the molecule is
asymmetric (*b*), it has excess positive charge in one place and equal excess negative charge in another; such molecules are *polar* and are attracted to each other
+ to −. (*a*) is non-polar methane, (*b*) is polar methyl alcohol. (*In all chemical diagrams,* C = a carbon atom, O = an oxygen atom, H = a hydrogen atom.)

asymmetrically, the molecule behaves as though there is a slight excess
of positive electrical charge in one place and an equal negative charge
in another. This arrangement is called a **dipole**. The tiny electrical
fields of these dipoles are attracted together—positive parts to negative
parts—in a somewhat similar way to the attraction which occurs
between magnets. These tiny forces are the main cause of adhesion and
cohesion.

Most substances do have molecules which are asymmetric in shape,
and so they do have some dipole forces. The effectiveness of these forces
will depend not only on how strong they are, but also on how frequently they occur in the substance. Molecules with six atoms are small;
those with a hundred are large. There are far more six-atom molecules
in a cubic millimetre than there are of molecules with many atoms. If
both kinds of molecule have the same polar forces, the six-atom substance will have much greater cohesion than the one with the larger
molecules. But a large irregularly shaped molecule can have several
places along its length where it is slightly more electrically positive or
negative, and glue molecules are like that.

## 9.4. *Water*

Water and carbon dioxide are very simple molecules, each having just three atoms (Fig. 9.4). Carbon dioxide has three atoms O=C=O in a line; it is symmetrical. It has no cohesion and it is a gas at ordinary temperatures. If the three atoms H–O–H of water were in a line, it would be a gas at very low temperatures indeed. It so happens that the water molecule is very asymmetric, and for its size, it has one of the strongest dipoles known. Hence water molecules are very strongly attracted to each other, giving water its high cohesion and making it liquid at ordinary temperatures. These strong polar forces also produce the adhesion of water to so many other substances, according to how strong and how many electrical polar fields they have. The attractive force of a single water molecule may be minute, but there are some million millions of them on a square millimetre of surface, and that adds up to quite a significant force.

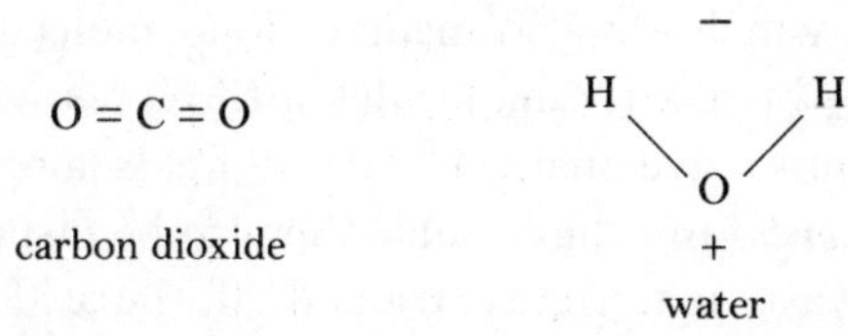

$$O = C = O$$

carbon dioxide

$$\overset{-}{\underset{\underset{+}{O}}{H\diagdown \quad \diagup H}}$$

water

FIG. 9.4. Water is very asymmetric and has a strong dipole, giving it strong cohesion and adhesion to polar substances. Carbon dioxide is symmetrical. It has no dipole and is a gas.

## 9.5. *Non-Polar Substances*

The major class of natural substances whose molecules are symmetrical in shape and have no dipoles are the oils and waxes (see Chapter 10.2). They have one of two basic structures: either a long chain of carbon atoms, each surrounded by hydrogens, and called 'paraffins' (the word means little affinity); or symmetrical rings of six carbon atoms, each with a hydrogen, called the 'aromatics'—because many of them are (see Fig. 10.1). Because they lack dipoles they have very low cohesion. A paraffin with as many as fifty atoms is a liquid; solid waxes have very little strength. They have little adhesion for polar substances like water. And since adhesion is concerned with the attraction of the very surface of things, a layer of oil or wax which is only one molecule thick will completely change the adhesion of surfaces, like those of wood or glass, from a very polar to a non-polar surface which will no longer have a high adhesion for glue—any kind of glue. Grease from fingers can spoil a surface to be glued, and the most important function of sanding or scraping wood before jointing is to remove a layer of the surface with any grease on it, rather than to make it rough or expose holes. In a discussion of glue, non-polar materials are only of interest for explaining why some things cannot be glued satisfactorily; they are, however, of great importance in varnish (see Chapter 10).

## 9.6. *Glue Manufacture*

Glue is made by boiling tendons, skin, and similar waste materials, usually in a dilute acid. The strength of tendons and hides is due to collagen, a substance which consists of enormously long molecules running in the directions which have to withstand tension. It corresponds in function in many animals to the fibres which give wood its strength along the grain, which are also made of long molecules, in this case of cellulose. Boiling breaks the molecules into pieces which are still quite long. These chains have many electrical fields along their length to which water adheres, and these cause them to be dispersed in hot water. Hair and other waste material is strained off, the acid is neutralized, and the glue solution is dried, either in sheets or often nowadays in globules called pearls.

## 9.7. *Glue and Water*

When dry glue is placed in water, the electrical poles of the molecules attract water. If a 5 mm cube is cut from dry sheet glue and left overnight in cold water, it swells about seven times in volume because water diffuses in until all the poles on the chains are linked with water. The 5 mm cube now measures about $7 \times 7 \times 18$ mm; this curious behaviour has a bearing on how the glue works in joints.

The surface of dry glue is not sticky. It becomes so immediately any water is applied. When it has taken up as much water as it can, it is slimy, but again it is not sticky. The adhesion of this glue to any surface such as wood, which has many poles, depends very largely on the long chains of glue molecules and the wood surface sharing an amount of water which is inadequate to satisfy their respective electrical poles.

There is some direct adhesion between glue molecules and wood molecules, but if a long molecule, with positive and negative poles along it at fixed places, lies on wood, which also has its poles at places determined by its structure, only some of the two sets can match. Water molecules can place themselves between opposite poles which are too far apart to provide adhesion on their own. In a sense, therefore, the water is a glue and may be the most important contributor to the adhesion. That is why a surface on which glue can be used effectively has high adhesion for water, and can be tested by seeing how drops of water behave on it.

In the same way, the cohesion: the internal strength of the glue depends on the sharing of inadequate amounts of water between its long chains. When glue is really dry, it is brittle because there is too little water to hold the chains sufficiently together. When glue is fully swollen with water, it is a soft jelly (gelatine is highly purified glue). It is strongest—both adhesively and cohesively—when it contains around 5 per cent of water: a fraction of the amount it will take up on soaking. That is the sort of water content the glue in a violin should normally have; hence if an instrument is kept in a dry centrally heated atmosphere, joints may open. The humidifying devices that some people put in instruments are also helpful to the glue (see Chapter 4.18).

## 9.8. *Liquids*

Although glue absorbs cold water, it is not dispersed. To distribute it on wood, it must be changed into a liquid, which is achieved by heating. In Section 2 above, we said that whether substances were solid, liquid, or gas, depended on the strength of the cohesive forces between their molecules. Why does heat reduce the cohesion of a solid and make it liquid? All molecules vibrate continuously. In solids the vibration is so small that the tiny cohesive forces are able to keep the molecules in fixed positions relative to one another. Heat increases the vibration and disrupts some of the forces; that is why a rib can be bent when it is hot, and why it retains that shape when it cools, because the cohesive forces increase again. When a solid is heated sufficiently (unless the molecules are changed chemically, e.g. they burn), the vibration becomes so great that the cohesive forces can no longer maintain the shape; it melts. A liquid has enough cohesive forces to hold the molecules together; our picture of a liquid is that cohesive links between some molecules are being broken by vibration all the time, but are forming between other molecules all the time too, so that at any instant, the total number of links between molecules remains the same. When a liquid is stirred, the forces are broken by the stirrer but reform immediately behind it.

When glue is heated after soaking in water, the vibration of the glue chains and of the water breaks more and more of the polar forces, and it becomes a liquid. The polar fields of the water are still just as strong and they can adhere to the surface to be glued, but only if they can reach all of the surface while the glue is still liquid. Warming the wood beforehand helps to keep the glue liquid for a longer time. It also allows the glue to wet and run into all the microscopic cavities in wood surfaces; this does form studs in sockets, but the more important matter is that cavities full of air contribute no adhesion, and many tiny air pockets added together reduce the area actually glued. Keeping the glue liquid also allows more time to set the parts in their exact positions in relation to each other.

In hot liquid glue the long chains run in every direction. When glue dries into flat sheets during manufacture, most of the chains come to lie in the plane of the sheet. An analogy is to compress a fluffed-up ball of cotton wool. It starts with the fibres running in every direction, but when it is compressed, the majority lie in the plane of the material. Hence when a cube cut from dry sheet glue swells, water goes between the chains which are lying flat on one another, and the cube swells more in that direction than in the other two dimensions. Similarly, as a glued joint dries, the chains tend to lie in the plane of the joint.

## 9.9. *Cramping*

If a glue does not wet a surface of its own accord, no amount of pressure will increase the adhesion. It may be sensible to fix the components relative to each other until the glue has set. But *joints should never be cramped tightly*. Tight cramps distort wood, which will endeavour to regain its original shape on removing the clamps. If the two surfaces to be glued do not fit exactly, and are forced together by bending the wood, the joint is in a state of stress, trying to pull apart. The strongest joints have minimal space for the glue (see Section 12 below).

## 9.10. *Rubbed Centre Joints*

While there are several reasons, given below, for using animal glue for most of a violin, it might be thought that a stronger synthetic glue would be better for joining the halves of two-piece fronts and backs. These joints have to withstand large forces during carving, and it is a serious matter should they open at any time. There is, however, more to this than mere strength. These joints should be made by planing the faces so perfectly flat that it is difficult to rotate one about the other when they are dry. They are warmed, and *rubbed together* with hot glue, squeezing out as much as possible. This produces an extremely thin layer of glue, and it is achieved because animal glue is so fluid; other glues are viscous. The virtue of the rubbed joint is acoustical. Glues have quite different properties from wood, and one does not want a large physical discontinuity in the middle of a vibrating front. The front may be made of two pieces of wood but it must behave as one; if it behaved otherwise there might be a significant difference between one- and two-piece fronts.

## 9.11. *Synthetic Glues*

Modern synthetic glues start as tiny molecules with strong electrical poles which adhere directly to a solid surface. Because the molecules are small and mobile, they can bind to many poles without using water. The ends of the molecules which are not adhering to surfaces then combine together chemically, forming long chains which run in all directions through the glue and give it great strength. But since the chemical change cancels all the free poles, any exposed surface of the set glue is non-polar. The chemical linking of small similar molecules to form very large ones is called polymerizing, and is also the process by which linseed oil varnish sets (see Chapter 10.8). Synthetic glues such as the epoxy glues, which include the varieties of Araldite, can make very strong joints. The so-called superglues also change chemically in this way; they are not necessarily super-strength, but they set almost instantaneously and there are no second chances. There are no solvents which can be used safely on fingers that have thus been joined together.

There are circumstances after major accidents, such as when the neck of a double bass has sheared off at the root, where the only consideration is to use the strongest glue in existence, and repairs of this kind would not have been possible before synthetic glues were available. But repairing is a relatively recent innovation in the ancient craft of the luthier—and so is an insurance policy.

## 9.12. *The Advantages of Animal Glue*

Many of the synthetic glues do not change in volume as chemical hardening takes place, and are called gap-filling glues; animal glue shrinks as it dries. That is one reason why all violin joints should be as good a fit as one can achieve. Before jumping to the conclusion that a modern glue would make careful craftsmanship unnecessary and have great strength, excellent adhesion to most woods, and other useful properties, we must consider what makes animal glue the choice for violin making.

One does not want a glue so strong that if there is an accident the one thing which does not break is the glue. It is far better for glue to give than for wood to break. If a repair or renovation, such as putting in a new bass bar, involves opening an instrument, animal glue will give to a thin knife (not to hot water, as one or two recent books suggest, for that risks ruining varnish); joints with synthetic glues are almost impossible to open without damaging wood. Any opened joint which has been made with animal glue can readily be re-glued because animal glue sticks to itself. This *cannot* be done with most modern glues. The chemical changes produce a material which, like many 'plastics' (synthetic polymers), have extremely few poles, and one cannot glue to them satisfactorily with any adhesive. An area covered with a synthetic glue must be scraped back to the bare wood. It is also difficult to get varnishes to cover many modern glues, because similar forces of adhesion are involved. If the parts of instruments are exactly fitted, animal-glued joints are so thin that they cannot be seen. There is thus no case for a gap-filling glue, and if gaps are inevitable in some repairs, they must be filled with real wood. Any excess animal glue around a joint can easily be removed after the glue has set; every trace of modern glue must be removed before it sets.

Three hundred years of experience have shown that animal glue is strong enough. This is not to suggest that modern glues will have a limited life, but time is the only test. There is also the mundane matter that glue is used frequently in small amounts. A glue-pot is always at the ready, whereas any two-component glue has a limited life after mixing. Animal glue has its problems, but taken together, its advantages for the violin family are so great that there are unlikely to be any contenders.

The properties of traditional glue are exploited in a different way in one of the commonest systems for constructing instruments. Initially the top, bottom, and corner blocks are temporarily glued to an internal mould around which the ribs and back are assembled. The glued joints between blocks and mould can then be broken and the mould withdrawn. Fronts can be lightly glued to the blocks to complete the edges, and then removed for purfling and cutting *f*-holes. Fingerboards are temporarily glued to the neck for shaping them and setting the neck in the mitre joint, then removed before varnishing the instrument. No doubt other ways of achieving these processes would have been developed if it were not so conveniently easy to make and break temporary joints with animal glue, but one could not do this with any other glue.

## 9.13. *Varieties of Animal Glue*

Rabbit glue is supposedly made by boiling down rabbit skin and tendon instead of waste from larger animals. It is much paler in colour than Scotch glue, because it has also been decolorized. There is no evidence that it has any different properties from ordinary Scotch glue as an adhesive, and there should be no places on an instrument where the glue actually shows, so the colour should not matter.

According to a major glue manufacturer, animal glue can be made liquid when cold by adding 30 per cent of urea and has reasonable adhesion when used, but slowly degrades. It is not known whether preparations of this kind are commercially available in the UK (but see Chapter 12.14). Adding 5 per cent of urea will slow the setting of glue without affecting its strength, but one must be a very slow violin maker to need this.

## 9.14. *Practical Advice*

Solid dry glue should be soaked in three to four times its volume of water, and then heated in an earthenware pot in a water-bath at around 70–80°C, ideally on an electric hotplate with a thermostat. Never boil it; it has the right mix of chain lengths when purchased, and boiling will slowly break the chains into smaller lengths and weaken the glue. Whenever possible take the work to the glue-pot, but if that is not practicable, use a ware pot which retains heat; and the classical metal pot often also makes glue go dark. Gelatin is an excellent medium on which to study the growth of moulds and bacteria. If the pot is heated every day, glue has a very long life, but if there are any visible or smellable signs that the glue has become alive, start again. Anything which attacks glue breaks up the chains and it will be less strong.

Although it is rare in temperate climates for instruments to be abandoned in conditions which allow micro-organisms to damage joints, there are moulds in the humid tropics which can even attack optical glass, and animal glue is quite high on the menu. Animal glue can be protected by adding formaldehyde to the glue when it is hot, just before applying it, but this links the chains together chemically, and in effect turns it into a material like a synthetic glue, thus losing the very properties which make it so valuable. Formaldehyde will do the same to your protein chains, and must be treated with the utmost respect. The vapour does no good to eyes, nose, lungs, or skin.

### 9.15. *Emergencies*

The best advice is: don't try to glue anything yourself, but whatever you do, never use any form of rubber-based glue. Apart from the difficulty of removing it to make a proper repair, rubber-based materials absorb vibration and may upset the behaviour of an instrument. This is also true of proprietary wood fillers.

### 9.16. *Playing In*

That a new instrument is improved by being played, is one of several long-standing beliefs; a hundred and fifty years ago Otto recommended that a new violin should be bowed across all four open strings for fifteen minutes, repeating this with a finger or a loop around the neck, stopping all four strings at successively higher positions. He thought a rosined wheel could be used. Carleen Hutchins recently suggested that a new instrument can be played in by vibrating the bridge for several days with a probe reproducing classical music. Science is not the only field in which the wheel is re-invented periodically. But is playing in yet another myth? The supposed changes are invariably judged by our notoriously unreliable memory of sound, which is so susceptible to suggestion. If playing in can be done mechanically, this eliminates the plausible explanation that the player has become familiar with the foibles of an instrument. But one has first to prove that there is such a phenomenon. When strings are put on an instrument, the state of the box is completely changed, nor should one expect the changes to be accommodated instantaneously. It is a possible if unproved idea that playing promotes changes, but when the changes are always said to produce an *improvement* one must be suspicious and, in the light of the things that hearing can and cannot detect (see Chapter 6), sceptical.

Popular description seems to assume that instruments are simply completed, strung, and then they all play happily ever after. Real life is not like that. Anticipation apart, instruments are strung before varnishing for good practical reasons. When stressed by strings for the first time, it is not unusual for a joint between a rib and the front or back to open; cellos and basses do so with a noise like a small explosion. Instruments should be left under full tension for a few days before stripping them down; it is much easier to re-glue a joint then than after they are varnished. The same joint rarely opens twice (or if it does one should be worried). An instrument should not be played extensively in the white, or it will need re-cleaning, but varnishing takes a considerable time. Detection of any change due to playing must start from the restringing after varnishing, but it is usually found that after a month or so of playing the soundpost is loose, and once the post is adjusted, one can no longer attribute any change to playing. If a soundpost was forced in to start with, one would certainly expect an improvement as the instrument accommodated it.

Suppose, however, we assume that there is something in the phenomenon. We have already discarded the idea that playing cracks the glue securing the purfling. A favourite idea that vibration 'rearranges the molecules of the wood' is ingenious in that it cannot be proved, but it is exceedingly unlikely. However, any theory that the initial playing produces some permanent improvement fails because of a second phenomenon. An old instrument which has been left without any string tension for some years is said to require playing in too.

The most plausible possibility concerns a more general behaviour of glue. A glued joint several inches long does not fail simultaneously over its entire length. It fails because there is excessive stress at one point; when that gives, the tension is transferred to the next part of the joint, and the fracture immediately runs along the joint. However exactly the parts are made to fit, stringing produces unevenly distributed stresses on all the glued joints compared with those when the joints are assembled. Animal glue is capable of a certain amount of plastic flow (unless it has been excessively dried). Provided it does not give way altogether, it will flow most where stress is greatest and may help to distribute stress more evenly. This will happen under static tension. It is just feasible that continuous vibration could speed up the flow of the glue. Redistributing tensions might make an instrument vibrate more readily and increase its responsiveness. The suggestion that the 'tone' improves is meaningless.

If glue can flow under stress, it is possible that it will also slowly flow back towards its original state when tension has been absent for a long time. An instrument should not be left unstrung for longer than necessary. Any change in glue will be greater if an unstrung instrument has been in damp conditions, but more commonly old unstrung instruments are found to have open joints when first put under tension, and after re-gluing they will behave like new ones anyway.

Even if one sacrificed an instrument by putting it together with an epoxy glue which does not flow, it is not clear how one could test whether or not it 'improved'. All we can conclude is that instruments change when put under string tension, change when soundposts are moved, and when different-tension strings are used. No one can detect slow change over time by hearing, but it is just remotely possible that a player could detect a change in an instrument's responsiveness, and there is no harm in people believing that they can. As Belloc wrote: 'Oh! let us never, never doubt What nobody is sure about.'

## 9.17. *Care of the Glue-Pot*

A visiting luthier from the southern hemisphere told me that he took pity on a despairing double bass player in a well-known orchestra touring his country and re-glued the bass bar for him in forty-eight hours. When the player returned and picked up the instrument, he more or less shot it to the ceiling. 'What the hell have you done?' he shouted, 'It weighs half as much as when I brought it in!' The luthier pointed to a large glue-encrusted iron pot. 'That', he replied, 'is what you've been carrying round for years, stuck on the strut across the back.' History does not relate whether the bass was improved, but up-market luthiers have been know to refer to double bass making as carpentry.

# 10

# Varnish and Varnishing

◆ ◆ ◆ ❖ ◆ ◆ ◆

## 10.1. *Introduction*

Violin varnish has excited enormous interest and is associated with
myths which are still promoted. This chapter may help to explain how
some of the nonsense came about. Varnishing—putting a protective
layer on a violin—would not be difficult but for the convention, established by classical makers, of making it look like furniture. Long before
violins were made, fine furniture was finished by colouring wood and
then protecting it with a clear varnish. Trying to imitate that causes a
multitude of difficulties for one simple reason. Furniture on which it is
worth producing a fine finish is made of hardwood. If colour is required,
the wood can be stained before applying the varnish. There are dyes
which, once attached to wood, are unlikely to fade under the conditions
in which fine furniture is usually kept. Coloured wood can be enhanced
by a clear varnish, the simplest of which is just boiled linseed oil.
Because it is transparent, it need not even be uniformly thick. The front
of a violin must be made of a softwood; if softwood is used anywhere in
good furniture it is never exposed. If softwood is stained, there is a
'reversal of stripes': the hard parts of the wood are naturally darker, but
the soft parts absorb most dye. That might be acceptable if a front was
a flat sheet with all the grain running exactly in the plane of the wood.
But carving the front in a way that exposes end-grain is essential, and
the end-grain of spruce is a multitude of tiny tubes and cavities which
mop up stain and produce dark irregular patches. That, in a nutshell, is
what all the troubles stem from.

The varnish must perform the most important role of protecting the
wood from dirt, water, and sweat and provide some resistance to
mechanical damage. It must transmit light so that the beauty of the
wood can be seen, but it cannot be transparent, because all the colour
must be in the varnish. The depth of colour is determined by the

thickness of the varnish, which must therefore be a very even layer, and since colour must not run into any micro-cavities, the surface has to be sealed. Varnish can also accumulate in larger cavities, such as those between the ribs and plates, and produce dark lines there. The number of suitable dyes, *soluble* in varnish materials, which are not affected by varnish chemicals, which do not interfere with the setting of the varnish, and which are light-stable, is very limited. And on top of all this, every maker harbours the thought that his creation will still be played three hundred years hence. One very good reason for using traditional varnishes is that they do survive. There is no way of knowing whether any modern synthetic varnish would.

Many who see a violin 'in the white' think it most attractive. It would slowly turn pale brown under a clear varnish, and this natural colour change is often accelerated by exposing instruments to the sun before varnishing them. The appearance of some pre-Stradivarius violins does suggest that all they have is a plain oil varnish over the wood, and that the wood and varnish have developed their natural brown colour. If only that tradition had been continued, makers would have been saved an enormous amount of adrenalin, for varnishing is the most difficult part of their work. It is, too, difficult to match and make an invisible repair in a coloured varnish, though that thought would probably not have occurred to makers until the nineteenth century.

There is one wicked thought which will appeal to scientists. The density of exposed end-grain will be greatest where the front is most flexible. End-grain strongly absorbs stain, and since the shell is of uniform thickness, a stained front would be a map of the variation in flexibility of the structure; it would reveal at a glance, things as interesting as any electronic devices could disclose.

## 10.2. *The Basis of Varnishes*

Mechanical protection apart, the major role of varnish is to prevent water and water-soluble substances from reaching the wood. The wood does and must contain water, or the glue would fail, and varnish does not prevent the wood from absorbing water from the atmosphere or losing it, because the inside of the box is not sealed. But wood swells unevenly when in contact with liquid water, and dries leaving a rough surface. Rough surfaces collect dirt more than smooth ones. Sweat is very largely water. Any piece of exposed wood which is repeatedly handled becomes dirty; dirt is an omnibus term for almost any unwanted substance, just as noise is any unwanted sound. Varnish is therefore primarily a preventive cosmetic. If it is a barrier to water, it will prevent many other substances from reaching the wood; the attractive aspect of the cosmetic is added to taste. Like beauty it is, and should be, only skin-deep.

In Chapter 9 it was explained that the adhesion of glue depends upon the attraction of polar substances to each other, and that water is a highly polar substance. The principle of polar and non-polar substances, explained in Chapter 9.2–5, is also the basis for understanding varnish, but here we need substances with the least affinity for water. Theoretically, varnish would be made of molecules with no polar forces: molecules with completely symmetrical structure. The commonest of these are the paraffin oils and waxes. They are long chains of carbon atoms with hydrogens symmetrically arranged around them (Fig. 10.1).

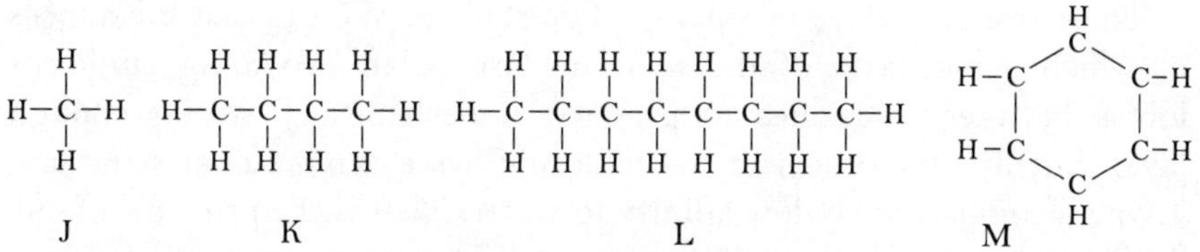

FIG. 10.1. The symmetrical non-polar paraffins: J, methane; K, butane; L, octane. Paraffin wax is a mixture of chains with 28–36 carbon atoms. M is the symmetrical benzene ring.

Crude oil is a mixture of such substances, ranging from butane (used as gas fuels), through petrol and kerosene (paraffin oil), to the long-chain petroleum jellies ('Vaseline') and hard wax, used for candles and, until the advent of polythene, for waterproof packaging. Crude oil also contains materials based on the other type of symmetrical molecule, a ring of six carbon atoms each with one hydrogen attached, the simplest of which is benzene (Fig. 10.2); multiple ring structures are important components of bitumens and pitch. White spirit, used for brush cleaning and as a paint-thinner, is obtained by distilling crude oil, and consists of about 85 per cent straight chain substances and 15 per cent ring compounds; it is entirely non-polar.

We cannot use wax as a varnish because of the very properties which makes it useful for waterproofing. Because they lack polar forces, the molecules are not strongly attracted to each other. A very thin layer of wax *over* varnish may be suitable for some purposes, but wax itself has

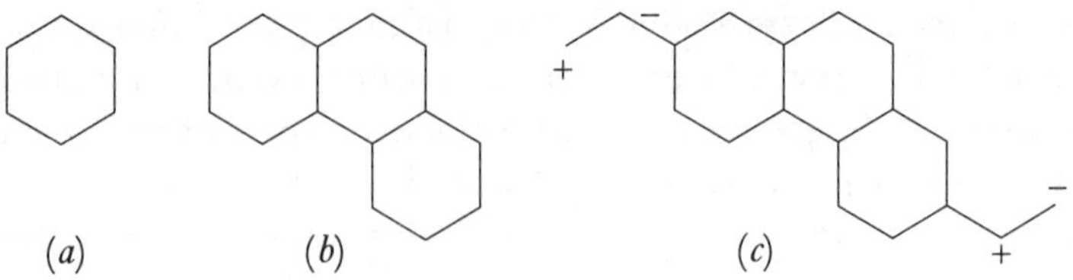

FIG. 10.2. Non-polar benzene (see Fig. 10.1) is usually drawn as a hexagon (*a*). Two or three rings sharing atoms occur in bitumen and pitch (*b*). Natural resins typically contain substances with two or three shared rings and one or two additions, producing polar regions (*c*).

almost no resistance to mechanical damage, and it has been known since biblical times that he who touches pitch shall be defiled therewith—the pitches and bitumens never set hard, as those who put them in varnish may discover.

There are two ways of solving the problem. We can use substances in which some parts of the molecule are polar, providing sufficient forces between molecules to produce a mechanically strong enough layer, but in which most of the molecule has a symmetrical structure, giving a comparatively low affinity to water. That is the principle of one traditional material: the **spirit** varnishes. The other approach is to use substances which are even less polar, but which will combine together chemically after they have been applied and provide mechanical strength that way: the **oil** varnishes. Both satisfy the need for water-proofing because low affinity to water also means that even if there are microscopic holes or pores in a waterproofing layer, water will not run into them (see Section 24 below).

Because varnish must be relatively non-polar, there is another problem. Varnish has to adhere to the instrument. Glue adheres to wood because wood has a myriad of tiny electrical poles on its surface. Therefore non-polar substances used in varnish will not. In practice, since the surface must be sealed to prevent coloured varnish from entering the spruce, the requirement is transferred to the sealer, which must stick to the wood and must also be something to which varnish sticks. Sealers must have special properties.

## 10.3. *Spirit Varnish*

Spirit varnish is made from slightly polar molecules. The molecules need also to be relatively large, because the larger the molecules, the more solid they will be. They must be dissolved in a suitable liquid to spread them. Solution in a liquid involves some of the liquid molecules adhering to the substance and forming a continuum with the rest of the liquid. Slightly polar molecules will not dissolve in water, which is highly polar, nor will they adhere to the molecules of completely non-polar liquids such as paraffin or benzene. They will be attracted to and dissolve in a liquid which, like themselves, has some polar and some non-polar parts. The solvent liquid must be volatile: it must evaporate after the solution has been spread, leaving the solid material. Liquids with the appropriate properties are the alcohols, and they provide an excellent example of how the balance between polar and non-polar property determines all the different features of materials which are important in understanding varnish.

## 10.4. *The Alcohols*

The word alcohol is commonly used for a substance in beverages, but that is only one of a large chemical family of substances. Fig. 10.3 shows

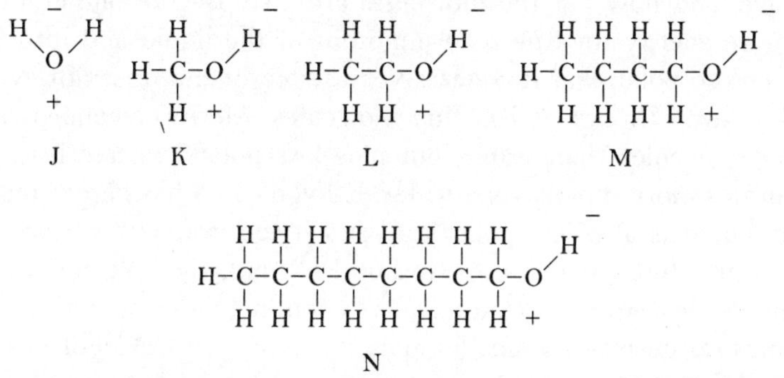

Fig. 10.3. The alcohols are non-polar paraffin chains with one asymmetric polar group at the end: J, water; K, methyl alcohol; L, ethyl alcohol; M, butyl alcohol; N, octyl alcohol.

one series of these; they all consist of a length of non-polar paraffin chain, with the ending –OH (an oxygen and a hydrogen), which is asymmetric and provides displaced electrical fields: a polar ending. In a way, water can be looked upon as the simplest of all the alcohols; it is extremely polar. As the length of the non-polar paraffin chain increases, so the substance becomes increasingly less polar; the length of the chain controls all the properties in which we are interested. Methyl alcohol, with the smallest paraffin chain, is still very polar. It dissolves completely in water. It is a good solvent for polar substances, but will not dissolve non-polar ones like waxes. Ethyl alcohol, the one which occurs in drinks, has a slightly longer chain. It is still sufficiently polar to mix completely with water, but it is a better solvent for substances with some non-polar regions, and is a useful solvent for solids which can make varnishes.

Butyl alcohol has twice the length of non-polar chain, which now begins to dominate the polar ending. It does not mix completely with water. It is a better solvent for substances which are more non-polar than polar and in some ways is a more useful solvent for spirit varnish solids than ethyl alcohol. Octyl alcohol, with a long non-polar chain, will hardly mix with water at all, and is soluble in completely non-polar solvents like white spirit.

Next, how does this balance of polarity affect evaporation? The evaporation of the liquid from a solution of a solid depends on three things: how much the solvent loves the solid, because to evaporate it has to unhitch itself; how polar the solvent molecules are themselves, because the more polar, the more they stick together as a liquid and do not want to leave; and how big the molecules are, because the bigger they are, the more energy they need to jump out of the liquid and into the air. Water is so polar that it coheres very strongly and does not evaporate quickly, even though it has tiny molecules. Methyl alcohol may have bigger molecules than water, but it is less polar, coheres less, and so evaporates more rapidly than water. Ethyl alcohol has bigger molecules again, but it is also less polar still, and it too evaporates more readily than water. But when we get to butyl alcohol, the size and weight of the molecule begins to count and is enough to slow down its rate of evaporation despite its smaller polarity. And octyl alcohol evaporates much more slowly.

For solids which themselves have the right balance of polarity to make varnish, the choice really is between ethyl and butyl alcohols. The solvent commonly used is industrial spirit, a mixture of about 90 per cent ethyl alcohol with 10 per cent methyl alcohol: hence the name spirit varnish. The methyl alcohol has little effect on the solvent properties of the ethyl alcohol. It is not put in; the manufacturing process produces the mixture, and there would be no point in an expensive process to separate them. Methylated spirit, the purplish liquid used for cleaning and in simple stoves, is industrial spirit with a dye and repulsive substances added, to dissuade people from drinking it. Methyl alcohol is harmful if drunk—not to suggest that excessive ethyl alcohol is

without an effect—and those who are granted an excise licence to purchase industrial spirit are expected to use it only for the purposes noti-
fied to the authorities. One can buy butyl alcohol without a licence. The
correct thing to ask for is *n*-butyl-1-ol because more than one substance
answers to the name 'butyl alcohol'.

An important rider follows: any colouring material for a spirit varnish must itself also have molecules of a shape which produces a balance of polar and non-polar properties, or it will not dissolve in alcohol
or be uniformly distributed in the solids after evaporation.

Industrial spirit will absorb water from the atmosphere; this sticks to
the polar endings, and as little as 5 per cent of water in the spirit ruins
its solvent properties for varnish solids. Spirit varnishes should be kept
in a sealed container, but the spirit itself must be water-free.
Manufacturers add quicklime to remove any water in the product, but
it is not a nice substance to handle, nor easy to obtain in small amounts.
There is a much safer way, using copper sulphate. This normally occurs
as bright blue crystals, which contain water. If it is heated on a piece of
metal over a flame, the water is driven off and white powdery copper
sulphate remains. It can be placed in a small glass tube with plugs of
cotton wool (not synthetic fibre) at either end, and kept in the spirit
bottle. It is totally insoluble in alcohol and absorbs any water present,
and when it has turned blue, it can be drained, reheated, and reused
indefinitely. The colour is a very sensitive test for water; to discover
whether spirit contains water, put a drop on a little white powder. If it
does, the powder turns blue.

### 10.5. *Spirit Varnish Solids*

Not surprisingly, all the solids used in traditional spirit varnishes are
natural products. There is no reason why alternatives should not be
synthesized, but this is not apparently commercially viable—yet. The
solids are called 'resins', but the term is an ill-defined descriptor for
almost anything natural or synthetic which starts life as a sticky mess
and eventually becomes a solid. Most of the substances used, such as
mastic, the copals, the elemis, sandarac, and benzoin, are secretions produced by trees to seal off some injury, in most instances a long time
ago. The trees had used them to do exactly the same thing that is
required of a varnish: to waterproof a damaged area and provide a layer
resistant to bacterial and fungal attack. The materials were naturally
selected to be sufficiently non-polar to prevent them from dissolving in

water and being washed off, but sufficiently polar to be mechanically strong. Also, since everything inside a living organism has to occur in a watery medium, the substances have to be transported to where they are needed, and even living systems find it difficult to transport something as completely non-polar as a paraffin wax. The plants produced the resins in volatile solvents which have long since disappeared.

The other widely used resin is shellac, obtained from a scale insect which lives continuously in one position on a bush, feeding through an inserted tube. It secretes the material over its surface for the same purposes: waterproofing and mechanical protection. Many insects make minute quantities of shellac, but this scale insect specializes in using it as a defence.

Copal and elemi are products of a number of different plants; samples may vary in physical properties and, so far as it is known, in chemical composition. The main components typically comprise two or more symmetrical non-polar rings with a few polar groups attached (see Fig. 10.2). Shellac, though also a mixture, is much more uniform in composition and behaviour, but it is sold in various grades of purity. It contains waxes from both the insect and the tree. The cleanest material normally available is orange shellac, but it should always be dissolved in industrial spirit and left to allow insoluble material to settle out; that will include the waxes which are too non-polar to dissolve. Decant the shellac solution; shellac blocks filters in no time. If wax is not removed, the varnish will be cloudy.

## 10.6. *Applying Spirit Varnish*

The evaporation of solvent from a layer of varnish is not simple. The alcohol molecules of the liquid in between the large resin molecules jump out into the atmosphere readily, but those adhering to the resins leave more reluctantly. During the evaporation of any liquid, huge numbers of molecules jump out but the majority fall back in again, which is why evaporation is faster if air is blown over it. Evaporation from a brush is rapid because it is moved through the air. For reasons which follow, the faster the varnish dries on the violin's surface, the better.

A layer of varnish dries from the outside, and if it is thick, the resin molecules form a nearly solid 'skin', not only making it difficult for solvent molecules underneath to get through and jump out, but keeping the liquid present for long enough for it to penetrate into anything underneath. And if underneath are previous layers of varnish solids, solvent will get between those resin molecules and swell the layers irregularly, just as water swells glue. This can result in wrinkles, cracks, or crazes. That is why spirit varnishes must be applied in several thin coats.

Spirit varnishes are comparatively easy to make: one simply dissolves the right resins and colouring materials (see Section 10 below) in alcohol. But they are difficult to apply. One problem with spirit varnish would be overcome if only each layer changed after it was applied so that the next layer could not affect it. That advantage is obtained with oil varnish.

## 10.7. *Oil Varnish*

Oil varnish is based on linseed oil, which has been used as a varnish and a base for paint for centuries and, usually with a slight modification of the natural oil, still is, in huge amounts. Linseed is called a **drying** oil, but the drying process is entirely different from the way in which a spirit varnish dries by solvent evaporation. 'Drying' implies that a liquid turns into a solid, and when people had no idea of what happens, they used the same word for both processes. Linseed and a very few other plant oils, such as tung and poppy, change chemically when exposed to the air and become solid; other oils do not, and some which are used as components of oil varnish are solvents which evaporate. 'Oil' is a general term, like 'resin'. The word comes from *olea*, the Latin name for the olive, and the liquids extracted from olives, linseed, and other plants were called oils for many centuries before the discovery of mineral oil, which has some similar properties such as insolubility in water and flammability. The two kinds of oil are totally different.

Plant oils, and also animal fats, are all of the general form show in Fig. 10.4. Don't be put off by the apparent complexity of the pictures. All we are concerned with is that the plant oils and animal fats all consist of three very long chains of carbons with hydrogens around them—just like the non-polar paraffin oils—linked by a short stem. They are therefore almost completely non-polar, insoluble in water and polar solvents such as industrial spirit, but soluble in non-polar liquids like petrol, white spirit, benzene, and turpentine. Molecules drawn on paper do not give a three-dimensional picture. The three long chains stick out from the stem at roughly 120° to each other as suggested in the diagram—and when the oils are liquid the chains are wriggling about all the time.

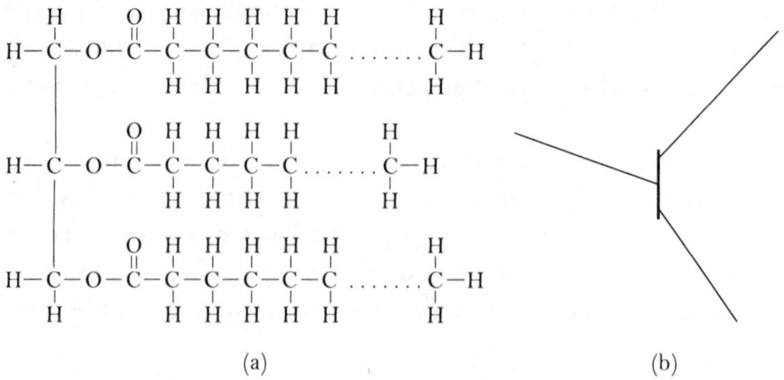

$$H-\overset{\overset{\displaystyle H}{|}}{\underset{\displaystyle |}{C}}-O-\overset{\overset{\displaystyle O}{\|}}{C}-\overset{\overset{\displaystyle H}{|}}{\underset{\displaystyle H}{C}}-\overset{\overset{\displaystyle H}{|}}{\underset{\displaystyle H}{C}}-\overset{\overset{\displaystyle H}{|}}{\underset{\displaystyle H}{C}}-\overset{\overset{\displaystyle H}{|}}{\underset{\displaystyle H}{C}}-\overset{\overset{\displaystyle H}{|}}{\underset{\displaystyle H}{C}}\ldots\ldots\overset{\overset{\displaystyle H}{|}}{\underset{\displaystyle H}{C}}-H$$

(a) (b)

FIG. 10.4. Plant oils and animal fats consist of three long non-polar paraffin chains attached to a stem of three carbons (a). The chains differ in length according to the plant or animal species. In reality the chains point in different directions from the stem (b).

These are quite big molecules. Animal fats like lard and dripping are liquid only at blood temperature. Plant oils have slightly different chains and are liquid at the temperatures at which plants live. The most important difference between plant oils and animal fats can be found on any carton of margarine (see Fig. 10.5). Every carbon of the long chains

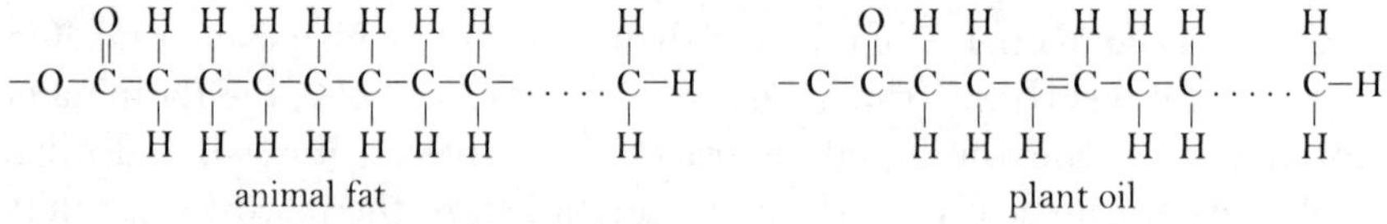

animal fat                    plant oil

FIG. 10.5. The long chains of animal fats are 'saturated' with hydrogens: each carbon has two hydrogens. The chains of plant oils are 'unsaturated': in at least one place, two adjacent carbons have only one hydrogen each.

of animal fat has two hydrogens on it; these are called **saturated fats** because every carbon has as many hydrogens as it will combine with. But the long chains of plant oils (or vegetable fats, as the food industry quite correctly calls them) have a few carbons with only one hydrogen attached to them, which is why they are called **unsaturated fats**. Most plant oils have only one place on their chains where two adjacent carbon atoms each have only one hydrogen.

## 10.8. *How Oil Varnish Dries*

The special thing about linseed oil (Fig. 10.6) is that two of its chains each have *two places* where adjacent carbon atoms have only one hydrogen each. And drying—turning into a solid—happens because carbon atoms in that situation prefer to be joined onto some other atom rather than be 'unsaturated', and given the chance, they will become 'saturated' by linking chemically to similar places on the chains of other molecules (Fig. 10.7). They form gigantic long molecules by polymerization, the same kind of chemical process by which the modern synthetic glues become solid (see Chapter 9.11). When linseed oil turns into such a solid it forms a tough mechanically resistant layer which is also waterproof, for it is still made up of non-polar molecules.

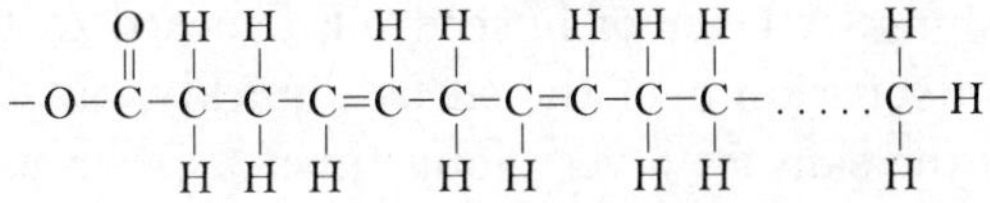

Fig. 10.6. Two of the three chains of linseed oil each have *two* places where adjacent carbons have only one hydrogen. These places 'want to be saturated',

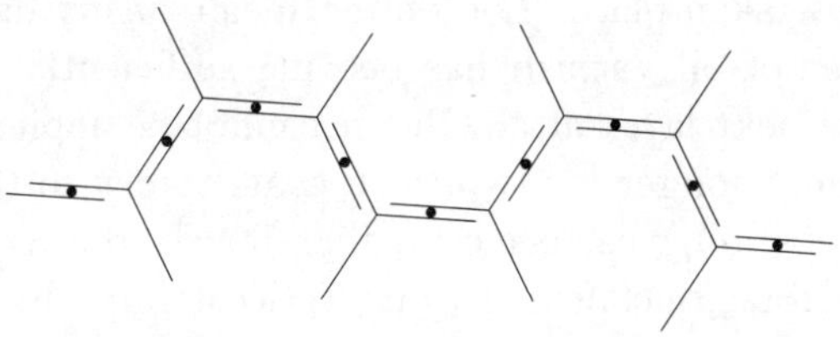

Fig. 10.7. When linseed oil is exposed to air, the unsaturated places on the chains join together, polymerizing—forming enormously long molecules in all directions through the oil.

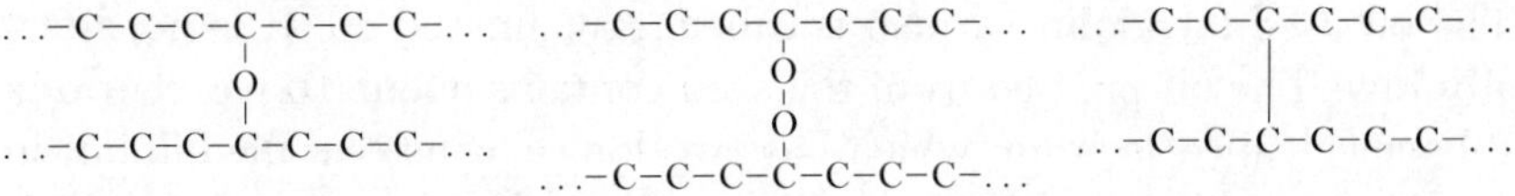

Fig. 10.8. Linseed oil does not polymerize fully until some chains join together through one or two oxygen atoms (*d, e*). Then chains can slowly join directly (*f*). Only the carbons of the chains are shown.

Fig. 10.7 may suggest that the linking of the chains is a simple process, but there is still some doubt about the detail of what happens, though we know more about this than about some of the natural resins. What stops linseed oil linking together and turning solid in the plant? It cannot do so unless it has a supply of oxygen. The plant prevents oxygen getting to the oil; as soon as it is exposed to the air it takes up oxygen, which starts the process off. Some of the unsaturated places *must* be linked by oxygen atoms first (Fig. 10.8). Only after that has happened can other chains join directly, in a much slower process. One result of this can be seen if linseed oil or paint is stored in a sealed container with a little air; a skin forms on the surface but when the oxygen in the air has been used up, no further change occurs and the oil or paint underneath is unaffected.

That property protects oil in a sealed container but produces a problem when varnishing. A layer of linseed oil, exposed to the air, forms an extremely thin soft skin over the surface quickly, but it does not go solid underneath the skin for a very long time. As soon as the skin has formed, it is quite impermeable and slows the rate at which oxygen can diffuse through into the varnish underneath to complete the first part of the process. The varnish does not become a tough solid until the direct linking of chains has also been completed, long after all the oxygen linking has taken place. 'Long after' means many days, not hours.

Once a layer of oil varnish has become sufficiently solid, it is not affected by the next layer at all. But it cannot be applied in thick layers. It takes much longer for two thick coats to dry to the stage where all the oxygen bonding has occurred than for six thin coats which produce a similar total thickness. Drying is accelerated by heat (which is not much use for musical instruments); ultraviolet light can be used, though that may produce snags of another kind.

## 10.9. *Varieties of Linseed Oil*

The oil used for violin varnish is called 'raw' linseed oil. It is not literally raw. The oil pressed from the seed contains about 10 per cent of a substance called lecithin, which has two long chains like the oil, but in place of the third chain there is a strongly polar structure. Lecithin is a natural detergent; its long chains adhere to the chains of the oil, but its polar groups stick to water. The plant uses lecithin to transport non-polar materials like the oil. Gentle heat causes the lecithin to separate from the oil, and it is removed. The lecithin is called the 'break'; warming makes the natural oil break into its two components. The lecithin-free oil is 'raw'. In some older paint recipes a little lecithin is put back in the mix after the pigment has been added, to act as a spreader (see Section 21 below). Boiled linseed oil is also sold. Boiling initiates the polymerization process, so that the oil has larger molecules. It is then more viscous and does not dissolve other materials so well, but used alone as a simple varnish it dries more quickly.

## 10.10. *Colours and Varnish*

The appearance of varnished wood is complicated. The colour of a varnish seen in a bottle is only a partial guide to its effect on an instrument. To understand what is involved, we need a little background about the properties of light and the nature of colour. Sunlight—white light—can be split by a prism into 'all the colours of the rainbow' just as a rainbow is produced by raindrops acting as little prisms. White light is a mixture of all those colours. When it falls on a white surface, the light of all colours is reflected: that is the meaning of 'white'. When we see a coloured surface, the light which is reflected consists of that colour (almost always a mixture of several rainbow colours), and all the other colours in the light are absorbed by the surface. That is how we see the colour of something opaque: that we cannot see through. In fact, whatever the material light falls on, even a sheet of glass, some of all the light is reflected. If the surface is very smooth, the reflected light produces shine. If the surface is matt, which means it has a very small-scale irregularity, just as much light may be reflected, but it is scattered in all directions and does not produce shine. Light reflected at the surface does not pass through the varnish; it does not contribute to the colour or to our seeing the wood underneath (Fig. 10.9a). To some, a shine may add glamour, but it makes it more difficult to see the colour and the detail of the wood, unless the instrument is held so that our eyes do not receive the shine.

The light which does pass through the surface of a 'transparent' material such as varnish is also partly absorbed. Blue glass, for example, allows the blue light to go through; how much of all the other colours in the light are absorbed depends on how strong the blue colour is. Thus the darker the varnish, the less light goes through. Of the light which falls on the instrument, the part which reaches our eyes has been through the varnish, has been reflected by the wood, and has travelled back through the varnish again. The varnish has absorbed light twice,

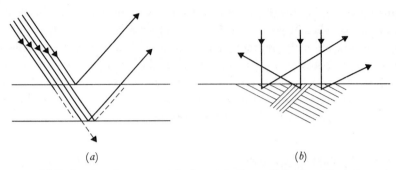

FIG. 10.9. (*a*) Reflection from varnished wood. Some light is reflected at the surface. Some is absorbed by the varnish. Some is absorbed by the wood. Some more of the reflected light is absorbed by the varnish. (*b*) The laminations of hardwood behave like mirrors, and the amount of reflected light seen depends on the angle of view.

once when going in each direction. However, some of the light which does go through is absorbed by the wood, and what is reflected depends on what colour the wood has. The condition which provides the maximum colour from a varnish, occurs when there is as much reflection as possible from the layer beneath the varnish—the wood—provided it has a colour which reflects the colours contained in the varnish. This does not mean that the wood must be the exact colour of the varnish; white would do. The wood may have been browned by sunlight, but that may not help. There is no brown colour in the rainbow. Several different mixtures of colour look brown. There is no guarantee that wood brown will reflect the colours which comprise a particular varnish brown, any more than a particular varnish red or orange.

The structure of the wood enters into the process too. Spruce is straightforward. It has darker hard parts and paler soft parts. They absorb or reflect according to their colour, and neither is a particularly good reflector. Figured hardwood, on the other hand, is made up of very thin plates stacked one upon another, and different areas have the plates facing at different angles, depending on how they have been cut through (Fig. 10.9*b*). One may think that wood is opaque, but light does penetrate its surface sufficiently for it to be differently reflected depending on which way the plates under the surface face. They act like tiny mirrors, in that those at a suitable angle reflect more light to the eye and appear lighter, while those at other angles reflect less and appear darker, with the result that the pattern changes as the instrument is rotated because the angles of the mirrors continually change. This is in addition to any actual colour differences between different parts of the hardwood. And in just the same way that roughness of the outer surface of varnish scatters reflected light in all directions, so also fine-scale roughness of the wood surface does some scattering; to obtain the combined effect of colour contrast and reflection contrast from hardwood, the wood must have a smooth finish.

## 10.11. *Colouring Materials*

Dyes must be soluble in varnish to be evenly distributed. The colouring material must match the varnish in its balance of polar and nonpolar properties. There are a few naturally occurring coloured substances which can be extracted from plants with boiling water and, after drying, can be dissolved in industrial spirit, but most substances which are very soluble in water are only slightly soluble in spirit. What sometimes happens is that boiling water extracts a suspension of fine particles from which the spirit dissolves a dye. It appears to be an absolute rule that one cannot extract a coloured material with spirit, evaporate the spirit, and get the dye to dissolve in oil varnish. To colour oil varnish by adding a dye, the dye must be virtually non-polar.

What causes colour? Unfortunately, what makes a dye coloured all too frequently also results in the colour disappearing when put in varnish. Colour usually occurs because some part of a complex molecule is under strain. The part under strain is actually vibrating at a rate which corresponds with the rate of vibration of light of the colour. One example of a molecule under strain is the unsaturated part of a linseed oil chain; it happens not to produce colour, but because it is under strain, it links with oxygen when it gets the chance. The same principle governs the stability of many coloured substances. They owe their colour to unstable chemical structures which, given the chance, will either take up oxygen or lose oxygen, so as not to be under strain—and the colour disappears. Chemists' fanciful word for this property is 'fugitive': the colour runs away. And like the drying of linseed oil and many other chemical processes, exposure to light containing some ultraviolet hastens the process. If colours survive extraction with boiling water, it is a promising start, but even some of them will still fade in sunlight.

One of the earliest successes of synthetic organic chemistry was the production of brightly coloured synthetic dyes, many of which are light-stable. The majority of them are utterly unsuitable for violin varnishes (there are some remarkable coloured instruments in the pop arena). An interesting thing about the first synthetic colours is that some of the more stable ones are based on a chemical structure which was subsequently found to be the same as in the most stable dye that can be obtained from vegetable material: madder, which has a long history in natural dyes, and has been used in violin varnish.

There are some stable dyes which can be used for spirit varnish. When we turn to colours for oil varnish, the problems are far more serious. A plain linseed oil varnish is colourless. It may darken a little with age, but that takes a very long time. Because linseed oil consists of large molecules it is a very poor solvent. There are few non-polar dyes: the part of the molecule which produces colour usually creates some polarity. But the biggest drawback is that linseed oil starts to change into a useful varnish by combining with oxygen, and if any oxygen in the colouring material can be stolen—and it usually can be from the part of the dye which produces its colour—the linseed oil will take it, and bleach the colour. There are some amusingly naïve suggestions about varnish colour, even in very recent publications: for example, that some of the redness of old varnishes might be due to iron from the pot in which they were made. In oxygen-demanding conditions, any iron would be in the ferrous state and produce a green colour; it would be more plausible, though improbable, that iron produced the slightly greenish tint of some Gagliano varnish.

Because we do not adequately understand how linseed oil becomes a hard tough varnish, we cannot predict whether, bleaching apart, any particular dye or other substance added to the oil will interfere with the processes by which it does becomes solid, for example, by linking with the chains and stopping polymerization. It is, like cooking, a case of 'suck it and see', or use a well-tried recipe and hope it will work. The situation is demonstrated by the painstaking work of Michelman, who made dozens of coloured oil-soluble substances for varnish. Out of over a hundred experimental recipes, only three or four produced a varnish which would set properly and had a light-stable colour which would also be acceptable on a violin.

Exactly the same thing applies to adding any solvent to oil varnish. The only safe thinner is artists'-quality oil of turpentine, which of course has then to evaporate and extends drying time. One can buy dyes to add to oil varnish. They come in a variety of unspecified solvents, some of which change the application properties of the varnish and the time it takes to set. Fashions change many times over the life of an instrument, and it would make things easier for everyone if we were content with the good natural colours produced by the traditional methods of making the oil varnishes which are available commercially. These are usually made by heating resins to temperatures of over 300°C, adding hot linseed oil, taking the mixture up to a high temperature, and adding hot real oil of turpentine. If you are ever tempted to try this sort of thing, check whether it is legal to do so. Such is the fire risk that some towns have centuries-old by-laws forbidding the making of varnish within their boundaries.

### 10.12. *Oil or Spirit?*

Oil varnish is very resistant to water and water-soluble substances, and reasonably so even to spirit and rosin dust. Spirit varnish is proof against water, water solubles, and rosin dust, but of course is ruined by alcohol. A well-meaning attempt by a student to remove rosin with eau-de-Cologne was an unmitigated disaster. Oil varnish is stronger and tougher: spirit varnish wears more rapidly where an instrument is inevitably rubbed while playing. Most amateurs find spirit varnish more difficult to apply successfully. But for those who have developed the skill, spirit varnish dries very rapidly. Even with ultraviolet lamps in a cabinet, varnishing with oil is a slow process, and it is difficult to judge when it is safe to start playing; the varnish may not reach its full hardness for six months. Never be tempted to add a commercial hardener to an oil varnish. It speeds up the drying process and it is often incorporated in paints. But it continues the hardening process beyond the point which makes a good instrument varnish, and commercial paints are made with the expectation that they will be stripped and replaced every ten or so years.

The other side of the coin is that if an instrument does get damaged, the repair will inevitably include touching in broken varnish. It is comparatively straightforward for a professional repairer to dissolve the edges of spirit varnish around the broken region, merge in matching varnish, and make a really invisible repair. Since oil varnish becomes large chemical molecules, it cannot be dissolved in anything (anything less potent than a paint-stripper, that is), making a repair more difficult.

### 10.13. *Other Varnishes*

Mass-produced instruments at the bottom of the market are often covered with cellulose lacquer. It can be applied with a spray-gun and dries rapidly. If there is any 'tinting and shading', look no further for clues. It can set with a glass-smooth surface giving a very high shine. It is durable and satisfactory for the instruments on which it is used, but much too hard for good instruments. The liquid varnish and the vapour are highly inflammable, and precautions must be taken against inhaling the vapour.

Modern synthetic varnishes such as polyurethane are easy to apply; they can be obtained suitably coloured, are unaffected by water and a wide range of chemicals, and have good abrasion resistance. However, they polymerize into a 'single molecule' and are almost impossible to repair. If any joint is not completely filled with glue, and synthetic varnish runs in and onto the gluing surface, one cannot glue to such a surface, just as one cannot glue to a synthetic glue's surface, should the joint subsequently come open. Oil varnish can produce a similar difficulty because it too creates a surface to which animal glue will not adhere. One other problem with synthetic varnishes is that the skin they form is very strong but their adhesion to wood is not, and if an instrument is bruised, the varnish can lift off as a 'blister'. But like any thin varnish, they do not affect the sound of the instrument. The isocyanate varnishes have similar properties, but they are very toxic and should only be used by trained people. Melamine-based two-pot varnishes are extremely durable and chemically resistant and have very good adhesion to wood. From personal experience, I add that a double bass varnished with a melamine-type varnish nearly forty years ago looks just as good today, after an enormous amount of use playing jazz.

All varnishes have their advantages and disadvantages. What is in favour of traditional varnish is that some have lasted three hundred years in good condition, but there are examples of old ones which have become cloudy, crazed, or cracked, and some have worn very badly. There is no substitute for time, and we have no idea whether any varnish invented in the twentieth century will maintain its properties for a hundred years. Painting pictures is similarly conservative, and some twentieth-century materials which have been used are already showing signs that they are not durable.

## 10.14. *What, no Recipes?*

No. Making varnish *is* like cooking; you can prepare meals apparently identically on separate occasions but the result will depend on the ingredients and their responses to the processes. Heron-Allen likened it to making claret cup, saying one added ingredients arbitrarily according to one's taste when one made it. Oil varnishes are usually made in large quantities at a time because that reduces variability, but commercial batches do vary, leaving aside that manufacturers may substitute one ingredient for another (as they have every right to do), which can completely alter the surface behaviour of the product. Resins vary so much that the same recipe can produce a hard or a soft varnish.

There are reasons why people make their own varnishes. Some like experimenting with chemicals, just as others enjoy the fun of finding out how violins work. Excellent oil and spirit varnishes can now be bought. Some of today's older professional makers prepare their own varnish out of habit because when they started making, no varnish suitable for instruments could be bought. Violin varnish was available before World War II. E. Spon's *Workshop Receipts* of 1895 describes how one was made. In part, the hiatus came about because of that war and in part because synthetic varnishes appeared; perhaps one reason why we lack detailed knowledge of traditional varnish resins and of how varnishes dry may be that the techniques of chemistry have been concentrated commercially on synthetic substitutes.

## 10.15. *Varnish and Tone*

There are apparently people who make their own varnish because they believe that varnish has something to do with tone, and one has the strongest suspicion that there are also a few who maintain that blarney about their own varnishes because there are people gullible enough to believe them. The entire syndrome starts from the fairy-tale that *the* secret which made the sound of classical instruments unique was their varnish; that we know is a nonsense—what we hear from them is not characterizable, let alone unique. That belief readily becomes the generality that the varnish has an effect on tone, even though adherents may no longer aspire to reproduce a classical varnish in the belief that it will make their instruments incomparable. It is at least consistent with this that if one believes varnish has an effect on tone, the tone of an unvarnished instrument must change when it is varnished, and I learned, while writing this chapter, that there are people who believe that an unvarnished instrument has a *characteristic* sound: that it is 'hollow' or 'woody'. Because of the extraordinary susceptibility of our hearing to suggestion, discussed in Chapters 5 and 6, I questioned some people who had never heard of this belief. Few people will have had my wife's experience of hearing about a thousand instruments in the white and again after they have been varnished, often played by professionals, some of whom are from national orchestras. She has never noticed anything unusual about the sound of a white instrument, nor have any of the players I have asked, and certainly I have not; they all sound like normal instruments before and after they are varnished. That view is supported by the classical scientific investigations of Meinel (see Wood, *The Physics of Music*) through to the conclusions of the authoritative physicist Cremer (see Cremer, *The Physics of the Violin*). Provided the varnish is neither thick, nor glass-hard, nor rubbery, it cannot have any detectable effect on what is heard from an instrument. Cremer puts it very simply. 'Varnish has one virtue; it is very thin.' My measurements give the average total thickness of fourteen coats of spirit varnish as 0.058 mm, or 2 per cent of the total thickness of an average violin front. The average thickness of a dozen coats of oil varnish is less than twice that. If a physicist can *measure* some change in the sound from an isolated instrument, which can be proved independent of unstringing it, the time involved in varnishing, and restringing it including resetting the soundpost, I will be impressed; but from what we discovered in Chapter 6 it is clear that no such conceivable change can have any perceptible effect on its tone when it is played.

The sound emitted is also not affected by whether a vibrating surface is polished or matt. The vibrating cones of many loudspeakers are made of quite rough-surfaced cardboard. A radiating surface must have irregularity on the same scale as the wavelength of sound before it affects the distribution of sound. The wavelength of the highest sound a young person can hear is about 20 mm in air and 100 mm in wood. The wavelength increases as the pitch goes down.

## 10.16. *Research on Past Varnishes*

The varnishes on some classical instruments are very fine, even to those who do not look at half a million pounds' worth of instrument through Venetian-tinted spectacles. It must have been implicit in the quest of earlier speculators that varnish was connected with tone, but the varnishes are still of consuming interest. All I can contribute is some questions. Is there is any evidence that Stradivarius or any of his teachers or contemporaries made any varnish? Almost everything the revered master used or wrote is preserved and described in greatest detail, but is there a single item associated with varnish making? These were skilled woodworking craftsmen; varnish making was a separate and distinctly down-market trade. It is more than likely that they bought their varnish from the shop round the corner, metaphorically speaking, which may also account for the colours used in different areas.

Suppose that, by the marvels of future science, the chemical composition of one of their varnishes is discovered; will that explain how it was compounded and how it was applied? And without daring to enter the argument about whether oil or spirit (or both) were used, has any author in the past hundred years questioned the availability of water-free spirit for varnish? Not until Coffey invented the compound still in 1890 could spirit comparatively free of water be obtained by distillation. Fermentation provides a maximum alcohol content of about 12 per cent. Simple distillation, the stock-in-trade of alchemy since the Dark Ages, may with luck concentrate the alcohol to something like 60 per cent. But one cannot use alcohol with as little as 5 per cent of water for varnish. If spirit varnish was used, the alcohol must have been dehydrated in some way, and if it was made from wine, it would have contained a variety of other alcohols, aldehydes, and esters, though it is doubtful whether they would have contributed any special properties.

### 10.17. *Preparing for Varnishing*

The whole of an instrument's surface must be really clean wood, which is often achieved by a final scraping. There are three possible initial processes, two of which may be combined. The spruce may be rubbed with finely particulate material called a 'filler'. A ground may be applied in order to change the adhesive properties of the wood surface. The surface must be sealed to prevent varnish colour from reaching the wood. The sealer may also act as a ground. The classical makers must have used sealers. Whether they used grounds or fillers is a matter of conjecture.

### 10.18. *Grounds*

The preparation of surfaces for oil-paint (linseed oil with added pigments) almost certainly predates the varnishing of violins. Canvas was sized with substances that filled holes, but they also 'prepared the ground' for the oil-paint. In domestic decoration, the undercoat is a ground for gloss oil-paint as well as a vehicle for most of the pigment. Wood has many polar groups, and the adhesion of an oil varnish is increased by reducing the polar nature of a wood surface. That is the objective of a ground. Some people apply a ground before using spirit varnish. For oil varnish, we do not want to make the surface entirely non-polar; that would be like coating it with paraffin wax, which would not have adequate adhesion either (see Section 2 above). The wood itself can come to our rescue. The special property of water is that it has a strong dipole. Where the wood has a positive pole, the water's negative pole sticks, and vice versa. If we apply something which has only one kind of exposed pole on it and the rest of it is non-polar, it will block half of the wood's poles and make a surface with reduced polarity which will provide better adhesion for varnish molecules (Fig. 10.10). There are many materials with those chemical properties, like soaps and detergents, but they cannot be used because they would lift off if water reached them.

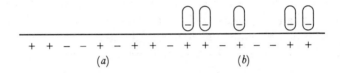

FIG. 10.10. Grounds. (a) Wood has poles of both kinds exposed. (b) A substance with polar ends of one kind adheres to the oppositely charged places, reducing the polarity of the surface by making it a patchwork of polar and non-polar areas.

The ideal ground material has less water affinity than a soap and can be spread as a liquid. One can get surprisingly close to coating a wood surface with only one layer of molecules adhering to one set of poles by wiping it with a clean rag moistened with an essential oil such as rosemary or lavender oil; these oils consist largely of substances with considerable non-polar portions and small polar groups. It does not matter if a little sinks into the wood, but one should be parsimonious. Ten milligrams or so will cover the entire surface of a violin. The name for these oils means 'essence', not vital. I once reviewed a machine-translated book with the intriguing title *Bulgarian Rose Concrete*; it was about the solid (concrete) waxes and resins left behind after the essence has been removed from flower extracts for perfume manufacture.

A clear spirit varnish can be used as a ground for oil varnish, and also a solution of propolis in spirit. Propolis is collected by honey-bees and used for several purposes, including blocking small holes in hives. Like spirit varnish solids, propolis is a mixture of substances with polar and non-polar parts: it consists of gums akin to those which in the past were secreted by plants and turned into some of the traditional spirit varnish resins. It is very variable in composition. The best material for use as a ground is said to be obtained by extracting with boiling alcohol for long periods. Propolis has been used in varnishes, but received wisdom is that often these never harden sufficiently. According to a recent book from a country which shall be nameless, propolis is also endowed with over a hundred different medicinal properties (none of which is apparent from the chemical composition, given in the same book), so one cannot discount its magical effect if included in violin varnish.

Other materials that makers are known to use include water-glass (sodium silicate), egg-white, and a mayonnaise of egg-yolk and linseed oil akin to the tempera of painting. Some of these may at least partly seal the surface too. They all have the same purpose of changing surface affinity, whether users realize it or not.

## 10.19.  Sealers

Sealing is usually achieved with two thin coats of clear varnish, whether spirit or oil is used. Applying two coats is important (see Section 24 below). A tiny amount of the transparent sealer will run a little way into pores in the front. It will assist in anchoring the varnish and will have no acoustic effect.

There are one or two makers who apply boiled linseed oil to the wood in sufficient quantity for it to permeate right through the thickness of the front, before using a coloured oil varnish, and who believe that classical makers did so. Some Victorians thought that oiling the wood lubricated the molecules or the fibres, allowing them to slip over each other, thus enhancing their ability to vibrate. Fibres don't slip over each other in vibrations, and linseed oil is not a good lubricant for any purpose. Boiled oil will gradually turn into a solid because oxygen can diffuse into the wood from the inside of the box. The most likely thing the treatment will do is reduce resonance. To my knowledge, no one has suggested that this surprising treatment affects instruments in the long term; perhaps it affects the behaviour of the wood such that any short term changes due to humidity are of minor effect.

## 10.20. *Fillers*

Paste fillers are widely used to fill the large holes in open-grained furniture hardwoods, but what does rubbing a mineral powder into spruce
do? It is naïve to think that this blocks holes completely because no
amount of rubbing mixed-sized particles into a porous surface will
select ones which will exactly fit each hole. It is even worse to think
that they will stop a sealer from running into the hole, because if the
filler has a surface which is wetted by the sealer—which is essential—
the smaller the gaps between the sides of the filler particle and the sides
of the pore, the stronger the forces which will suck sealer into the gap
(see Section 24 below). If the surface of the filler is not wetted by the
sealer, there is a prospect of one of the horrors of varnishing: a spot
which will not coat and goes on not coating, layer after layer.

There are other possible roles. Glass-like substances such as quartz
or alumina form an optical boundary with varnish. Tiny particles of
such materials in a filler would reflect light and add apparent bright-
ness. Finely powdered glass has been used for this purpose, though
never, so far as I know, in the varnish put on instruments. Quartz and
alumina are also polishing materials. 'Polishing' is an omnibus term for
several different processes which make a surface shine because it is flat.
On metal, polishing is cutting: removing any metal which sticks up.
On varnish, friction melts the very surface and it then resets. Wood,
especially softwood, can be polished by compressing projections, but it
does not necessarily stay compressed; fillers and abrasives used on
wood must not be applied with excessive pressure. One cannot treat
the surface of wood with a particulate abrasive without leaving
some of it in and on the wood. Silica, alumina, and some other abrasive particles adhere to the surface of wood very strongly by polar
forces.

Thus one cannot tell whether any mineral particles which are in or
on varnished wood are there as a result of abrasion or filling, or for
reflection. Prepared abrasives such as sandpaper are recent inventions;
they too leave particles behind. If makers of earlier periods did use an
abrasive, they probably used the best material of all, which does not
shed its cutting elements—dogfish skin. The denticles on this are enam-
elled teeth, immensely strongly attached and exceedingly hard, and the
material is naturally graded from fine to coarse from the back to the
belly of the fish. Nowadays the dogfish is euphemistically called the
rock salmon; its skin is still a valuable tool. One thing of which we can

be sure is that any silica in old varnish has not come from fish skin; denticles are composed of calcium and magnesium compounds.

## 10.21. *Spreaders and Surface Tension*

Spreaders are substances which can be added in very small amounts to 'improve the flow' of liquids. This description unfortunately gives the impression that they lower the viscosity. Spreaders work by changing the surface in a rather drastic way. They can be added to oil varnishes, but whether one should do so needs careful consideration. To understand what is involved, apply some oil varnish to a piece of wood which has been wiped with essential oil and watch the edge of the brush. A brush distributes varnish rather arbitrarily; you may brush it out into a more even layer, but the varnish itself produces the smooth surface. Provided they wet adequately, varnish and gloss paint produce a smooth even layer on flat and convex-shaped surfaces. Liquid is sucked into corners and hollows; this is not a case of liquids flowing downhill, because it would happen if a violin was held upside down.

Spirit varnish spreads in the same way, but everything happens much more quickly. The varnish appears streaky if the solvent evaporates so quickly that the liquid becomes too viscous before spreading makes it even. This is why a solvent like butyl alcohol, which evaporates more slowly, can be helpful.

When discussing water, liquid glue, and grounds, we have thought only about a liquid against a solid; liquid spreads if its adhesion for the surface is greater than its cohesion. The liquid has another surface, in contact with air. Within a liquid, every molecule is equally attracted in all directions by the cohesive forces of the similar molecules around it (Fig. 10.11). A molecule at the surface has molecules on either side and below. Above there is only air. All the molecules in a liquid's surface are being pulled inwards. If a liquid is disposed in any shape, its cohesive forces try to pull molecules back into the bulk of the liquid until no more can be pulled in; it tries to have *the minimum possible surface area.* That is why gloss paint, spread on a flat panel in an uneven layer by a brush, produces a flat surface on itself; if the liquid were in any other shape it would have a larger surface area. Before the phenomenon was understood it was unfortunately called **surface tension**, because it appears that the surface is trying to shrink. But liquid spread on a surface will only form a flat layer if it has enough adhesion to the solid. If the adhesion is poor, surface tension will break the layer up, usually into

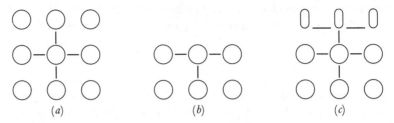

FIG. 10.11. Surface tension. (a) A molecule within a liquid is attracted equally to all molecules around it. (b) A molecule in the surface is attracted on both sides and inwards, but has no attraction outwards. Molecules are pulled in to make the surface as small as possible. (c) A spreader provides some attraction outwards, and decreases the surface tension.

separate droplets, and the total surface area of the droplets will be smaller than that of the flat area. This can be prevented by lowering the surface tension, and that is what a spreader does. An everyday example is provided by soap. Water has low adhesion for a non-polar surface like polythene and shrinks into isolated droplets because of its strong cohesion. Anything which floats on the water and which produces a small outward attraction for the water, reduces the cohesion force pulling the water molecules inwards (Fig. 10.11). The surface tension is reduced, the water spreads and has a larger surface area. We have not changed the viscosity of the water or the adhesion of the water for the polythene; *spreaders do not increase a liquid's adhesion.*

Only a layer of spreader one molecule thick is required. The actual shape and size of molecules is known, and one can work out how much soap, for example, is needed to form a layer one molecule thick on a surface. About ten million million soap molecules—a two-hundred-thousandth of a milligram—will pack onto a square millimetre. Less than two milligrams of soap would form a packed coat one molecule thick over the smooth surface of a varnished violin. This indicates how little essential oil is needed for a ground, and how much spreader might be needed for a layer of oil varnish. For the ground we have to allow for the micro-roughness and cavities of the wood. We may need to apply ten or so milligrams of essential oil from the rag, but only two or three milligrams of a spreader is needed.

Lowering surface tension helps to produce smooth flat and convex surfaces, but concave situations are different. Consider the 'corner' between a rib and the overlapping plate, with varnish available from the brush (Fig. 10.12). The two sides of the corner represent a bigger area

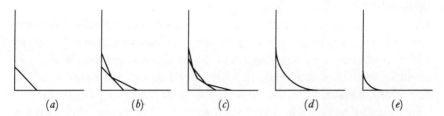

FIG. 10.12. Surface tension would make varnish in a corner have a flat surface (*a*), but adhesion pulls the edges out (*b*, *c*). The resulting surface is an arc. High surface tension pulls more liquid in (*d*); low surface tension encloses less liquid (*e*).

than a straight line drawn across the corner. If we draw a line diagonally across it, we create two new corners, across which we can draw straight lines which represent a smaller surface still. If we repeat this we arrive at the shape which actually forms: a continuous curve which has a lot of varnish behind it. The stronger the surface tension, the shallower the curve, because the shallower it is, the smaller is its area. The stronger the adhesion of the varnish for wood, the further the edges of the curve are pulled out. If surface tension and adhesion are both strong, they try to pull a large amount of liquid into the corner. The only controlling factor is how much varnish can be obtained from the brush. There are three options: decrease the adhesion of the wood surface, use a spreader, or have only a little varnish on the brush when doing corners and concavities, which is good technique.

If a spreader is used with varnish, it is added to the liquid. It only works if it gets to the surface, so how does it get there? The explanation is one of the most convincing demonstrations that the molecules of a liquid are always in movement. Spreaders must have less adhesion to varnish molecules than they have for themselves, or they would not work. If a molecule of spreader comes up to the surface, there is less attraction to pull it back in than to pull molecules of the varnish back in. Once spreader molecules get there, they stay there and accumulate until the surface is full of them.

We now come to the cause for concern. Since a spreader covers the varnish surface when it is liquid, it is there when the varnish sets. A spreader accumulates on the surface because it has low adhesion for the varnish, but arranges itself with the ends which have some adhesion next to the varnish. Its other ends—facing outwards—have least adhesion for varnish. And when the next coat of varnish is applied? Either there will be extremely low adhesion between the two coats; or the spreader will dissolve in the next coat, which then contains two portions of spreader. Some years ago a one-coat gloss paint was produced which contained a silicon compound. Some silicon compounds are very effective spreaders and this paint had excellent covering powers and a fine gloss surface, with the added advantage that it was very easy to clean because very little would stick to it. Unfortunately that included paint. The only way to redecorate was to strip it with a paint-stripper.

There is a way of dealing with a layer of spreader on a coat of oil varnish. When it is dry enough, rub it down with fine abrasive paper until every scrap of the surface has been removed. Traditional oil varnish is known to last for hundreds of years. It is an interesting question whether oil varnish applied with a spreader will do so. Perhaps the doctrine of perfection would be to add a trace of a silicon-based spreader only to the final coat of oil varnish. It should ensure a superb gloss finish without polishing, and the instrument should be very easy to keep clean.

### 10.22. *Unwettable Spots and Orange-Peel*

When applying varnish one sometimes finds an unwettable spot. It may be small, but successive coats will not cover it, and if untreated it produces a dimple with the entire thickness of varnish forming a rim. The patch has the wrong surface property—it has little adhesion for the varnish. The simplest cause may be failure to cover the area with the ground; the most likely one is that the wood has absorbed a highly polar substance such as a salt; sweat contains salts. If a spot appears, as soon as it is practicable, clean the surface of the spot with finest-grade abrasive paper and smooth out the rim of varnish. Rub pure beeswax hard into the area and wipe thoroughly with a clean cloth to remove any wax which will come off. Touch in the area and leave to dry. Paper the whole area gently and complete the varnishing. A spot of this kind can occur, though more rarely, with spirit varnish, and similar treatment with rosemary oil should cure the trouble.

But an irregular pattern of patches (unkindly called the 'English orange peel effect') is probably due to water in the spirit. As little as 5 per cent of water completely changes its solvent properties, and as the alcohol evaporates from a very thin layer, the surface tension rises, pulling the liquid away from areas of least adhesion. This is most likely to happen when varnishing cellos, because the varnish pot is exposed to air for a long time. The typical English climate is no doubt the culprit;

there was no orange-peeling in the long dry summer of 1995. Since we do not control the weather, we should keep the spirit stock dry with copper sulphate (see Section 4 above), keep the varnish in closed containers with as little air above the liquid as possible, and expose it for the minimum time while varnishing. Butyl alcohol absorbs water more slowly from the atmosphere and is much less likely to cause orange peel problems in damp conditions.

## 10.23. *Rubbing Down*

It is valuable to rub down with finest abrasive after every coat of varnish. Natural resins and commercial varnishes may contain substances which act as spreaders, and if any of the lecithin occurring naturally in linseed oil is left in, it acts as a spreader too. But papering has a further advantage. If a liquid will spread on a smooth surface, it will spread more on that same material if it has a micro-rough surface. There is an explanation for surface chemists in advanced books on surface chemistry.

## 10.24. *Porous Surfaces*

The principle which explains why varnish accumulates in corners—a tug of war between surface tension and adhesion—applies also to liquids in a tube (Fig. 10.13). If a liquid has good adhesion for the walls of the tube, it runs along them. This makes a curved surface on the liquid; surface tension pulls it flat. The edges run further along the walls, and surface tension shrinks the surface again. The liquid is sucked into the tube, whatever shape it is; this is how a sponge works. The smaller the hole, the stronger the suction; but the *speed* at which it happens

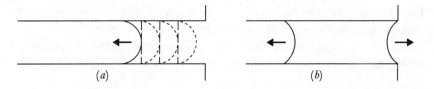

(a)                                  (b)

FIG. 10.13. (a) If liquid wets the walls of a tube, it spreads along them, extending its surface. Surface tension pulls the surface flat, and the process repeats, sucking liquid in. (b) When the supply ceases, the liquid has the same shape at either end and has a pit on the surface.

depends on how viscous the liquid is. The suction may be strong if a sealer or varnish wets the walls of the tubes in spruce, but if the liquid is viscous, the smaller the hole, the slower it will go in. If a liquid does not wet the walls of a tube, exactly the opposite effect occurs. It is very difficult to force water into a wax- or silicone-lined tube, and the smaller the hole, the more it resists being filled; that is the principle of the proofed canvas tent.

A filler particle must be wetted by a sealer, so that it runs into the hole whose sides are partly wood and partly filler. The first coat of sealer will be sucked down the hole. It stops when there is no more liquid on the surface; the liquid in the mouth of the hole is pulled into a shape which exactly balances the shape of the liquid/air surface in the hole (Fig. 10.13). The sealer becomes solid, and its outer surface will have shallow pits over all the holes. By reducing the size of holes to the gaps round a filler particle, a filler helps to make these pits as small as possible. But a second coat of sealer fills the pits because they are concavities, and makes a smooth surface over them. Two coats of sealer should be applied, both to ensure that the surface is covered and to fill the pits.

If an essential oil is used as a ground for clear varnish, there should be enough for a little to run into the micro-cavities. That will line them with a surface over which clear varnish will run in. Glue sticks to wood by polar forces, and a mechanical key is not important, but varnish and sealers never adhere as well as glue, and any keying of the material into pores helps to fix it to the surface.

### 10.25. *Brushes*

The same forces which cause tubes to take in liquids operate between the bristles of brushes. A brush with many fine bristles, well wetted by varnish, holds a lot of varnish and parts with it reluctantly, allowing the experienced user to control the flow. Some natural hair has excellent properties for spirit varnish, and synthetic bristles are too non-polar. On the other hand, being non-polar, some synthetic bristles are quite practicable with oil varnishes.

### 10.26. *Polishing?*

In theory surface tension ought to leave varnish with a perfect glass-smooth surface if the whole operation has been carried out in a dust-

free atmosphere. Some makers do not like such a flashy surface and tone
it down with the finest abrasive. Some polish it at length. It makes no
difference to the sound, but time must be added to the price.

## 10.27. *The Varnish Myth*

Science explains the principles of varnish; it cannot explain what might
happen in mixtures of natural substances of unknown composition, and
the minutest amount of some substance in a natural component can
change the behaviour of a well-tried recipe. No one knows how a violin
will behave until it is tried, and the same is certainly true of a varnish.
The classical makers must have solved the problems just as empirically,
for they can have known no more about why varnish worked than why
their wooden boxes did. But whereas any skilled woodworker could
copy a wooden box exactly, he could not fathom the varnish or the
process, and nor apparently, at the time of writing this, can we. Was it
a very clever idea to disseminate the rumour that the secret of tone was
in the varnish? The 'secret ingredient X' is the stock-in-trade of cos-
metics today, as the cosmetic, violin varnish, became. Whoever did start
the clever myth, we can be fairly sure the classical makers themselves
did not believe it. They must have had very good hearing as well as
being superb varnishers.

# 11

# Real Strings

♦♦♦❖♦♦♦

## 11.1. *Introduction*

We have only obtained some idea of how violins work in the latter part
of the twentieth century. The basic laws which determine the pitch of
strings have been known for more than three centuries, but the technology which made it possible to apply them fully has only been developed in the past fifty years, producing a string-making revolution. A
wide range of strings with very different properties is now available; it
has proved to be a mixed blessing. Few people would dream of modifying their instrument or bow, but strings are changed and mixed with
abandon. Players need not know how a violin works, but there are several things they should know about strings.

## 11.2. *Catgut*

Gut, often called 'catgut', is made from the membrane surrounding the
small intestine of animals, for which purpose it needs to be strong and
elastic. It is possible that it was even used in Egyptian times, and making catgut was a flourishing industry in Europe by the sixteenth century. It could not have come from a cat; only vegetarians need a long
gut to complete the digestion and absorbtion of food low in nutritional
content. Apparently, lute strings were divided into minnikins and
catlins, and the 'cat' prefix was transferred to gut. Strings have been
made from several herbivores, but today it is invariably sheep gut which
is used. The principle of making gut strings has hardly varied.
According to the size of string required, a number of lengths of the
membrane are wound tightly together while wet, and held stretched
under tension for several days; the strands cohere well when they are
then dried. Nowadays the string is ground to make it uniformly cylin-

drical throughout its length, because uniformity is essential for high-quality sound. Irregular gut strings are required for authentic early-instrument sound—and one can hear that they are.

Gut strings are expensive and have a limited life; that is why steel strings were introduced. Strings are now produced which more closely imitate gut, and since they are also more durable than gut, it is to be hoped that their use will spread, for they are kinder to both instruments and ears. Strings are also now made with appropriate tensions for children's small-sized instruments and to match more exactly the different sizes of viola and double bass. String tensions are important to bridge pressure and to the balance of forces between the two sides of the bridge. The harmonicity of strings made of different materials is also largely determined by their tensions. To understand how string makers can manipulate the properties of strings to improve harmonicity and behaviour, we need to know how pitch, length, weight, and tension are related. The principle of these relationships was discovered independently by Galileo (who invented the first telescope) and by the ever-surprising Mersenne; of course they had to express their findings in terms of musical pitches, for the concept of frequency was not known.

## 11.3. *The Basic Laws*

The relationship of the pitch to the playing length of a bowed string is apparently more complex than the standard law given in acoustics books (see Chapter 2.14), but the principle that pitch is inversely proportional to length is sufficiently accurate when selecting strings for an unusual size of instrument. How is pitch related to tension? When one tunes a new string, a small increase in tension raises the pitch rapidly at first, but as the required pitch is approached, a large force is required for a small increase in pitch. Suppose a composer requires an instrument to be tuned up a tone; this was common for double bass concertos, though they were probably played on a small chamber bass. What roughly is the increase in tension? Tension is proportional to the frequency squared. Sorry to be mathematical, but I'm afraid there is no alternative way to state that. 'Squared' means 'multiplied by itself'. When a string is tuned up a tone, for example from G (392 Hz) to A (440 Hz), the tension will increase by 440 × 440 divided by 392 × 392, which is almost exactly 1.25. Raising four strings by a tone is equivalent to adding another string, and increases the bridge pressure on a typical gut-strung bass by more than 10 kgm.

How can two strings have the same tension but one sound a fourth higher than the other? Mersenne said that the pitch is inversely proportional to the diameter of the string; for example, if one gut string is 3 mm in diameter and the other 4 mm, the thinner string will have 4/3 the frequency of the 4 mm one—a fourth higher. That is a theoretical example: one does not have plain gut strings of 4 mm diameter nowadays. Mersenne's work was brilliant science in 1636, but the relation of diameter to pitch only holds for strings of uniform material such as plain gut or wire. Pitch is determined by the weight of the string per unit length, and the weight can be made up of different materials provided that they are uniformly distributed along the string. Since the pitch is also determined by the tension, increasing the weight allows a string to have a low pitch with a reasonably high tension. By 1660 gut was being wound with wire to make lower-pitched strings, and by 1700 strings made this way were available for violins as well. At what stage this changed from being an empirical to a scientifically calculated process is unclear. The law which the string maker uses is that for a given length and pitch, the tension is proportional to the weight per unit length. (Frequency is inversely proportional to the square root of the mass per unit length. Mersenne's luck was that diameter is a measure of the square root of mass for a string of uniform material.) When my wife made me a violone thirty years ago, I went to a well-known shop in the West End of London specializing in double basses, produced a spring balance, and asked to weigh a large number of strings to find the six nearest to those it required. They were very interested and extremely helpful.

### 11.4. *Damping in Strings*

The violin family was evolved with gut strings. It is still the best material, and string makers have yet to produce any alternative which matches the superb inherent properties of gut. That is not just my taste in string tone; the statement was made by the physicist advising one of the major manufacturers of strings. The first reason concerns damping. One of the important properties of spruce is its high internal damping (see Chapter 5). Gut is ideal for the same reason. A string has a very sharp resonance at the pitch it sounds. Most of the energy put in, in each vibration of a gut string, is used up in deforming the string. Thus the string responds to the instruction of the bow; it does not, for example, continue to vibrate at large amplitude when the player wants a sudden diminuendo. Steel and synthetic materials have almost no internal damping; they are suited to instruments like the guitar, which rely on vibration from energy stored after they are plucked.

## 11.5. *Stiffness*

The second reason for choosing gut is its **harmonicity**: how closely a string's harmonics approximate to whole-number ratios. The only force restoring an ideal string to its resting shape after it is displaced, is its elasticity. Strings are also stiff. It requires more force to bend a violin steel E than a gut A string, whether under tension or not. A steel string as thick as a gut A would be very stiff. Stiffness resists bending by plucking or by bowing, and *the stiffness of a string makes its harmonics sharp*.

The force produced on the bridge by a given bowing is the same whatever the tension of the string (see Chapter 2). The higher the string's tension, the less it is bent, the smaller will be the effect of its stiffness on its vibration, and therefore the nicer the sound. But high tension produces high pitch. The only way to offset higher tension is to make the string heavier. If we use plain gut, we are now in a catch-22 situation. The string can only be made heavier by making it thicker; the thicker the string, the stiffer it becomes, and we lose what we have gained by high tension. For a plain gut string there must be a compromise between tension and diameter, or the string must be loaded with metal. Tension and thickness affect the bow/string interaction, and players choose strings to suit their bowing; needless to say, they do so empirically.

## 11.6. *The Gut String Compromise*

On average, gut breaks when loaded with 14 kgm on each sq. mm of its cross-section. If a plain gut string is to have a reasonable life it must be used well below that loading. Suppose we have a string with a cross-section of 1 sq. mm—a diameter of 1.13 mm—and apply a safe tension of 10 kgm, which is about right for a violin E. The pitch will be around G♯. To obtain E at 10 kgm tension, the weight must be reduced by making the diameter about 0.7 mm, but the cross-section of the gut will then be sustaining 13 kgm per sq. mm, which is very close to breaking-point. Since very thin strings are particularly susceptible to sweat and wear, one can understand why the gut violin E went out of use. A plain gut A is practicable; it can have a diameter of 0.8 mm at a tension of 5.8

kgm on a violin, or 6.5 kgm on a viola, with a loading on the cross-section which will ensure a reasonable life and good harmonicity.

## 11.7. *Weighting and Diameter: Gut*

Once a metal casing is used, the string maker can decide what tension a string should have at pitch, select a safe core diameter, and apply a suitable layer of metal to obtain the open string pitch. Provided the metal does not contribute stiffness, the string has good harmonicity and high damping, giving good bow control. A metal casing also reduces the string's overall diameter and reduces the twisting of the string as it is bowed (see Chapter 2.16). Twisting is unavoidable, but the smaller the diameter, the less twisting occurs. If one has never eaten strawberries one would not miss them, but now that strings are available in a range of diameters, professional players get used to a particular diameter and can certainly sense the difference between an 0.7 mm and an 0.8 mm string. This is a personal choice; certainly some violaists prefer the thicker plain gut A to the thinner metal-covered one. The string surface is different, but there should be no difference in friction (see Chapter 8). A gut core only 0.6 mm in diameter wound with silver wire 0.15 mm in diameter makes a violin G half the diameter of a plain gut string of the same weight; they have the same desirable tension at pitch, but the wound string's gut core is under ten times the tension per unit cross-section of the plain gut string. The metal wound string has enormously improved harmonicity, and twisting is much reduced.

Even so, the player relies entirely on the string maker. All the player can do is bring a string up to pitch and hope that the maker has adjusted weight and core size to give the right tension with minimum stiffness. There is a real element of paying your money and taking your pick with strings. The finest tone comes from using a gut core as close to breaking-point as one dares, but the life of the string is then correspondingly shorter. A professional soloist is concerned about reliability, and changes strings as an insurance policy. The lack of durability of gut, as well as its actual cost, produced the pressure to develop alternative string materials for ordinary players.

## 11.8. *Solid-Metal-Core Strings*

About the only things to be said in favour of a solid or solid-core steel string are that it will have a much smaller diameter than gut for corresponding tensions, and a longer life. Steel has little internal damping, making it more difficult to control. It is enormously stiffer than gut and cannot be used at anything like the tension per unit cross-section which would be required to give it reasonable harmonicity. The one practicable exception is that a plain steel violin E can be used, because a combination of the properties of hearing and the lack of resonance of the violin ensure that one cannot hear the sharp high harmonics which it produces. There is no accounting for human likes and dislikes; those who like bowed instrument harmonics to be as pure as possible may find the twang of the steel-strung folk guitar and banjo attractive and yet be repelled by the sound of the low-tension strings of Eastern ethnic instruments.

Steps are taken, as explained below, to overcome the lack of damping in solid-steel-core strings. Their sound would be worse if they were not used at much higher tensions than the corresponding gut strings. They put excessive pressure on the arch of the instrument and require a lower bridge and often, a stronger bass bar. Those who learn with high-tension strings encounter a different problem. The strings are nearer the fingerboard and are easier to play with poor technique; once players get used to this, they find it difficult to play on proper strings. The problem is serious with the cello and bass. There is the excuse of economy in particular circumstances, but not amongst professionals. There is a very real fear that steel tone will become the norm, and the wonderful sound of Casals will be lost for ever.

## 11.9. *Flexible-Core Strings*

String makers have to some extent reduced stiffness by using a multi-stranded steel core with seven or nineteen wires of 0.05 to 0.12 mm diameter. Seven wires make a close-packed hexagon round a central member; a further twelve will pack in a circle round them, and either number produces a core which is stable and cylindrical. The harmonicity is somewhat improved, but the tensions are still high. The damping in steel is no greater whether it is stranded or solid.

Some forty or so years ago, solid synthetic strings were tried for double basses; they have been very successful on acoustic guitars. The bass strings were stiffer than gut but, more seriously, their surface was very difficult to bow (see Chapters 9 and 10). Nylon-type cores have now been developed in a multi-stranded form which can be arranged to have tension and flexibility quite close to that of gut and therefore agreeable harmonicity. Several hundred fibres 0.0075 mm diameter are used. They are by far the best substitute for gut so far produced, with the added advantage that they are humidity- and temperature-stable. For obvious reasons they have to be cased.

The lack of damping in steel- and polymer-core strings would best be mitigated by inserting damping material between the strands, and some makers use waxy materials between the elements of steel cores. However, the main method is to wrap cores of both types in a spiral of material with heavy damping properties before the metal casing is put on.

## 11.10. *Making Cased Strings*

The earliest method of adding metal to gut was to wind wire round it. It has been suggested that at a still earlier date, gut was soaked in salts of metals to increase the weight, but the effect which that could produce is minuscule, and the salts of heavy metals which would have been available, such as of copper or iron, could have combined with the gut and made the strings stiffer. Many substances were applied to gut at various times for a different reason—in modern language, as disinfectants—and salts of heavy metals would be quite effective.

Winding gut with wire has several advantages. Wire makes its own tight spiral if it bears against the previous turn as it is added. The same method is used by bow makers when adding wire lapping. The round surface of the wire also beds slightly into the gut so that when the core is stretched, the spiral is evenly extended and weight continues to be uniformly distributed. Such extension of the spiral produces a regular gap between the coils and prevents one turn from pressing against the next when the string is bent in playing; in this way, the covering does not interfere with flexibility. However, a wire-wound string has a corrugated surface which produces a whistle when a finger slides over it, and it is a less efficient surface on which to bow than a flat one. The better-quality wire-wound strings were therefore 'polished': a euphemism for removing the outer part of the wire and making the surface much flatter so that in effect the winding became almost semicircular cross-section wire. Polishing removes metal and reduces weight; in theory the maker allowed for removing material when selecting what diameter of wire to use.

The ideal covering is a flat metal ribbon, and suitable techniques have now been developed to use it. The strip has to be applied as a spiral so that it will gap slightly when the string comes up to tension. Strip does not bed into a core like a round wire, but the casing must expand evenly. A virtue is made of necessity with steel and polymer cores, because strip will bed to some extent into the soft damping material on which it is actually wound. On larger strings there may even be a woven coating of damping material between core and cover. The hexagonal or polygonal cores of multi-stranded steel will help to locate damping material, and one presumes that when solid steel cores are made from hexagonal wire, this is for the same purpose.

The major problem in winding a flat strip is that it does not make its own spiral. It must be fed at exactly the correct angle, or it will either gap increasingly, or pile up. In addition, a covering must be wound tightly, which means pulling hard, sideways on the core. Cores must therefore be stiff in order to apply the winding but, obviously, they cannot be held at greater tension than when used for playing. They are therefore stiffened dynamically by winding them at speeds of up to 20,000 r.p.m. The potential for catastrophe if the feed angle is incorrect or anything goes wrong is worthy of an animated cartoon. Things have come a very long way from the days of minnikins and catlins.

## 11.11. *Metals for Windings*

Winding with metal has other problems. When copper wire was wound on bass strings for keyboard instruments it was soon discovered that copper work-hardens: copper and aluminium are amongst those metals which are soft after they have been heated and allowed to cool, but become stiff and hard during any bending. If either metal is very tightly bent it becomes so inflexible that it cracks. One object of casing is to reduce string diameter, but the smaller the diameter, the more the strip is bent and the greater the hardening of the metal.

Aluminium is light (density about 2.5) and adequate for the casing needed on violin and viola gut A, but it is soft and it wears. Silver (density 9) is used for the lower strings of these instruments. It does not work-harden. Pure silver is too soft, and its resistance to wear is increased by incorporating a little copper. Silver is not inexpensive. To get enough weight on strings for cello and bass at an acceptable price, iron alloys are used. The largest strings may be made with multiple layers of thin strip and with damping layers between each. String makers are now trying tungsten alloys, which have twice the density of silver, but they are difficult to handle. Such is the increasingly sophisticated technology now used for large gut-imitating strings, that we may even contemplate a return to real gut cores, which, as yet, have the best properties.

## 11.12. *String Gauges*

As Mersenne originally discovered, the diameter of a string of uniform material determines the pitch at a given tension. Plain steel or gut strings can therefore be selected by the width of the slot they will pass through on a gauge plate which is standardized, and normally used to specify piano wire. When strings are covered, the gauge tells one nothing about their tension at pitch. It is the proud boast of at least one well-known firm of string makers that they will produce strings of any gauge and tension if requirements are not found amongst the dozens listed in their catalogue in steps of a quarter of a string-gauge unit, albeit no tensions are given, and a test of one retailer's large stock with a micrometer revealed that accuracy to a quarter of a gauge unit was more evident on the packages than on the products inside them. String tensions are important for harmonicity, for the right balance across the bridge, and for the right pressure on the bridge. One does not get this information from a gauge, and at the very minimum, the tension for a stated playing length ought to be in the catalogue and on the packet.

## 11.13. *Coda*

Amateurs may not be able to string their instruments with the most expensive gut strings, but it is hoped the reader will be convinced that one cannot not get the best out of an instrument by using an arbitrary mixed collection of gut, gut-imitating, and steel strings. Good makers will usually suggest what type of string should be used on an instrument—and if you happen to break a string on a borrowed one, do replace it with one of the same kind. Any reasonable supplier can recognize what it is from the bit between the bridge and tailpiece.

# 12

## Purchase, Maintenance, and Children's Instruments

♦ ♦ ♦ ❖ ♦ ♦ ♦

### 12.1. *Introduction*

Most products arrive complete with manufacturer's instructions, though often written in pidgin and always more concerned with protecting the makers against litigation than with helping the user. Violins don't. There are a few big and many little things which need to be checked when buying an instrument, especially perhaps a small-size one for a child, some of which make all the difference to using it. There are things which have to be maintained, and there are symptoms of trouble, large or small, which will usually get larger if they are not dealt with when they are small. Even so simple a thing as winding a string on a peg has a best way and a way which can do serious damage. This chapter describes some things which ought to be in the instructions—not the maker's instructions, because it includes things which should make one reject an instrument on sight.

### 12.2. *The 'Stop'*

On a fretted instrument the places for the left-hand fingers are fixed; on the violin family, the player relies on ear and one indicator: the top of the body where the hand 'stops'. The ratio of string lengths either side of the top of the body *must be correct*. One should be able to assume that the ratio is correct on new professionally made instruments; factory-made instruments from Eastern Europe and the Far East usually are correct. One cannot do so for second-hand instruments, especially amateur-made ones, whether full-size or for children. The outline and the general proportions, particularly of children's cellos, can depart considerably from the conventional. Violas and basses come in all sizes, but the 'stop' must be right. Check that the top of the bridge is opposite the inner nicks on the *f*-holes. Using a cloth or plastic tape so as not to scratch the varnish, measure the distance from the top nut to the edge of the body where the neck joins, and the distance from there to the bridge. The ratios of these distances must be 2 : 3 within a very few millimetres on violins and violas; within a centimetre or less of 7 : 10 on cellos and basses. If the neck length is very incorrect in relation to the bridge position, there is little which can be done about it, for there is a limit to the distance one can move the bridge. If the ratio is wrong, the player will be thrown or confused when moving from or to an instrument which is correct.

## 12.3. *Pegs and Pegbox*

Pegs taper and fit into tapered holes. They should turn smoothly but grip sufficiently by friction without having to be forced in excessively. A new instrument or a commercially sold second-hand one described as being in full working order should have pegs which do work like that. In theory, pegs fit exactly on both sides, but in practice they grip on the peg-head side. Strings should normally be arranged so that they wind round the peg in a tight spiral towards the peg head. If the peg-box has been properly designed, and the pegs have string holes in the right places, this will ensure that strings do not interfere with one another. The wound spiral must not be allowed to reach the side of the box. If it does, the first indication will be that it will pull the peg into its conical hole and make it much harder to turn, and the peg may seize in the hole. If one attempts to force the peg to turn, the pegbox may split. The sideways force which can be applied by the wound string in this way is very large. But the mechanical advantage of a machine head on a bass is greater, and one does not get such a warning because the winding barrels are cylindrical and cannot seize. Inspection is essential. On the other hand, a string must not be allowed to pile up on itself in one place if the clearance behind the peg is small; it may split the side by pushing the peg away from the back of the box. Alternatively, any of these things may break a thin string—by far the least expensive catastrophe.

Because the pegbox is made of grained wood, the holes eventually wear oval and pegs will not grip. The holes can be reamed to make them circular and larger pegs fitted, or the hole can be drilled larger, a wooden lining called a 'bush' glued in, and the original peg refitted.

Finally, when changing a set of strings, change one at a time so as

to maintain as much normal pressure on the bridge as possible and prevent the soundpost from moving. This will also help to limit the extent
to which a new string will pull the top of the bridge towards the nut,
because it will be held by the other three strings. But do check and if
necessary pull the bridge upright very carefully after putting on any
new string.

## 12.4. *Adjusters*

Tuning by pegs requires practice, and getting the pitch right is not easy
for children anyway, let alone by using pegs. Fine tuning by a screw on
an adjuster on the tailpiece simplifies the process. It is essential for a
violin steel E, and for steel strings on all instruments except the bass.
Metal tailpieces with four adjusters are available for full-sized and children's instruments.

## 12.5. *Nuts and Fingerboards*

The height of the nut and depth of its grooves should have been
adjusted precisely to determine the correct height of the strings over
the fingerboard in relation to the height of the bridge. Instruments with
an arbitrary bridge usually have strings at the wrong height. The
height is different for steel and for gut-equivalent strings. Too-high
steel strings need excessive finger pressure; too-low gut-equivalent
strings buzz. Strings can be damaged if the grooves in the nut are too
narrow. The grooves should be lubricated with graphite. The fingerboard itself is 'dished': skilfully planed so that it is slightly concave
along its length. After several years of playing, a fingerboard develops
grooves where the strings are hammered onto it. A luthier can remove
these by planing, called 'shooting', but eventually a new board has to
be fitted.

## 12.6. *Bridges*

Enough has been said in Chapters 2–7 about the absolute necessity to
have a bridge of correct height, shape, weight, and fit. Many second-
hand instruments have poor bridges. The tops of bridges always creep
slowly but relentlessly towards the nut, and bridges should be inspected
regularly and pulled upright. If they are not adjusted they warp and
eventually break.

## 12.7. *Tailguts*

The tailgut attaches the tailpiece to the endpin. (In some older books the endpins of violin and viola are called buttons; the tab at the top of the back, glued to the neck, is the button.) For all but basses the tailgut is now usually of nylon with screw-threaded ends to adjust its length; there should be minimal distance between saddle and tailpiece, but it must not project beyond the edge of the table. Basses need wire. Solid steel wire is not sufficiently flexible; other metals work-harden, fatigue, and break without warning (I have had one very lucky escape). Multi-stranded wire solves all these problems, and a simple trick overcomes the difficulty of securing it. Remove the wood between the two holes in the tailpiece through which the wire is normally threaded, making a slot. Obtain a closed loop of the requisite length of high-tensile multi-stranded cable, such as is used for sailing-boat rigging, by compressing an alloy sleeve around the ends of the cable. Push the loop through the slot and over a grooved aluminium saddle placed in the recess of the tailpiece (Fig. 12.1); the other end of the loop goes round the endpin. Two of these loops show no sign of degradation after over thirty years, but should a loop be damaged, replacement is extremely simple.

FIG. 12.1. A closed loop of multi-stranded wire inserted through a slot (A) in a double bass tailpiece is retained by an aluminium saddle.

## 12.8. *Endpins*

Spikes need not be lethally sharp: they should *always* have some utterly fixed projection or ring which makes it impossible for them to get loose inside the cello or bass. It is not just the Chinese puzzle of coaxing them out; sharp ones have come through ribs. Luthiers are certainly not metal-workers. The most abominable feature of the entire violin family is a steel wing-screw that runs through a thin brass ring surrounding the wooden boss. There appears to be no way of persuading players, least of all children, that only light force is needed to secure a spike; the miserable amount of thread inevitably strips. The most elementary improvement would be to use a brass screw in a steel ring, for it is simpler to replace a stripped screw than to rethread a hole and make a larger screw. The state of the endpin holder on a second-hand cello or bass should always be examined, by undoing the screw half a turn and checking the side-to-side freedom of the screw; if it slops about, its life is likely to be short. Thin steel spikes whip; hollow aluminium ones are far more rigid. If held by a screw, the spike should operate on a shoe below the screw hole, shaped to spike diameter. The most sanitary device for holding a spike is a ring collet; such a thing is available.

An endpin has a cone, which should fit the hole in the bottom block exactly. It can sometimes be exceedingly difficult to remove, and a new one has to be individually fitted; time is expensive.

## 12.9. *Chin Rests*

There are many designs of chin rest, and they are very personal things. Most luthiers have a range which can be tried, and they are the best people to fit them, since they can ensure that they are entirely supported by the bottom block and do not damage ribs. Some people's skin can react to some chin rest materials; man-made substances are usually more inert than wood.

## 12.10. *Edge Protectors*

During rehearsal and concert intervals, violins and violas are either retained or stored safely; cellos are often and basses are invariably laid on their sides. The edges of fronts and backs are damaged and gradually worn away. Small hardwood blocks glued to the ribs close to the front and back edges at the widest part of the instrument above and below the waist, and projecting slightly beyond the edges, will prevent wear. They ought to be a standard fitting on all basses, and the cost of having a set fitted is minute compared with that of making, fitting, and varnishing new edges.

## 12.11. *Care of Strings*

Strings with metal casings need particular care. The casing is easily damaged if pinched by the grooves in the nut. If strings are supplied coiled, that is probably the limit to which it is safe to bend the playing length without damaging the cover. If they are provided straight, they should be stored straight. A manufacturer assumes that the gap in the windings which is produced at pitch, is sufficient for the sharpest bending to which the string will be subjected in playing it. Steel-core bass strings are sometimes supplied with a curved shoe to go between string and bridge to prevent too acute an angle over the bridge. They may also have a 'tone filter': a thick rubber band to press against the string either side the bridge. This reduces the higher harmonics somewhat, but it is an admission of defeat, and does nothing to mitigate the fundamental problem of sharp harmonics.

*The practice of pulling a covered string*, especially a new one, *away from the fingerboard* in order to tune it or equilibrate tensions either side of the bridge *bends it excessively*, and if the gaps in the casing meet on the inside of the angle, the core is excessively stretched on the other side. This can produce a false string or a crack in the core.

Heavily wound strings are usually made so that the metal stops before the peg, and only the core has to be inserted. Do not disturb any binding around the string at either end. Apart from the damping which it is meant to provide between bridge and tailpiece, a binding may be securing the ends of windings, and once released this can undo onto the playing length.

If you are lucky (or affluent) enough to have some plain gut strings on a double bass, you can extend their life by wiping the fingered region with a cloth dampened with almond oil before playing. The oil reduces sweat-penetration; it has a fine aroma too.

## 12.12. *False Strings*

Occasionally a string will suddenly produce an unattractive tone. Careful examination may reveal a small imperfection somewhere along the playing length where the mechanical property of the string has changed: almost any imperfection in the covering will do this. Such a string will vibrate in a complex manner, which is a combination of its normal harmonics and the harmonics of two strings which are the lengths respectively from the bridge to the imperfection and from the imperfection to the finger stopping it. The string will not necessarily break, but unfortunately it must be replaced. If a new string behaves in this way, expect a free replacement.

## 12.13. *Routines*

After playing, remove rosin dust with a soft cloth; rosin has a high affinity for varnish. Never clean an instrument with anything other than a very soft cloth. Always release the tension of the hair on a bow. However soft the lining of a case, there is wear on the edges whenever a violin or viola is taken out and put in. Wrapping the instrument in a silk or equivalent synthetic cloth prevents such wear. And do remember to remove any shoulder rest first; commercial cases always provide places for bows, strings, and rosin, but it is remarkable how few allow anywhere for a shoulder rest.

## 12.14. *Accidents*

Accidents will happen: actually they are always caused, but that doesn't help. If you value an instrument at all, take it to a *professional* repairer for an estimate. Repairing is an entirely different craft from making, requiring specialized training and tools. Serious damage has often been done by amateur repairers, and their efforts invariably make it much more difficult—and expensive—to effect a proper repair. You may be puzzled that some craftsmen describe themselves as repairers and others as restorers. Very few people want an old instrument converted back into the baroque form, or varnish added to make it look like its original pristine state; occasions when two instruments can be cannibalized to create one with all the parts by one maker are rare. If you are a person of modest means with a modest instrument, it is suggested that you go to a modest professional repairer.

So: do not try to glue anything together again—and at all costs do not attempt a temporary repair with epoxy, rubber, resin, or instant adhesives. In an absolute emergency there is a liquid fish-based glue called Seccotine, which can be used. If any pieces have come adrift, save them in a plastic bag. It is much more difficult to match grain and colour than to replace the original. It is worth searching for every splinter. A fine old English cello has been reconstructed into a reasonable instrument after a large blackboard fell on it, but only because almost every one of the fifty-odd pieces was saved. A broken bridge cannot be mended, but take the pieces to the luthier. He may be able to explain why it broke and what maintenance to carry out in future.

### 12.15. *Repairs*

A repairer should provide a written estimate and, if required, a receipt for the instrument. He should explain what has to be done. He may suggest or advise other things an instrument may need, but the customer decides what work is to be done. Once a repairer has undertaken the work stated on the estimate, he does it, regardless of the problems which may arise, unless he warns that he cannot divine what may be revealed, such as woodworm damage, when an instrument is opened. A customer has a right to refuse to pay for any work carried out without permission. The luthier will expect repaired instruments to be collected promptly and can retain an instrument until he has been paid. The following gives some indication of what the repair of typical accidents involves, and is *not* intended to explain how an amateur might carry them out.

Instruments inevitably become unglued around the edges where the ribs meet front or back. This fault is the first thing to look for if there is a buzz when playing. People sometimes suggest that their instrument has developed a wolf note; a wolf is usually resident from the start, but sets of steel strings often come with a free wolf (see Chapter 5.12). When instruments are brought in for service, unglued edges are often found. Mending is usually straighforward, but requires special clamps; when the box is glued together during making, there is no varnish to complicate the situation. Fingerboards may come loose. Regluing is simple unless the reason is that it has warped, but the fingerboard contributes considerably to the strength of the neck, and if it is seen to be unglued, the strings should be slackened by about a fifth; if they are slackened completely the soundpost may fall over.

The commonest serious accident is the soundpost crack; this occurs because the instrument has been crushed and the post driven into (one hopes not through) the front or back, or both. The crack will often run the length of the body. The strings should be let down completely. The repair usually requires taking the front off and gluing studs—pieces of exactly fitting wood—across the crack throughout its length, and then paring these down. A patch of new wood must usually be put in to support the post. This involves thinning an area of the plate, gluing in an exactly fitting piece, and thinning that down so that in the end the area is brought to its original thickness. It is an expensive repair.

Bass bars can become unglued; not only can this produce buzzes, but also the bridge tilts, the pitches of the lower strings slowly fall, and the gap between bottom string and fingerboard disappears. The strings should be let down completely. The front must be removed to reglue the bar, and it may be advisable to fit a new one. On the other hand, though a crack along the line of the bass bar (usually caused by a blow on the bridge) requires studding as with a soundpost crack, it is less likely to degrade the instrument than any other large-scale damage to the front, because the repair will be along the line of greatest stiffness anyway.

It may be possible to pull together and glue some cracks, depending on position and severity, without removing the front. The underlying problem with most repairs is that an object which curves in every direction cannot be gripped in some of them, and when it also has a varnished surface, this requires a collection of special cramps and tools which no amateur has.

## 12.16. *Warnings*

The smaller the instrument, the more easily it can be damaged, but the larger it is, the more likely it is that it will be. The most dangerous place for a bow is the bow pocket of a soft case. A hard case protects—but only if the lid is deep enough. Old violin cases can be most attractive but inspect them for signs of woodworm, and if there are any fragments of old bow hair, look even more carefully for a pale grey-brown hairy grub which eats it. The distance between the top tread and the ceiling of some escalators is an inch less than the length of a full-size double bass; the damage when one is shortened by an inch is horrendous.

## 12.17. *Purchasing: From a Maker*

Most makers are honest people trying to make a not very lucrative living and making because they love it. You should expect a price on the basis that a craftsman might be able to produce a dozen to fifteen violins or violas, or six cellos a year if he does nothing else; apart from machines, tools, and overheads, the price has to include wood, strings, and fittings. It will also reflect how much time has been given to polishing. Most makers cannot afford to wait to be paid but may accept instalments.

Makers do not necessarily have instruments to choose from. Some of those who have are either asking too much or are not making good instruments, but be suspicious of anyone who purports to have hand-made instruments and makes more in a year than can reasonably be made. There is nothing in principle against instruments which have been roughed out by copy-routing machines, but if there are large numbers in circulation by one maker, they may not hold their value or appreciate. It is not thought that anyone in the United Kingdom imports instruments from Eastern Europe and puts their own label in them, but it is widely believed that one 'maker' on the other side of the Atlantic does so.

Allowing intending purchasers to take instruments on approval for a couple of weeks is standard practice, but unless you are known, some form of surety is expected. If you do take an instrument to try, take the very utmost care of it in every respect. You will probably be asked to insure it.

If a maker produces any gimmicks, such as special ways of ageing wood, or varnish which is good for tone, or claims that a 'scientific' method of any kind has been used in making, be suspicious. A new instrument may not have been played in, but do not buy anything which has shortcomings in the belief that playing it will produce a significant change.

A maker should offer advice on what strings to use, and if gut or gut-equivalent ones are recommended, the instrument may not have been constructed for high-tension steel strings. It is very worthwhile to take a new instrument back to be checked after a month or so; caring makers usually suggest this.

A maker who has won a prize for making is probably a good craftsman. A prize for 'tone' means nothing. Some makers disapprove of competitions, and some do not have time to participate. Some amateurs can make very good instruments, but these may not appreciate like those with a professional's name in it.

## 12.18. *Purchasing: From a Dealer*

Dealers are indispensable to many makers; they sell instruments. They often provide the only opportunity for players to try a selection of instruments. Most dealers are honest tradesmen. The amount they know about instruments varies from zero to international expertise; those in general music shops are usually close to the bottom end of that scale. If, remarkably, a professional player says that a dealer is reliable, he is bound to be. If a dealer starts talking about tone and Italian instruments, old instruments, or similar moonshine, be suspicious.

The name on the label inside an instrument is not necessarily that of the maker. Technically, it is an offence even to sell a pre-1914 trade fiddle with the standard 'Stradivarius fecit' label in it without making clear that he did not. If a dealer says that an instrument was by a specific maker you are entitled to a signed statement to that effect. If there is any uncertainty, the law requires the statement to be qualified by 'probably', or 'believed to be', or 'from the school of', but it also requires that such uncertainty must be clearly expressed when the instrument is first described, before any statement is written; if otherwise, Trading Standards officers are interested.

## 12.19. *Casual Purchases*

Bargains and discoveries are very rare these days. Current English law gives no protection or compensation to the purchaser of an instrument which subsequently proves to have been stolen. Such instruments do occasionally turn up even in illustrious auction houses. In most other European countries, the purchaser is protected and the seller bears any loss. Nevertheless, our police are interested in anyone who offers a stolen instrument for sale. Thieves are usually one of two kinds: either they know the value of an old instrument and have ways of getting it out of the country quickly, or they have no idea of the value and the ease with which individual instruments can be identified. If an instrument of any reasonable value is lost, presumed stolen, apart from reporting to the police and your insurance company, it is worth telling a reputable dealer. Such dealers have an excellent private network and liaison with the police.

## 12.20. *Instruments for Children*

The sizes of children's violins and cellos are designated by fractions with a sublime disregard for both mathematics and measurement. Originally they were called 1/4, 1/2, 3/4, and full size, though the increases in length between them are somewhere between 1/10 and

1/40. For those who learn when very young, 1/8, 1/16, and 1/32 sizes are now made, with similar small differences in length. Unfortunately with a similar disregard for mechanics, many are exact reductions of a full-size instrument, and it is sad though not surprising that two pages of detailed dimensions for small instruments in an impressive-looking book from a teacher in one of the best known European schools of violin making are merely figures so derived (see Section 22 below). Occasionally a child discovers that a thing called a viola exists, and a violin can be adapted appropriately. Small factory-made basses are now available: a welcome development because their tuning and fingering are completely different from those of the rest of the family, and relearning is necessary if someone starts on the cello.

For further confusion, 7/8 is used for 'small full-size' instruments, bearing in mind that the violin is the only member of the family which has a commonly adopted standard length anyway; the 7/8 is not a normal step in the series for children, but an instrument comfortable in size for some people to play. For the same reasons given in previous chapters, which show that the size of a viola makes no difference to its sound, 7/8 violins, cellos, and basses can be excellent instruments in every respect. A smaller cello is often called a 'lady's' (despite legislation against such discrimination).

If a child is receiving lessons, the teacher will advise when a pupil should change to a larger instrument, but the already arbitrary nomenclature is further confused by the existence of 'large quarters' and 'small halves'. A parent seeking an instrument might be much happier if given a length in inches or millimetres! All the points to check on full-size instruments apply to small ones, with a rider. Skilled repairers may be able to sort out most of the shortcomings of a small instrument and make it a reasonable one on which to learn, and they may also improve the sound, especially by fitting a properly cut bridge, but whether they are prepared to spend time doing it, and whether the instrument is worth the remuneration of a craftsman, is another matter. Some repairers do not stock small-size fittings.

It is difficult to play on low-tension strings and not straightforward to cannibalize strings from full-size instruments (see Chapter 11). Strings suitable for small-size instruments are available. And since three-quarters of the art of playing is using a bow, a reasonable bow is important and becomes more so, the more advanced the learner.

## 12.21. *'Plywood' Instruments*

Many factory-made cellos and basses, both small and full-size, have laminated backs and ribs: sheets of very thin wood glued together in the required shape. This is often described as 'plywood'; it is stronger and more rigid than solid wood and less costly to make. If the front is of suitably carved spruce, such an instrument can be quite satisfactory, especially for educational use. A laminated instrument appears to have a one-piece back with no centre joint, which is fairly rare in cellos and almost unknown in double basses. It is often possible to see the laminations at the edge of the back. The cheaper instruments have a high-gloss cellulose lacquer with 'shading put in'. The glue used in laminating is more dense than wood, and the instruments are usually heavy. Laminated wood withstands blows which would break a solid structure, but if it is broken it is usually unrepairable, and it is not economic to attempt it. The choice rests upon balancing the cost against the risk of writing the instrument off in the event of an accident.

## 12.22. *The Sound*

Very small instruments make a very small sound; this is a blessing. But from half-size upwards, most could sound better than they do. If the thickness of a beam is reduced by 10 per cent, its stiffness is decreased by much more than 10 per cent. One should not simply reduce proportionally the dimensions of the front and bass bar, whose compliance is an integral part of sound production. Linearly reduced instruments are usually 'soft', and their sound corresponds. I applied simplified formulae to this problem, and Christopher Beament made some instruments with the resulting dimensions to test them. The violins produced an attractive sound for their size and had a good response to the bow; a half-size cello, played by a professional, could be mistaken for a full-size instrument on casual listening.

Unfortunately there is an economic snag. Making a small instrument to a reasonable standard takes about the same proportion of the time needed for a full-size one as its nominal size; a 3/4 cello requires three-quarters of the time it takes to make a full-size one. But the price people expect to pay is little more than the cost of the wood, because the benchmark is set by the astonishingly low cost of outfits from the Far East, some of which do not exactly emulate the song of the birds (with one exception) after which they are named. It would be a very real contribution to future generations of string players if amateurs made small instruments—with the right dimensions. In the Cambridge classes several have been made by parents and grandparents.

Bowed instruments of a different design can be made relatively rapidly by hand. Savart designed a trapezoid-shaped violin, with a flat front and back and straight ribs, economical of both time and materials. Two of these have been made in the Cambridge classes; they have a powerful very violin-like sound, to the disappointment of those who believe in the magic of the traditional shape. Other time-consuming parts such as the scroll can be simplified. The reaction to all such instruments is predictable: a child, particularly playing with peers, wants an instrument which looks right.

### 12.23. *Left-Handed Instruments*

These do exist, and normal ones can be converted by moving the bass bar across and preferably changing the pegs round so that the lowest peg head faces the other way to the norm. The fingerboard has to have reversed camber, and a different bridge is required. *But never even suggest* to a left-handed child that such things exist, except in the unhappy circumstance that the child has a damaged left hand, but which is capable of holding a bow. Expect a beginner to play a normal instrument the normal way round. Most left-handed people do. Playing left-handed is likely to create problems throughout life, especially in orchestras.

### 12.24. *Musical Advice*

Playing any instrument, apart from keyboards and some percussion, requires a sense of pitch, and bowed strings demand this more than most. Hearing can develop a good sense of pitch, but it is naturally more inherent in some than others, and can be observed in many ways at a very early age. Do not judge pitch sense by an ability to sing in tune; controlling the voice is one of the most complex things humans have to learn (apart from bowing), and many children have been condemned as tone-deaf when all they lack is voice control. But if a good sense of pitch does not develop, give up—and please don't recommend the bass, because it requires just as good intonation as its smaller relations.

One of the shortcomings of playing an entirely melodic instrument is that it does very little to develop a sense of harmony. Despite the risk of being seduced into pop music, there is no better way of developing a harmonic sense than to play the guitar beyond the 'three chord' stage. Any form of harmonic appreciation, however subconscious, will improve intonation as string playing develops; lack of it is apparent in some quite well-known soloists and chamber music ensembles. If a child starts playing 'by ear'—playing melodies without ever having seen them as music—it is a most promising sign of natural musicality. Curiously, this does not seem to be correlated with an ability to sight-read music; music notation is a form of displaying information with less redundancy than any other that man has devised, except some branches of mathematics—a point which perhaps some teachers do not fully appreciate.

Playing music should be for pleasure, and children should play for their own pleasure, not for that of their parents. The music profession is overcrowded, and very few get to the top. The life of an orchestral player is tolerable if unmarried. Teaching is a worthy and rewarding profession in every way except financially. If a child wants to play, give every encouragement. Teenagers may lose interest, but muscular memory is of long duration, and an ability to play as an amateur can usually be recovered quite rapidly after a few years' lapse, when people begin to appreciate music again. Mature people can successfully learn the cello and bass for amateur playing, but it is more difficult with the violin and viola. This is largely concerned with muscles and tendons, and few people have the time or incentive to maintain all of them adequately by suitable daily aerobics. But if one parent in an otherwise string-playing family feels left out of things, learning to make instruments as an amateur is a sure way of recovering esteem.

# 13

# Conclusions

♦♦♦❖♦♦♦

THE production of sound by a violin might be represented by the sequence: player → bow → string → bridge → body → sound → hearing → perception. If we assume uniform bowing, we can obtain a generalized picture of the vibration of the string and of the events up to the point where sound is produced in the air. But these physical steps are not independent because the string interacts with the bow, and the body interacts with the string via the bridge. We can relate basic aspects of bowing to basic features of the sound. The picture is limited to sustained sound because that is what uniform bowing produces.

When we include the player, complications arise even in this simple picture, because the player monitors his playing by what he hears, and adjusts his bowing accordingly. In this way a skilled player can coax worthwhile sound out of almost any instrument by making it behave; he adjusts rapidly and to a degree subconsciously to an orthodox wellmade one. And on top of all this, a player plays by what *he* hears, but listeners hear something different.

While players and makers do not need to know how instruments work, both need to be aware that because the components interact, changing any one of them could cause changes in how the mechanism behaves. String tensions modify almost every part of the system. Every feature of the bridge is significant; its behaviour even enters into where the player puts a left-hand finger to obtain a desired pitch, and how effectively an instrument can be heard in an auditorium. Changing a component may cause something which can be measured physically on an isolated instrument, but whether it has any effect depends entirely on whether it produces any reaction by the player, and it can only be judged by the result when he plays. The one exception is the harmonicity of a string; that is immutable, and appears in the sound independently of player and instrument.

To obtain any real understanding of the bowed instrument we have to apply knowledge of the peculiar way our hearing works. The sound is changed even before we sense it, and what is presented to the brain from which the sensation is created is a surprisingly different version of the vibrations which enter the ears. This explains some relatively straightforward things, such as how bowing is related to musical dynamic and why a double bass does not drown a violin, but our hearing has one property which has profound implications for almost everything discovered or believed about bowed instruments. Hearing evolved to sense natural sound, and natural sound is continuously changing sound. We attach significance to any change in sound. We characterize, identify, and memorize sounds almost entirely by the way they change while they are changing. A musical note played by a stringed instrument consists of continuously changing sound, usually followed by a sustained sound, though it may be entirely transient. The only thing we can describe adequately in terms of mechanism and of the physical sound produced is the sustained part.

'Tone', a word used in so many vague ways, is widely considered to be the vital property of the sound. Loudness and pitch are more complex than we may think, but tone does not mean anything unless we say what it describes. Fortunately, it was defined precisely in 1870 by Helmholtz, who discovered that pitched musical sound consists of a specially related set of harmonics; this is an artefact created by man. Tone is the sensation produced by which harmonics are present and how big each is in this sound. The only thing we can discuss meaningfully is the tone of the sustained part of the sound, for in any transient sound, the sizes of the harmonics are continuously changing, and the way in which they change is due to the way the player bows the string. In comparison, sustained string sound provides relatively little by which it can be characterized. Unlike some sustained instrumental sounds, the violin family produce no particular patterns; they produce a complete set of the harmonics, and in the sustained sound these are somewhat irregular in size. The irregularity is slightly different at each semitone pitch of any one instrument, and it differs between notes of the same pitch on any two instruments. That irregularity is the only thing in the tone which can be attributed to the instrument—the box—and is due to its many resonances. All well-made instruments have different irregularity, but because of the way we hear, that creates nothing we can characterize and remember. The characteristics of bowed tone are simply determined by how many harmonics we can hear and the balance between the lower and higher ones, which depends upon where the string is bowed, how the string is bowed, and which string is bowed.

Hearing processes bowed sound in interesting ways. The tone of most notes may be determined by only the first six harmonics, plus some indistinct signals. Below the bass staff the harmonics are all somewhat indistinct; above the treble staff fewer and fewer contribute. The characteristic roughness or gruffness, most pronounced in low bass notes, is manufactured in our hearing and is not present in the physical sound. At least at low dynamic, we cannot hear the fundamental of low notes; we can perceive the pitches, because they are created by our hearing from the other harmonics present. It is almost miraculous that centuries before any of this was known, the entire violin family were made with upper limits of resonance roughly such that no purpose would be served by raising it because we could not perceive the effect, nor would anything be gained by making large cellos and basses to produce fundamentals we need not hear. Violas can be of whatever size is comfortable to play; their size has nothing to do with their sound or sound output.

None of those things, however, are responsible for an essential sensation produced by the bowed string. Its ostensibly constant-pitched sound is overlaid by continuous small random changes of frequency, a phenomenon we have described as creating the timbre. A major part of this is due to the inherent continuously irregular vibration of a string when expertly bowed. The explanation in physical terms of why that irregularity is produced by the bowed string is exceptionally complex, but what the irregularity actually is, is unimportant—we must sense that the frequencies are continuously varying, but not how they are changing. The changes are not identifiable, but they transform the monotony of constant-frequency tone into sound which interests hearing. It is the behaviour of a string when expertly bowed that creates the unique sound of the violin family.

The only sounds a listener can try to use to characterize or identify an instrument are the sustained parts of notes. Every listening test confirms the conclusion reached from considering our hearing system, that we are incapable of remembering this sound over quite short periods. It cannot be used to determine change in an instrument over time, or to identify an instrument when played. But if people believe they can remember this sound, they will persuade themselves that they can, and that is why the sound is so subjective and susceptible to suggestion, belief, and myth. Tell a listener that something about an instrument has changed, and he will believe he can hear something different, whether a change has occurred or not. The fallacy of attributing *tone* to an instrument is that tone only exists in our hearing when an instrument is played; when it is played, what we perceive and how we characterize the sound are entirely dominated by how the particular player bows it.

So where does the instrument that the maker made—crudely, the box—come into all this? It is a vehicle through which the string's vibration is made audible. The great majority of well-made orthodox instruments resonate adequately, because if such shaped objects made of the peculiarly structured material: wood, are stressed and vibrated asymmetrically, they have a large series of irregular resonances—that, in a nutshell, is what the early makers discovered empirically by making violin-shaped boxes with a suitably shaped spruce front. There are no secrets about this. Make an orthodox instrument—violin, viola, cello, or bass—by good craftsmanship, and a good player will make it sound like one. It will tolerate a reasonable amount of variation before it starts to show anomalies. The detailed shape of some features such as *f*-holes, which have commanded much attention, appear to have no effect on behaviour. To some, an instrument's outline can be a thing of beauty; instruments shaped like a guitar work just as well. The orthodox outline can vary. Stradivarius experimented continually with outlines, but no particular shape is specially associated with anything we hear. What characterizes his instruments is outstanding craftsmanship; one definition of genius is an infinite capacity for taking pains, but we have no evidence that his infinite pains produced special behaviour. Cremer, a great authority on the physics of the violin, concluded that the only significant factors are the total area, average thickness, average wood properties, and inner damping of the front. The fronts of many prized classical instruments on which players can produce wonderful sound bear this out, for they may have an average thickness of three millimetres, but they vary irregularly from their average thickness by as much as half a millimetre in either direction. Did Guarnerius know that such variation does not matter? With all this evidence, there is no justification for suggesting that electronic devices can be used to make 'perfect' fronts; that is inventing new fairy-tales to replace the old ones.

None of these arguments provide any excuse for poor construction. There are good practical reasons why parts should fit perfectly before they are assembled. Those which are well shaped where it matters for playing, and, for violins and violas, have a suitable weight distribution when held only by the chin, commend themselves to players. But there is not the slightest evidence that thin varnish can change anything we can hear, or that polishing an instrument makes any difference to the sound.

Every instrument is physically different, even when made in identical shape and from the same trees. But the only aspect of that difference which matters, is how each reacts to an individual player's bowing and hearing. Players call that responsiveness. There are instruments on which players must use more restrained bowing and others which require more work. Some prefer one kind, some the other. The resonances and internal damping must enter into this, but that is only the tip of the iceberg. An advanced player chooses an instrument which is responsive to his particular way of playing, in all the different ways in which he bows to obtain the great variety of sounds which are such a feature of the family—and by what he hears very close to the instrument. Playing is a continuous interaction between player and instrument. No doubt auto-suggestion enters into this too. But all the elements involved in an instrument's responsiveness can only be determined when we know the corresponding elements of a player's responsiveness, and then it is questionable whether makers could ever tailor an instrument to match a particular player. Until that day, it is essential that a variety of instruments be made, from which the greater variety of individual players may hope to choose one that suits each.

Do any of these things argue against the great value set on old instruments made by famous names? Not at all; as with all such artefacts, the price is determined by supply and demand. They do not make any different sound, and no audience can tell what instrument is being played. But if a player thinks he plays better on such an instrument, he will. Certainly an audience will think the sound is better if they know, and publicity agents are very aware that audiences are even more susceptible to suggestion than players. Because of their rarity, few artefacts have proved such an appreciating investment. What this does argue against most powerfully is the nonsense that any old instrument which might have been made by some obscure person with an Italianate name has any better performance properties and is worth any more than a good modern instrument.

Science has been able to explain how these instruments produce their sound, but it has produced nothing which might be of use to skilled makers. That is as it should be; it is not the business of science to tell traditional craftsmen what to do. Where it has appeared possible, with apparently simpler kinds of instrument, to specify an ideal and apply high technology, the outcome has by no means been a resounding success, for it implicitly assumes specifying what human hearing should like and what players should want to play on. Even if it were possible, which fortunately it is not, the last thing we want is a scientifically standardized violin for a standardized violinist in a brave new world in which there are standardized performances of music. We do not play by physics; we play by hearing and by that mysterious facility, musicality, which can be developed, provided there are natural properties of the brain to start with, and which is infinitely more complex than a violin.

What we have learned by applying the enormously powerful methods and concepts of science to these artefacts is both surprising and humbling. The violin was evolved and refined by trial and rejection without any of our concepts, without any knowledge of how it worked, three hundred years ago. Those made then are neither better nor worse than those that can be made today; there is nothing we can do to improve anything. All that science has achieved is to replace one kind of wonder by another. It has exploded most of the myths and superstitions. It has shown how instruments of the violin family work. But why they work? That lies in the extraordinary properties of trees and waste material from animals, of hearing, and of musical people. There are very few other things like that in the world today.

# Further Reading of Several Kinds

♦♦♦❖♦♦♦

BEAMENT, J., 'The Biology of Music', *Psychology of Music*, 5/3–18 (1977). The original report of many of the principles on which Chapter 6 is based.

BEKESY, G., *Experiments in Hearing* (New York: McGraw Hill, 1961). The discovery of the behaviour of the ear's coding membrane.

CREMER, L., *The Physics of the Violin*, trans. J. S. Allen (Cambridge, Mass.: MIT Press, 1985). The comprehensive account, but comprehensible only to mathematical physicists. Contains extensive references to the research work of Hutchins, McIntyre, Schelleng, Schumacher, Woodhouse, etc.

DINWOODIE, J. M., *Timber, its Nature and Behaviour* (Montreal: Van Nostrand Reinhold, 1975). About the best book there is on wood as opposed to trees.

FRY, G., *The Varnishes of the Italian Violin Makers and their Influence on Tone* (London: Stevens, 1904). Early investigation of varnishes and much else.

GILTAY, J. W., *Bowed Instruments, their Form and Construction*, trans. author (London: Reeves, *c*.1930). Pioneer physical investigations.

HALL, D. E., *An Introduction to Musical Acoustics* (Belmont, Calif.: Wadsworth, 1980). Written with musical understanding; for those with a little science.

HELMHOLTZ, H. L. F., *Die Lehre von den Tonempfinfungen als Physiologische Grundlage für die Theorie der Musik*, 4th edn. (Vieweg: Braunschweig, 1887). Trans. into English, with notes, by A. J. Ellis as *On the Sensations of Tone* (New York: Dover, 1954). The classical work; the origin of all modern ideas on acoustics and the scientific investigation of music.

HERON-ALLEN, E., *Violin Making as it Was and Is* (London: Ward Locke, 1895). A verbose account of how to make a violin, with entertaining historical information.

HERRINGHAM, C., *The Book of the Art of Cennino Cennini* (London: George Allen, 1930). A unique account of the art of *making* paint and varnish in 1550, when the violin was just emerging.

KIANG, N. Y.-S., *Discharge Patterns of Single Auditory Fibers* (MIT Research Monograph, 35; Cambridge, Mass.: MIT Press, 1969). The pattern of the pulses that code pure tones to the brain.

MACE, T., *Musick's Monument* (London: Ratcliffe, 1676; facsimile, Paris: Centre National de la Recherche Scientifique, 1958). A perceptive and charming account of ideas about instruments and music then.

MICHELMAN, J., *Violin Varnish*. 1946. Privately published, N.Y., USA. Describes over one hundred experiments in making oil varnish.

OTTO, J. A., *Treatise on the Structure and Preservation of the Violin* (London: Reeves, *c.*1875). A wise and honest account of the work and views of a master luthier of the period.

PICKERING, N. C., *The Bowed String* (New York: Amerion, 1989). An authoritative account of making strings. Not quite as accessible as the author suggests.

SAVART, F., *Mémoire sur la construction des instrumens à cordes et à archet* (Paris: Leblank, 1819; facsimile, Geneva: Minkoff, 1979). Savart's account of many of his experiments on violins.

SCHELLENG, J. C., 'The Physics of the Bowed String', *Scientific American*, 54 (1974), 87–95. An excellent elementary description.

TAYLOR, C., *Exploring Music* (Bristol: Institute of Physics Publishing, 1994). Actually, exploring elementary acoustics, and very readable.

TURNER, G. P. A., *Introduction to Paint Chemistry* (London: Chapman & Hall, 1988). A comprehensive review, including a reasonably accessible account of linseed oil, and of how light interacts with surface coatings.

WOOD, A., *The Physics of Music* (1944), rev. J. M. Bowsher (London: Methuen, 1961). Though dated, this classic created the subject, and its approach by a passionate lover of music has never been equalled.

# Index

♦ ♦ ♦ ❖ ♦ ♦ ♦

accidents 225
adhesion 166
adjusters 221
air resonance 84–6
alcohols 183
amplification 140
amplitude 7
arching 36, 52, 56, 67
armonico, *see* touch harmonics

back 61
bass bar 60, 227
beeswax 206
black boxes 139, 142
bitumen 181–2
bow:
   baroque 157
   modern 158
   position 14, 18
   pressure 14, 17, 22, 34
   speed 16
   steel 160
   synthetic 159
bowing angle 37
brazil wood 159
bridge:
   bending 41, 44
   creeping 49
   forces 35–40
   position 65
   pressure 35, 50
   ratio 38, 135
   resonance 88
   shape 44
   weight 45
butyl alcohol 184

Cambridge classes vii, 64, 89, 232
catgut, *see* gut
C-bouts 60, 67

cello:
   resonance 77, 86
   size 85–7
Chanot 48, 84
children's instruments 229–33
chin rests 223
Chladni patterns 64
cohesion 166
competitions 141
cramping 172
Cremer 32, 51, 64, 67, 74, 138, 198
cycle 7

damping:
   in strings 212, 216
   in wood 70, 73, 93
decibel 148
design 66, 138
double bass:
   resonance 77, 86
   roughness 100–3, 117
   size 86, 121
   tailgut 222
double stops 48, 121
dynamic 5, 98
   range 108
   scale 109–11

ear 97
electric violin 139
electronic testing 64, 139
endpin 222
energy:
   in sound 3
   transfer 73

feedback 91
false string 224
*f*-holes 65–7,
fingerboard 221
fillers 202

Fletcher–Munsen curves 109
friction 22, 49, 162
Fourier analysis 9
frequency 7, 14
    irregularity 31
    and loudness 111
    sensitivity 123
frog 163
front:
    balance 60
    flexibility 54
    thickness 62
fundamental 9
    and pitch 121
    virtual 120, 123

Galileo 7
glue:
    animal 165, 170, 174–6
    casein 165
    synthetic 173
Grappelli 130, 140
grounds 199–201
gut 210, 213
Guarnerius 55, 75, 90, 94

hair 160–5
    beetle 227
handedness 156, 164
harmonic:
    balance 112–6
    enhancement 111
    logic 120
    loudness 104–11
    richness 114–17
    series 9
harmonics perceived 99–103
    of real strings 117
    see also touch harmonics
harmonicity 126, 213
hearing:
    coding 97, 99, 107, 119–21
    directionality 149
    evolution 97, 105
    frequency 109
    loudness 109–11
    range 14, 98
    sensitivity 99, 109
    subjective 140, 143
Helmholtz 8, 58, 75, 122, 143
Heron-Allen 48, 84
Hertz 14
holography 42, 51, 78
Huggins 27, 58, 75, 95
humidity 68, 201
Hutchins 87, 137, 176

individuality of instruments 142
industrial spirit 184
ivory 163

laminated instruments 231–2
lapping 163
left-handed instruments 232
linseed oil, see varnish
loudness 5, 98, 104–7
    measurement 147–9
    variation 130

Maggini 75
maple 62
masking 101
Mersenne 7, 28, 212
mother-of-pearl 163
mute 46, 88

node 11
noise 23, 103
nut 221

oil varnish, see varnish
old instruments 88–91, 93
old varnishes 197–9, 209
orchestral sections 153
Otto 43, 46, 176

pegs and pegbox 220
perception 109–16, 127–9
pernambuco 159
pitch:
    definition 7, 121
    of bowed string 27, 96, 124–6
    origin 119–21
    sensitivity 124
    of touch harmonics 26
    virtual 120, 123
pizzicato 12, 29
plate tuning 62, 71
playing in 67, 176–8
polarity 167–70
polishing 198, 208
portamento 129
precession 30
projection 152
propolis 200
pure tone 8, 23
purchasing 227–9
purfling 67

repairs 226
resins 185
resonance 70–3
    body 75, 85–8
    curve 77

ear tube 106, 111
  limit 114
  and tone 74, 122
response curve 76
responsiveness 90–4, 142
rosemary oil 200
rosin 162
roughness 100–4
rubbed joints 172

Saunders 75, 87–8, 137
Savart 7, 63, 89
sawtooth wave 20, 104
scooping 54
sealers 201
setting up 91, 137
shellac 186
size 229
snakewood 159
sine wave, see pure tone
sound:
  distribution 144–7
  energy 3
  identification 122
  production 94
  quality 133
  speed 3,
  wave 2
soundpost:
  crack 226
  material 43
  mechanics 40, 56–60
  pressure 58
spiccato 130
spirit varnish, see varnish
spreaders 203–6
spruce 51
starting transient 7, 24
stop ratio 219
Stradivarius 35, 55, 90, 94, 95
string:
  casing 214, 216–18
  diameter 214
  effective length 26–9
  gauges 218
  harmonics 20, 117
  laws 211
  stability 82
  stiffness 213
  tails 83
  tension 34, 50, 58

twisting 29
  vibration 18
strings, care of 224
  steel 214–16
  synthetic cored 215
surface tension 203–6
symmetry 63
synthesized tone 120, 122

tailgut 222
tailpiece 47, 83
theft 229
timbre 97, 122–5, 131–3
tone:
  and bowing position 18
  definition 10, 96
  and harmonics 104, 112–16, 122
  of individual strings 133–6
  and resonance 74, 137
  richness 116
tortoiseshell 163
touch harmonics 11, 25–7
Tourte 158
transience 122, 127–31
triangle of forces 35

varnish:
  basis 180–82
  cellulose 195
  colour 191–5
  hardeners 195
  myth 209
  oil 169, 182, 187–91
  orange-peel 206
  spirit 182–7
  synthetic 196
  and tone 197
vibrato 124, 129, 140
viola:
  resonance 77, 86
  size 65, 85–8, 137
  tone 136

water 169
water-free spirit 185, 207
waxes 169, 181
wave form 19
wolf tone 79–82, 121, 226
wood resonances 85–6
woodworm 64, 226, 227